...nally published in hardcover in the United States by Crown
...ers, an imprint of the Crown Publishing Group, a division of
Random House, Inc., New York.

...ul acknowledgment is made to Ear Booker Enterprises for
...mission to reprint lyrics from the song "eBay," lyrics by
...ovic. Reprinted by permission of Ear Booker Enterprises.

...Library of Congress Cataloging-in-Publication Data

... Meg.
...wer of many : values for success in business and in life / by
...man ; with Joan O'C. Hamilton.
...m.
...ss in business.   2. Success.   I. Hamilton, Joan O'C.

...4934 2010
...2   2009045331

ISBN 978-0-307-59122-7

Printed in the United States of America

Design by Gretchen Achilles

10 9 8 7 6 5 4 3 2 1

First Paperback Edition

More Acclaim for
the POWER *of* MANY

"Meg Whitman's charming and candid book translates the spirit behind eBay's growth into lessons every business leader needs: how to earn profits by investing in bonds of trust with users and a culture that inspires high performance."
—**ROSABETH MOSS KANTER**, HARVARD BUSINESS SCHOOL;
AUTHOR OF *SUPERCORP: HOW VANGUARD COMPANIES CREATE INNOVATION, PROFITS, GROWTH, AND SOCIAL GOOD*

"What Meg Whitman created and developed at eBay is truly extraordinary. This book chronicles how her vision, dedication, hard work, and focus on results created the opportunity for millions of Americans to form their own businesses and secure their families' futures. As a direct result of Meg's leadership, eBay has contributed to tremendous job growth both here in Silicon Valley and beyond; I believe she has the ability to further develop and shape our future economy."
—**JOHN CHAMBERS**, CHAIRMAN AND CEO, CISCO

"Meg attacks problems. Meg knows how to make tough decisions, how to cut through complexity and uncertainty . . . and find solutions to challenges. Meg knows how to lead, and this book reflects that: it is both authentic and inspiring."
—**MARY MEEKER**, MANAGING DIRECTOR, MORGAN STANLEY

"This book is inspiring. Meg Whitman steered a tiny start-up through the dot-com frenzy and emerged running a multibillion-dollar global pillar of e-commerce. *The Power of Many* demonstrates that integrity and values in business are not just 'nice to haves,' they are essential for leaders to succeed in running modern, high-impact organizations."
—**CAROL BARTZ**, PRESIDENT AND CEO, YAHOO!

"*The Power of Many* will be a crucial resource for women looking for both inspiration and practical advice on achieving success and fulfillment within all areas of their lives. A dazzling accomplishment."

—**MOIRA FORBES**, PUBLISHER, *FORBESWOMAN*

"Meg Whitman has had a remarkable business career, culminating as CEO of eBay. She weaves a compelling story about family, education, successes, failures (not so many), mentors, the power of teams, and the systematic acquisition and application of wisdom. She develops a coherent model for high integrity and high-performance leadership that should be emulated by everyone."

—**WILLIAM A. SAHLMAN**, PROFESSOR OF BUSINESS ADMINISTRATION, HARVARD BUSINESS SCHOOL

"In *The Power of Many*, Meg's great insight is that running a successful organization in the Internet Age requires constant reinvention. Advances in technology drive a lot of that, but Meg understands that the emotional connections of a community networked together can give even a simple idea global reach. This is a great discussion of the importance of listening and harnessing that energy in order to create positive change."

—**TERRY SEMEL**, CHAIRMAN, WINDSOR MEDIA; FORMER CHAIRMAN AND CEO, YAHOO! AND WARNER BROS.

"Meg Whitman makes a compelling case for the Power of Many, but she makes an even stronger case for focus, vision, and integrity. She repeatedly demonstrates all three in this refreshingly candid guide for leaders, taking us through her good and bad decisions to demonstrate that expecting the best from people is not just a philosophy; it is a winning business strategy."

—**NELL MINOW**, CHAIR AND COFOUNDER, *THE CORPORATE LIBRARY*; COAUTHOR OF *CORPORATE GOVERNANCE*

the PO
of MA

Pub
of the

Three

Origi
Publish

Grate
pe
Al Yan

Values
in Busine

MEG W

with JOAN

Whitman
The po
Meg Whit
p.
1. Succe
II. Title.
HF5386 W
650.1—dc

THREE

For my husband, Griff, and my sons, Griff and Will

CONTENTS

the POWER *of* MANY

INTRODUCTION

The first question

W hat is the *right* thing to do here?"

Looking back, I don't think I would have had to ask the question if my team hadn't been so exhausted. It was June 11, 1999, and I was walking down the hall at eBay when I saw and heard a noisy group of my senior staff in one of our conference rooms. It had been, to put it mildly, a rough day and a half, and most of us still looked like the walking wounded—gimlet-eyed, glum, both wired and tired from stress and coffee and lack of sleep. We had just experienced a twenty-two-hour system outage that had nearly propelled us to a prime spot on the list of the most spectacular business failures of all time. The crisis was far from over still. We had been publicly traded for only a short time but had a market capitalization larger than that of Sears, Roebuck—a fact one news commentator pointedly noted when he explained that our system shutdown was the equivalent of all the Sears stores in the country locking their doors simultaneously and admitting they didn't know when they might reopen.

Our technical team had at last brought the system back up. Sort of. We'd finally been able to pull down the huge sheets of brown paper that we'd taped over the first-floor windows to avoid the hordes of camera crews from CNN and the local stations. Unfortunately, our system was still unstable, still crashing intermittently, still desperately in need of a thorough overhaul. The even worse reality was that we had thousands of frustrated and angry eBay community members. Our system crash had closed their doors as well.

I poked my head into the meeting room and asked what was going on. The group was discussing our service agreement with eBay sellers—those fine-print details that govern a transaction but which people tend not to read. One of the things spelled out in the fine print was that, under certain conditions, eBay would refund the listing fees on auctions that were disrupted by a system outage. At the time, eBay had more than 2 million active auctions. What did we owe those sellers? According to the agreement, we owed refunds only to the sellers in auctions scheduled to end during the period in which we were down. But we realized that all auctions, not just those scheduled to end during the outage, had been disrupted. The team figured that the difference between adhering to the letter of the agreement and offering a refund to every single seller could amount to almost $5 million—a significant number for a company whose total revenues the previous quarter were $34 million. A full refund to all sellers would mean we would miss our quarterly earnings projection, which could very easily cause Wall Street to lose confidence and the stock to plummet.

Listening to the conversation, it was clear to me that some voices in the group were trying to rationalize the smaller refund.

"What is the *right* thing to do here?" I asked, and then I left the room.

Rajiv Dutta, who was in our finance group at the time and later became our chief financial officer, subsequently told me that the debate ended immediately. We would refund listing fees to *all* sellers who had active auctions when the site crashed. What's more, we decided that going forward, we would refund fees anytime we had an outage that lasted more than two hours. We also sent a letter to our users that said, in part, "We know that you expect uninterrupted service from eBay. We believe that this is reasonable, and we know we haven't lived up to your expectations." And we apologized.

"People almost always know what they *should* do," Rajiv recalls. "But sometimes they need the leadership to remind them."

Now, this is a nice story, but it is not a story about the importance of always making the customer happy and worrying about the bottom line later. This is, after all, a book about success in both business and life. The reason I wanted to share this story is that while eBay's stock price was unstable during this crisis, it did not collapse. After we explained our decision, Wall Street did not panic at the prospect of our missing our earnings targets as a result of the refund. Our users did not abandon us. Instead, and in part due to some other measures we took that I will talk about later in this book, we forged an even stronger bond of trust with our users all over the world, and a better working relationship with our technology partners. We vowed to fix our computer system, and in short order we did that, too.

I believe all this happened because we were a company that had made a clear and deliberate choice to behave according to a set of values.

In the course of the next decade, time and again I found that managing eBay by what might be called old-fashioned, basic values unleashed a remarkable twenty-first-century phenomenon— what I call the Power of Many. A Power of Many company or organization utilizes the communication and networking powers of modern technology to do things that otherwise would be impossible. But the point is to use technology not only to save costs and improve efficiencies but also as a way to engage the energy, ideas, and goodness of people, their desire to team up with others who share their interests and work together to make their own lives and life in general better. It demands a style of management and leadership that emphasizes communication and openness, and when difficult decisions loom, it demands that everybody consider this question: What is the right thing to do?

IN RETROSPECT, I have come to believe that all the career steps I took on my path to eBay prepared me to run and build what we became. From day one, I could see that eBay had all the ingredients of a great company at a remarkably young age. But I will not try to suggest that I had a true sense of the Power of Many when I agreed to take the job.

Early in my career, I worked as a management consultant. I was like a paratrooper, jumping into all manner of difficult and complicated situations in many kinds of companies—banks, cruise lines, high-tech instrument makers, beer companies, and airlines, to name a few. My job was to solve problems. As consultants, we were summoned to help companies that needed to forge a new strategy, reorganize after bad business decisions, or retool to more effectively battle the competition. Later, as an executive with a number of large corporations, including Disney and Hasbro, I worked with some of the most creative marketing minds in the country to develop new products and sell brands that millions of Americans use and rely on, even play with, every day. As the former head of Hasbro's Preschool Division, I can even say that I was on a first-name basis with Mr. and Mrs. Potato Head.

But eBay demanded all the skills and experience I brought with me and more. The results wildly exceeded our expectations: we turned a tiny start-up into a revolutionary economic engine that now provides a livelihood for people around the world and fuels tens of billions of dollars in transactions.

The "and more" part is what I want to talk about in this book.

There is a myth—at least I believe it's a myth—that great success demands that we give up, or at least fudge, our relationship to what most of us recognize as decent, commonsense values. Honesty. Family. Community. Integrity. Generosity. Courage. Empathy. As we climb the corporate ladder, the myth tells us, we have to step on people, stretch the truth when it fits our agenda, and make heartless decisions based only on the bottom line. We are not supposed to ask what is the right thing to do, but rather what is best for our careers or to burnish our reputation.

I have never bought into that myth. I respect ambition, but not ruthless ambition. I watched the "greed is good" philosophy of the eighties play out, eventually landing some wheeler-dealer executives in prison. More recently, we've seen self-dealing and fraud undermine our entire economy. I've seen self-absorbed strivers trample colleagues to get ahead. But what I realized after ten years running eBay was that if eBay had been the kind of company where we held no core values and followed no ethical compass, where we treated our community members and each other like pawns or assets to be exploited, we never would have succeeded at all.

Many companies go through the exercise of creating a list of "corporate values," invariably featuring platitudes such as "Always put the customer first." Too often it doesn't go much deeper than that. But just talking about values doesn't mean anything. Not long after I joined eBay, the founder, Pierre Omidyar, said something that hit me like a two-ton truck. He said, "We don't have to invent values. This community already has values. We need to align ourselves with their values or it's not going to work." Pierre sat down and wrote out what he thought those values were. They happened to deeply reflect his own personal values. From then on, eBay employee name badges carried these statements:

We believe people are basically good.

We recognize and respect everyone as a unique individual.

We believe everyone has something to contribute.

We encourage people to treat others the way they want to be treated.

We believe that an honest, open environment can bring out the best in people.

These values resonated deeply with me. They reflect the optimism and open-mindedness that I see in my most treasured friends. They are the values I saw in my parents' friends, who worked together, played together, volunteered together, prayed together, and treated one another with respect and compassion. There is nothing complicated or fancy about these values. But don't mistake their hopefulness or simplicity for naïveté.

Values-focused management is not the only way to lead a company. There are many different approaches to motivating and empowering employees. Andy Grove successfully ran Intel for many years with the mantra "Only the paranoid survive." Jack Welch became one of the nation's most respected business leaders with an informal but highly combative style designed to break down bureaucracy and banish what he called "superficial congeniality." Other successful organizations reflect the unique sensibilities of an iconic founder, such as Steve Jobs, Oprah Winfrey, or Michael Bloomberg.

But by the end of the twentieth century, the Internet had created entirely new possibilities. For the first time, businesspeople began to routinely talk about "transparency," as the secrecy around certain kinds of transactions or activities fell away. Technology drove this: information that used to be difficult to obtain or communicate, or reserved for a chosen few, was suddenly available on every computer screen and could travel around the globe in seconds. It became easy to provide detailed information about products and services and invite users to share information and issues with one another. Investor chat rooms suddenly featured leaked memos and internal rumors about companies and pending deals.

This transparency not only accelerated the flow of information and streamlined many of the traditional relationships between businesses and their customers but also began to suggest entirely new kinds of business relationships. Almost single-handedly, for example, eBay created a global mechanism to value secondhand goods by creating transparency in what collectors were willing to pay for certain items. It leveled the playing field. A shrewd collector had to bid against other knowledgeable collectors in the open on eBay, even if the seller was not an expert in the true value of an item being listed. Sellers had to fully and accurately describe their items or risk negative feedback that would hurt their reputation and discourage future buyers.

What I came to believe at eBay was that, far from dehumanizing our interactions, technology, properly managed, can amplify our humanity in extraordinary ways. It actually can help a company connect more deeply with what its customers want and need and partner with its community in pursuing shared interests instead of just dictating terms. However, this is not just a function of clever software or powerful computers. To be effective in creating this kind of community, leaders need to approach the challenge with optimism, openness, discipline, and courage. They need to use technology to institutionalize listening and enfranchising. Doing this can be noisy, even a little chaotic at times. As we learned at eBay, you will never please everyone. But if you are cynical or dishonest about your values, you will be exposed. In fact, when you start down this path, you need to realize that your stumbles and missteps, even some of your soul-searching, will occur out in the open, for all to see. That is the reality of transparency. Private e-mails become public. Customers post angry complaints. Competitors can move quickly to exploit any perceived weakness.

But if you follow an ethical and true course, you can unleash what I call the Power of Many. From the start, Pierre saw the connection between managing by shared values and creating trust within the community of eBay users. He exquisitely understood the extraordinary potential of a community that aligned and pulled together. The business challenge was to show that community that we intended to empower them, not exploit them, and that together we could all be successful.

We gave eBay users tools, structure, and minimal rules, and we tried to stay out of the way. That is why I have always said that we did not build eBay; our community of users did. As managers, we held ourselves accountable to deliver on our promises—to our investors and to our customers. We trusted our users to figure out the best way to use our services and to tell us how to improve our offerings. Ultimately, eBay developed because millions of people bought into the idea that they could trust each other. They came to take for granted that they could find a stranger with something they wanted to buy and conduct a satisfying transaction that benefited each of them. And those of us managing eBay believed we could build loyalty by actually listening to our customers and seeking their involvement.

That shared covenant is what ultimately propelled us far beyond where any of us initially dreamed of going.

The idea that our success would hinge on this shared covenant was not obvious at the time. We took a lot of heat from outside eBay for the emphasis we put on our values. People said they seemed like utopian ideals, not business values. Manage by asking what is the right thing to do? How naive, critics sniped. "That's nice, but what about your numbers?" asked some investors.

Well, we also had other values that were equally important. At the top of the list was the conviction that results matter. We knew that we needed to deliver on what we said we'd deliver. We vowed to be frugal and treat shareholder resources as something to be conserved for the best possible use. We made it a habit to constantly take stock and jettison projects that were interfering with our core focus. I had relied on these values throughout my training and career in business, and they were just as non-negotiable as the ones Pierre had established. What seems to surprise people is that these two sets of values—the hard-nosed business values and the "softer," ethical values—were complementary.

I believe eBay's success proved that values are not abstract ideals but essential tools. What strikes me most deeply as I reflect on my ten years at eBay is that both sets of values were as relevant and useful to me when I took over a $4 million company with thirty employees as they were on the day I retired from eBay in 2008, when we had grown to a nearly $8 billion company with 15,000 employees around the world. At that point, more than 1 million people who were not employed by eBay made most of, if not all of, their living selling in our marketplace. Time and again people would come up to me and say, "eBay changed my life." The company helped people be successful doing something they loved, and sometimes it even empowered individuals with disabilities who simply could not do in the land-based world what they could do in the eBay marketplace—compete on an even footing.

eBay was a unique place where many ideas and constituencies and dynamics converged. Today, across the landscape of business, more and more companies are talking about the importance of using the Internet to build a community, not just a customer base, whether they are selling hybrid automobiles, pharmaceuticals, gardening tools, or even diapers. Apple was once a fiercely independent boutique; today, by enfranchising thousands of outside application developers it has created an incredibly dynamic and powerful innovation engine. Members of its larger community have developed tens of thousands of applications for the iPhone. That is a classic Power of Many endeavor. In the best of these communities, you will find people who are basically good, working together in areas of shared interest, listening to one another, but also looking to create meaningful products and services with tangible value.

We faced many different kinds of challenges, and the path was not always smooth, but our performance and our reputation as a company of decent, good people who tried not only to be effective in delivering business results but also to be responsible citizens of both their eBay and real-world communities was something I was deeply proud of.

I began to ask a bigger question: If these guiding principles worked so well for eBay, shouldn't they work for other challenges in or beyond business? Don't we crave a government we can be proud of and feel part of, one that empowers us but also one that gets out of the way so we can innovate and invent our own futures? Don't most of us feel that people are basically good, that they step forward in difficult times with great courage and come up with new ideas that make all of our lives better? Shouldn't we make it easier for those ideas to see the light of day?

I'm writing this book in part because I believe that we have the opportunity today to use these values to help us reinvent our future during a time of great stress and economic anxiety. There are those who see a focus on values as a luxury for prosperous times when we can "afford" to sit back and think about making the world a kinder or nobler place. I want to make a different argument: that it is precisely during difficult times that we need to take a step back and align our priorities and actions with the fundamental principles that ultimately create stability, efficiency, energy, and even prosperity. Navigating by essential values can have a force-multiplying effect.

I don't recall a time in my life that we as a nation have so needed to tap the Power of Many. I believe the eBay experience vividly shows that businesses will best prosper by inviting customers and partners into their thinking and decision-making processes. Technology advances are giving us ever more exciting and powerful ways to do that, and to amplify the power of the communities that result. Combined with a values-based approach to management, this is a new model for success with lessons that go beyond business.

1

Trust that people are basically good.

The classic training of a business executive has little to do with trust. In fact, it's almost the opposite. You're trained to look for an advantage. When you analyze a business opportunity you learn to ask: "What is the competitive situation? What is my strategic advantage? What are my competitor's weaknesses?" That extends to managing one's own career: "What job do I want and who else wants it? Am I moving along this path at sufficient speed or do I need a better, bigger, more visible position?" That mind-set for waging the daily battles of business begins early.

On my first day of class at Harvard Business School in 1977, one of our professors issued a warning that is legendary in competitive, pressure-cooker environments: "Look to your left. Now, look to your right. One of you may not be here by the end of the first semester."

I looked to my left. He was a banker who'd been working on Wall Street for several years. He seemed to know everything about accounting and was very self-assured. I looked to my right. He was a U.S. Army major who had led men into battle. And me? I was only twenty-one years old (I had skipped a year of high school).

My main work experience was selling advertising for a college magazine. And I was one of only 138 women in a class of 754.

My first thought was, "Well, it's not going to be one of those two guys."

My next thought was, "I'm going to work so hard that it won't be me, either."

I survived.

Two decades later, in 1998, after I had held a number of senior executive positions at large corporations, I found myself in Silicon Valley on my first day on a new job. I walked into a room filled with computers, beach chairs, cables, coffee cups, and a crew of intense, bright, young employees in jeans, shorts, and T-shirts. It was a far cry from the stuffy marble and mahogany conference rooms full of pin-striped suits that Harvard prepared us to navigate and command. But I was there because this exciting but overwhelmed young company called eBay needed a CEO to take it to the next level. I also was there because when I'd met the founder of this company I had an epiphany of sorts.

I had been blown away by the power of trust.

Just a few months earlier, I had told the executive recruiter (or "headhunter," in the relentlessly aggressive lexicon of corporate America) that I was not interested in the start-up online auction company. At the time, I was living near Boston and was a division general manager at the toy company Hasbro. It was a terrific job. I ran the Preschool Division, and we were in the middle of a very exciting period, injecting new life into brands millions of American families loved, including Playskool, Barney the purple dinosaur, Weebles, and Mr. and Mrs. Potato Head. My two sons, Griff and Will, then twelve and nine, were signed up for Hasbro's toy testers program and got to play with new Nerf guns and Star Wars gear before their friends could buy them, which made my Hasbro job second in coolness only to the several years I spent as a Disney executive. We had family nearby and liked the boys' school. You didn't need to be a brain surgeon to understand why I was not anxious to move, but it didn't hurt, either: my neurosurgeon husband, Griff Harsh, understood because he was happily ensconced as executive director of the Brain Tumor Center at Massachusetts General Hospital.

However, one thing you learn as a business executive is that you always want to keep your head up and your eyes open. You always want your résumé well known among recruiters and companies working on exciting new ideas. So, to be perfectly honest, the main reason I finally agreed to go to Silicon Valley to talk to this tiny company's founder and lead investor was that I didn't want to alienate David Beirne, the executive recruiter who was helping them staff up. The next time, he might be calling with a job I really did want. I was skeptical, I told him, but I would fly out for a visit.

Before my trip, I pulled up the Web page for eBay. (Pierre originally called it Echo Bay Technology, but since that URL was already taken when he went to register the company, he shortened it to eBay.) Now, remember, this was 1997. Like most people, I was only spending a fraction of the time online that I now spend, and much of the Web still had a crude feel to it. The eBay site, then called AuctionWeb, was kind of ugly, confusing, even a little strange. The first time I looked at it, there were three parts to it: Pierre's girlfriend's home page, which featured information for San Francisco–based alumni of Tufts University; a compilation of current research and writing on the Ebola virus, which had terrified the entire world and fascinated Pierre; and then the section devoted to Pierre's online auction business, originally called AuctionWeb. The colors were black, gray, and white, with a little purple here and there. The design was busy and the text hard to read, and in the auction area there was a hodgepodge of items listed—Beanie Babies, Depression glass, secondhand modems. I thought: "Oh, great. I'm about to fly across the country for this."

But it would have been unprofessional to back out of the meeting, so I sighed and resigned myself to learning as much as I could and then, probably, politely passing on the job. I arrived at the San Francisco airport and took a cab to Silicon Valley's famous Sand Hill Road, where early-stage investors known as venture capitalists have offices on a knoll above Stanford University. At Benchmark Capital, David Beirne introduced me to Bob Kagle, the lead Benchmark partner who had invested in this little company, and to Pierre Omidyar and Jeff Skoll. Pierre was a thirty-year-old computer programmer who, in those days, sported a ponytail and sandals. He had been born in Paris to parents who had relocated there from Iran in the 1960s. The family moved to the United States when he was a boy. Brilliant and philosophical, he had worked at some of Silicon Valley's most creative companies, including Apple's Claris subsidiary and General Magic. Pierre actually created eBay; he wrote the original code and launched it from a computer in his apartment. Jeff was the company's president and first real employee, an intense, analytical electrical engineer and Stanford MBA who had left Knight Ridder, then the second-largest newspaper chain in the country, to help Pierre build eBay.

I was immediately impressed with Pierre and Jeff. Pierre explained that his motivation for starting eBay was that he thought the Internet had the potential to create the ideal trading market—one where buyers and sellers had equal access to information and together could set the appropriate price. He initially had experimented with putting items such as a broken laser pointer online, and he was startled when bidders bought the items, often for far more than he had dreamed anyone would pay. He figured an auction was an excellent tool for rationalizing the trading of items that are hard to price, such as used items. But it also was an effective tool to price brand-new items that are relatively scarce, such as the latest video game console, tickets to an event, or even the highly coveted Beanie Babies of that time, which were expertly marketed with an unpredictable distribution strategy that made people fight to get them.

Pierre explained that eBay's auctions were particularly appealing to collectors and hobbyists whose emotional attachment and passion for certain types of objects would motivate them to seek out other like-minded people. His girlfriend (now wife), Pam Wesley, for example, was using it to trade Pez dispensers.° By the time I came to look at the site, it was jam-packed with all sorts of collectibles—autographed items, vintage lunchboxes, pottery, and glass. But it also featured assorted equipment, for example, older-model computers and items such as broken record players that hi-fi hobbyists might buy to get parts to make repairs.

In part because of the users' shared hobbies and interests and their ability to actually communicate before and after the sale, Pierre was finding a high level of trustworthiness in the community, he said. Users sent money to total strangers to pay for an item that they trusted had been advertised accurately. The people selling the items actually cared about where their old cameras or silver

---

°The "Pez story" has become the stuff of lore. I was not there when the story began to circulate, but I'm told that around the time Pierre was starting eBay, he and Pam were driving through France and in a small country market Pam found a large cache of collectible French Pez dispensers. She snapped them up, but after they left the shop and drove on, she realized she had missed one, so they went back for it. When he retold the story to eBay's then-marketing manager, Mary Lou Song, he told her, "See, if we had a fully functioning online trading platform, I would not have had to turn around and go back. She could have found one online." Mary Lou loved the story and started telling reporters that Pam's Pez collection was part of Pierre's motivation to build eBay. He did not invent eBay so that Pam could trade Pez, however.

teaspoons went, and they often offered advice to the buyers about how to use or care for them, or shared the stories behind them.

What's more, the parties in eBay transactions usually resolved any disputes that developed without eBay getting involved, and to each party's satisfaction. Pierre had set up a feedback forum, and he urged me to check it out. There, he said I would see how what began as a sort of complaint forum had evolved into a community. Far more positive things were being said about trading partners than negative things. eBay users not only talked about their transactions but helped one another with personal problems and business dilemmas, traded gossip, and even played funny little games. (One of their favorite games was called "Tuz." Every post to the bulletin board was date-stamped. So every evening at exactly twenty-two seconds past 10:22—22:22:22 in military time—many users would try to post a comment. They kept track of who managed to do it, and they swapped techniques, such as using a metronome, for how to time hitting "send.") Many talked openly of having met their best friends on the service's online chat boards. Most remarkably, they gave the company feedback that helped the whole enterprise run better and more efficiently—and Pierre and the young team listened and often made changes based on that feedback. I had not imagined that such a rich world lay beneath the crazy-quilt home page.

Then Pierre and Jeff offered up something that was not so common to hear executives in start-ups talk about—the company's philosophy. I'm not talking about the brash "get big fast or go home" war whoop that soon would be the calling card of dot-commers. Rather, Pierre carefully explained that he believed eBay was thriving because it was based on the idea that most people are basically good and that the users could be trusted to do the right thing most of the time.

If the meeting had stopped right there, I would have admitted that I was deeply intrigued. It was plain that Pierre and Jeff were bright, thoughtful, and passionate about their company. They also had the humility to realize that to succeed they needed to hire people with skills they didn't have—a quality that can be rare among entrepreneurs.

But what really got my attention were the numbers they shared with me. At this stage of my career, I had seen a lot of financial reports. But despite launching new business lines and brands, I had never seen numbers for a young enterprise that could match eBay's. The two-year-old company's revenues were growing at 70 percent *per month* and their costs were so low that their profits were 85 percent of revenues. Even my pin-striped Harvard MBA classmates would have done a double take.

Let me repeat the two key words in that last paragraph, as they will become important themes throughout this book. The first is *revenues*—money coming in from real customers. The second is *profits*—the difference between the revenues and your costs, otherwise known as the point of being in business. From the very beginning and throughout my tenure at eBay, unlike 99 percent of the dot-com start-ups with which we would be lumped together for the next several years, eBay was profitable. This was not a co-op, not a user's group, not a gimmicky effort to attract traffic in hopes of selling advertising. This was a moneymaking business.

Suddenly I was glad I'd made the trip. The potential of this company began to shimmer in front of me. At the time of my first meeting, you have to realize that online commerce was an interesting idea—Amazon, for example, already had received a lot of attention—but most of the business world was still scratching its head about what the Internet was going to mean. That was certainly true back at Hasbro, a company that still was firmly grounded in what the Silicon Valley Internet folks called the "brick-and-mortar" world. (Later at eBay we used the odd term "land-based" to describe non-Internet businesses). Hasbro was a classic consumer products company. We designed and built toys such as Mr. Potato Head, sold them in toy stores, and advertised them on television and in magazines and newspapers. We had manufacturing agreements with overseas companies, we had warehouses, and we dealt with distribution channels and inventories.

But as I spoke with this young team, I realized that eBay had such extraordinary financial results because it did *not* do most of those things. Tiny eBay consisted of nothing more than a few computers and thirty people sitting in an office in San Jose. eBay's business was electronically connecting buyers and sellers in a way that had never been possible before, and then providing the tools to manage bids and run the auction. The company never saw or touched what it helped sell; it didn't much care what it helped sell (that came later); it didn't even demand that users keep a credit card on file. Sometimes eBay's small cut of the sales arrived in the office in envelopes with coins and small bills.

Because of all eBay *didn't* have to do, because of everything it didn't have to physically build, maintain, or warehouse, eBay could make a healthy profit on low fees, thanks to the high volume of transactions. The more I thought about all this, the more the potential of the Internet to turn classic business structures upside down seemed obvious. The Internet could do what almost all significant business innovations do: exploit inefficiencies. Just as trains exploited inefficiencies in covered-wagon travel and planes exploited the limitations of trains and ships, eBay's innovation was making inefficient markets efficient. It was going to connect people who wanted to sell things with people who wanted those specific items, wherever they might be, and it was going to let them determine the right price for the sale. And the whole process was going to be transparent, with anyone who might be interested seeing the same information and having the same opportunity to bid. Jeff

Skoll has said that he initially was skeptical about whether people would want to buy and sell online. "But what turned me around," he noted, "was seeing the classified ad people at Knight Ridder who were digging their heels in trying to protect their revenues and saying there was no way they were going to let that business go online." Jeff was prescient: he saw that an online marketplace actually stood to make the kind of transactions that people were using classified ads to complete much more efficient. "I realized, somebody will capitalize on this."

I LEFT THAT FIRST MEETING with Pierre and Jeff surprised and excited by what I'd seen. I'd only planned to spend a few hours with the team before heading home, so I wasn't able to visit their office. (I later heard they were just as happy about that because they worried the general disarray might have scared me off.) Even so, I called my husband from the airport and said, "This is pretty amazing, honey. We might want to move back to California."

I planned to come back in a few weeks. Meanwhile, I spent a lot of my evenings on the eBay site. Right around this time, the company switched the auction site to the eBay.com home page and removed Pam's home page and the Ebola virus material, so it was beginning to look more professional. More important, I read the e-mails and user comments on the message boards, all of it pulsing with human connection. eBay already had something that was highly unusual for a tiny start-up with a couple of dozen employees: a powerful brand.

A great brand delivers not only meaningful features and functionality but also an emotional connection. Think Coca-Cola, Nike, Levi's jeans, Crest, Pampers. Procter & Gamble really does deliver whiter whites and cleaner cleans from its laundry products, and a shampoo like Pantene feels richer than the drugstore generic. But they also sell you a *feeling.* Your family's clothes will look the best they can look. Your hair will be softer and will please you with how it feels. Your adorable little baby will be more comfortable in Pampers. A pair of Levi's is about not just a look but a feeling— comfort, practicality, casual style. "M&Ms melt in your mouth— not in your hand!" Great brands empower, they solve problems, and they please in a deep way. From the response and interactions of the community, it was clear that eBay stood for trust, fun, and opportunity, and for many users it had come to occupy a unique place where their financial and personal lives came together. They enjoyed being with one another online, so much so that users voted to call their online social discussion area the "eBay Cafe."

Now, not everything was touchy-feely and Kumbaya. The eBay Cafe tended to be an upbeat, fun place where users enjoyed interacting, but the bulletin boards where feedback was posted brought into sharp relief malfeasance and gaps in how the system was working. If you were selling a vintage Captain Kangaroo lunchbox and described it as being in mint condition but it arrived at the buyer's home with a rusty hinge and a broken thermos, well, you heard about it instantly. If you did not make things right, everybody else would soon hear about it, too. Users who might be too intimidated in a real-world restaurant to send a cold dinner back felt empowered online to demand an explanation and restitution for anything that seemed fraudulent or unfair. Buyers accused sellers of shady tactics such as shill bidding, which involved strategies for inflating bidding by using fake third-party accounts. People had arguments and they insulted each other from time to time. They had pet peeves.

But what was obvious was a level of caring by the community that I had not really seen before. They wanted—indeed, expected—to be consulted. They wanted their particular situations to be understood. They didn't complain and stomp off; they suggested solutions. It was obvious the community wanted this to work, and that they were willing to invest their own time in suggesting ways it could work better. And they invested in one another's success and lives in fascinating ways.

Later, I would learn about a user our early community managers knew only as "Darts." A frequent visitor to the eBay Cafe, she quickly made friends who looked forward to her posts. Why, they wondered, did she post only during the day? Well, it turned out that she could only post during the day from work because she didn't own a computer. Her new friends quickly set to work. Two eBay members collected parts for a computer and sent them to a third member, who assembled them and drove a couple of hours to deliver their gift to her in person. Finally, Darts could post at night and on the weekends. Eventually, Darts and the members who helped her all became part of our remote Customer Support team.

GRIFF AND I TALKED about the possibility of my taking the job, and we started thinking about that inclusive, anything-is-possible, everyone-is-invited spirit that we had so loved about California in the early 1980s. And right away we both had a feeling that another adventure for us was afoot.

I first met Griff when I was a sophomore at Princeton and he was a senior at Harvard. My older sister, Anne, was a tutor in the dormitory where Griff lived. Anne told me she had a hunch I might like him, so I went up to visit her one weekend. Sure enough, Griff and I hit it off right away.

I could instantly see that Griff was smart and charming, but it was also plain that he had his feet planted firmly on the ground. He was raised in Birmingham, Alabama, but had spent summers on his mother's family farm in Sweetwater, Tennessee, where he learned to ride horses, aim a shotgun, and do other chores around the farm. He inoculated cows, dug post holes, stacked hay, and "bush-hogged" (mowed) fields, earning $5 for a twelve-hour work-day. These experiences taught him both the fulfillment that can come from good hard work in the outdoors and the value of a dollar. And despite his subsequent academic achievements (he graduated summa cum laude), Griff has always had an understated, modest demeanor. He dislikes anything ostentatious or showy, and he is very serious about living an authentic life focused on things that matter—family, faith, friends, health, the stewardship of land, important ideas. In his personal style, Griff is meticulous and detail-oriented, traits that run in his family. His father and brother are both neurosurgeons, and from a young age, Griff sensed that he wanted to be a surgeon as well.

I liked him right off, but we did not start dating. Griff was about to leave to study in England on a Rhodes scholarship, and then he was headed for Harvard Medical School. I finished Princeton and then went off to Harvard Business School. We saw each other from time to time after he came back for medical school, but both of us were pretty busy.

What finally brought us together was Griff standing me up! When my sister got married in 1978, I helped make up the guest list, and we invited Griff, who called to say he'd love to come. I was in the wedding party and busy with the festivities, but I never saw him. It turned out he was out with friends celebrating his brother's birthday and had lost track of time. By the time he realized his mistake, changed course, and arrived at the reception, the band was carrying its instruments out the back door.

He called me, apologized profusely, and presented a list of five options for how he'd like to make it up to me: dinner and a play, watching the crew races, and several other dates that sounded fun. He didn't really need to do that—what I did not confess at the time was that my sister and I had also invited five other attractive, unattached men to her wedding. Nonetheless, I picked an option from his menu, and the rest is history.

Despite his reserved demeanor, Griff has a wonderful sense of humor and is always game to do something interesting or unconventional—like, say, taking up with a Yankee girl at Harvard Business School. Griff was still in medical school after I finished up at HBS and moved to Cincinnati to work for P&G. However, he found a way to do some month-long rotations at the University of Cincinnati, and we managed to see each other quite a bit. We got married the day after he graduated from medical school.

I enjoyed my job at Procter & Gamble and I learned a lot, but my commitment to Griff required a change. For his neurosurgical residency, Griff had his pick between two excellent programs: Massachusetts General Hospital in Boston and the University of California, San Francisco. By then, my mother, who had not concealed her concern that "your southern fiancé will drag you back to Alabama," had moved to Boston from New York. They are close friends today, but at the time Griff said to me with a wink: "Your mother's in Boston; let's go to San Francisco!"

It took me a few months of commuting, but I eventually landed a job with Bain & Co., based in San Francisco. We packed up and moved west and found a small house on a hill above the Haight-Ashbury district (where yuppies were just starting to displace hippies) that we just loved. San Francisco was diverse, interesting, and full of possibility. Even though I was working for a very traditional, East Coast–based consulting firm, both the San Francisco business community and Silicon Valley, just thirty-five miles to the south, felt like real meritocracies. The Bay Area was a place where all sorts of people from all sorts of backgrounds—from Levi Strauss during the gold rush to A. P. Giannini and the Bank of America at the turn of the century—could make it big on hard work and smarts. Inspired individuals had created great companies such as Apple and the biotech powerhouse Genentech. As fond as we were of the East Coast, Griff and I loved the risk-taking optimism of California (not to mention the weather).

So when the eBay job offer materialized, it brought back a lot of great memories of California. We talked about the opportunities our sons would have to be exposed to all sorts of interesting technology, ideas, and people. We are a family that loves the outdoors, and the prospect of living half an hour from the beach and four hours from the ski slopes had a lot of appeal as well.

A few weeks later I came back and spent time in the eBay offices in the Greylands Business Park in Campbell, California. I later learned that the company had scrambled to hire a temporary receptionist just so potential CEO candidates would be greeted by at least one familiar sign of a real company. At age forty-one, I was clearly going to play the role of the business veteran. On that visit, I pored over the company's books and saw that the momentum we'd discussed just a few weeks before was reflected in those numbers.

Our negotiations moved along pretty speedily from there. And then, after consulting with Griff and the boys, I decided to take the job.

FOR THE NEXT DECADE, eBay continued on a remarkable path. In a 2005 article in *Time*, Sallie Krawcheck, then Citigroup's chief financial officer, compared the marketplace we built to the stock market itself. "eBay is essentially doing the same thing," she wrote. "The men [at the time they were all men] who ran the stock market in its early days had to write the rules as they went along. It was messy and must have been thrilling." Morgan Stanley Internet analyst Mary Meeker once likened what we did to the challenge Peter

Stuyvesant of the Dutch West India Company took on when he came to Manhattan in the early seventeenth century: "He laid out the basic plans to meet the needs of the community—planning and building the streets of lower Manhattan, ramping up fire and police protection. He fostered an environment in which the community conducted commerce in a somewhat orderly fashion, prospered, and grew to become a powerful commerce hub for the New World."

It truly was only "somewhat orderly," especially in the beginning. But building eBay was unfailingly thrilling. The company became the hub of virtual commerce and changed the lives of millions of people around the world. And, most important to me as the CEO, we kept our heads down, kept working, and delivered results, even as flash-in-the-pan dot-coms crashed all around us. Our revenues, our profits, our transactions, and the size of our community grew steadily. It was exciting to change the world, but at the end of the day we were a business, and our first responsibility was to make a profit for our shareholders. That was job one, and we delivered those profits. This was true when I joined, when we were doing about $4.7 million in revenues annually; it was true the day I retired in 2008, when we would close the year with almost $8 billion in revenues and more than $2 billion in net income.

I will talk more about the values, the ideas, and the tools we used to shape and fuel that growth, but, more than a decade later, I still believe that Pierre was right: the fundamental reason eBay worked was that people everywhere are basically good. We provided the tools and reinforced the values, but our users built eBay. Our community's willingness to trust eBay—and one another—was the foundation of eBay's success.

I KNOW THERE are those who think trust or values were just happy sidecars to a clever and effective business model at a unique time and place. And I can assure you that there are those in boardrooms and on Wall Street who simply reject the idea that people are basically good. They see the business world as a zero-sum game where for one person to win, another must lose. They believe that customer service is important but that it has nothing to do with respect or a belief in the goodness of people. Their litany of negatives is long, and the evidence they present that people are not good is endless—from the seemingly constant reports of identity theft and Internet fraud to the 2 million Americans in prison. It's easy to read the daily parade of global horrors in the newspaper, witness the criminal or stupid behavior of a small number of executives or elected officials, or even just see the bizarre scheming and antics on reality shows and become very depressed. How can I talk about people's goodness?

Well, let's back up and look at what Pierre actually said. Pierre's premise was not that *all* people are good; it was that *most* people are *basically* good. I agree that it is an optimistic statement, but let's be clear: we did not build eBay by sticking our heads in the sand. We did not ignore or deny that fraud, distasteful behavior, or unlawful activities occurred on eBay from time to time. Quite the contrary: we invested significantly in eBay's Trust & Safety division, which policed the site. We created software that looked for patterns that might be signs of trading in counterfeit goods, illegal bidding, or even behavior that was simply inappropriate, such as one user stealing a digital photograph from another user's auction page. But from day one it was clear to us that such behavior involved only a tiny minority of people.

As time went on, we realized that we had to take seriously the task of protecting the vast, lawful, honest majority from the dangerous few. In 1997, for example, eBay sold its one millionth item. By 1999, we had more than 2 million items listed for sale *at any one time*. Today, at any given time, there are more than 113 million listings on eBay worldwide, and approximately 7.9 million listings are added per day. It's important to realize what a small percentage of transactions—a fraction of 1 percent—is cause for concern. However, as we grew, in absolute terms even a fraction of 1 percent was a significant number that merited constant vigilance. We moved aggressively to shut down fraudulent activity, and we suspended users from trading if they violated our rules. We also found that we had to change our rules over time. Sometimes these moves generated angry responses and vocal criticism. Naturally, the huge numbers of eBay community members whose auctions were going along just fine were not very noisy. This was simply an aspect of governing this new kind of community, just as in a city or town you are always going to have individuals who are outraged when they get a jaywalking ticket or don't like a governing body's decision about how to manage a park or where to build a cell tower.

We were not the only company to recognize that the majority of people on the Internet were there to do no harm. The Internet movie-rental company Netflix had a similar experience when it launched. At the time, its entire business involved sending physical DVDs back and forth, and some investors and industry observers said Netflix was taking a huge risk by trusting its customers. The worry was that people would pretend the DVDs they had ordered had never arrived and just keep them, or that many would be stolen out of mailboxes. After all, there is nothing so conspicuous as a bright red Netflix envelope bearing a DVD. But, somewhat surprisingly, the DVDs they mailed out came back in such high numbers that Netflix proved these fears were unfounded. *Most customers were basically honest.* The DVDs were not pilfered from mailboxes in large numbers. Customers didn't routinely pretend that a disk never arrived. The Netflix community, like the eBay community, has proven itself to be, by and large, an honest partner in the shared interest of renting and viewing movies at home.

Companies such as eBay and Netflix don't just cling to their optimism and write off the problems that do crop up as a cost of doing business, however. Over time Internet companies collect so much information that unusually high losses among a very small set of customers stand out and trigger an investigation and other consequences. All Internet companies have become increasingly sophisticated at identifying signs of fraud or illegal activity, often by using software tools. At eBay, we monitored our seller and buyer feedback to find patterns of unhappy users, and that some-times led us to fraudulent operators we had to shut down. At Net-flix I have read about odd cases where, say, a rogue postal worker steals Netflix DVDs in large numbers—the fraud revealed in part by the community, when multiple customers in the same region report that their disks aren't arriving. I think eBay and Netflix have shown that you can engineer smart, effective antifraud mea-sures without making your customers feel like they have entered a maximum-security prison.

I choose to believe, especially during the difficult economic times that our country has confronted recently, that realism is vital, but cynicism and negativity are deadly. I believe that inspired individuals can change the world. If the founders of eBay, Netflix, and many other Internet-based companies had had a dour and suspicious view of human nature, they never would have bothered to start these enterprises. It would have been too easy to fret that the few would ruin everything for the many. As Jeff Skoll notes, "If you set the right tone from the beginning, like Pierre did and like [Netflix CEO] Reed Hastings did, and you give good people a chance, they will figure it out."

At eBay, Pierre's beliefs about trust and transparency aligned with my own personal values and with how I choose to behave as a leader, but I had never thought about being so explicit in communicating them as *corporate* values. Pierre showed me that choosing to view our community as full of good people who generally wanted to create an honest place to do business was essential to our enterprise. So I ran with that notion. It became deeply woven into our culture—a fundamental component of how we treated one another internally as well as how we treated eBay users and partners. If someone sent a customer or a colleague a flame (Internet slang for a nasty e-mail response), we'd say, "Wait a minute, hold on. How would *you* feel if you received this?" This is not just a trite lesson in e-mail etiquette. When you believe people are basically good, your starting position in a conflict is that you have a misunderstanding that you can probably resolve, not that you need to intimidate or hurl insults. When you show respect, you become partners in seeking a solution. If eBay users didn't believe we were reading their feedback and learning from it, they wouldn't have given it and we would have been the poorer for that. If we'd replied defensively and shut down discussion, people would have bailed out.

Companies develop a tone and personality all their own, and it starts at the top. Every time I fly Southwest Airlines, I marvel at how the personnel of that airline so consistently demonstrate an attitude toward their jobs and their customers that stands out among the airlines. The vast majority of Southwest employees are friendly and energetic, and they do not treat their passengers as some kind of necessary evil. It would be easy to gloss over these qualities and believe that Southwest is just good at hiring particular personality types for the job. I don't buy that. You can't assemble an army of consistently friendly, energetic, customer-oriented people simply through screening. Rather, I believe Southwest executives live and breathe the value that their customers are valued partners, not simply flying wallets. They model this attitude, and employees come to see it as the right way, the only way, to behave. The upshot is that they create an experience in which even when the plane is late or there is some inconvenience, the customers are more patient; we see the Southwest flight attendants working hard to solve problems and we trust that they are doing their best. This is a triumph of management, and I believe it underscores the power of trust.

Good values are never a guarantee that you won't have setbacks and challenges. I know Southwest has recently grappled with some maintenance issues, for instance, but it's been my impression that they have addressed them in a forthright and open manner. Johnson & Johnson's immediate, full-scale response to the Tylenol poisoning in the 1980s remains a model of ethical corporate behavior. And I remember working in the field as a sales trainee at Procter & Gamble when the first reports linking a new P&G product called Rely tampons to a potentially lethal condition called toxic shock syndrome appeared. In those days we did not have e-mail or cell phones; I recall getting a paper note in my mailbox in the office that essentially said to every salesperson (and there were many thousands): "Drop everything, go to every account large and small, and pick up every single box of this product, from shelves, from storerooms, from trucks, and refund the retailers' money." This was not just about corporate liability. I admired the urgency management conveyed in making our customers' safety a priority.

RECENTLY I DISCOVERED a bit of family history in Google's repository of out-of-print books: a book titled *A Brief Outline of the Business of William Whitman & Co.* Originally published in 1910, it talks about a company started by my great-grandfather William Whitman. William came to the United States from Nova Scotia in the 1850s at the age of fourteen. He was a penniless immigrant who had run away from home and found work in a textile mill. The textile business was booming in the late nineteenth century, and after only a few years he started his own company, which served as an agent for major mills along the eastern seaboard and grew to be quite large and successful. Written by his son Malcolm, the book goes into detail about everything from grades of cotton to the mercerizing process, and it is illustrated with photographs of sour-faced alpaca sheep and woodcuts of ladies sitting at spinning wheels. But this comment in the beginning of the book struck me: "The successful development of the business is due largely to the co-operation of our friends among buyers, consumers, and associates. If this little book will help to promote that spirit of co-operation and to spread its influence among new friends and associates, it will have served its purpose."

There is something very eBay to me in those words. I think it's probably safe to say that nobody ever accused William Whitman of being soft or New Agey. The textile business was a competitive, intense, and difficult one and it took a lot of determination, shrewd strategy, smarts, and sweat for a young guy still in his teens to succeed as William did. But I think those words convey something very fundamental about business and life that perhaps we've lost sight of. Success happens when good people with good intentions cooperate and work together over a shared interest. Believing that people are basically good is what fuels most inspired individuals. Cynics and pessimists do not change the world.

My own father, Hendricks Hallett Whitman (he went by Hal), taught me a great deal about the power of a shared sense of purpose. During World War II, my father was in the U.S. Air Force, stationed in Guam. He was a big man (six foot eight) who didn't fit in fighter plane cockpits. Instead, he managed the Air Force's supply chain in Guam—behind-the-scenes work that was also critical.

They kept track of the assorted jeep tires, ball bearings, sleeping bags, wrenches, radios, fuel, cables, sacks of potatoes, giant drums of peanut butter, and bundles of boots that ultimately are as necessary to any war effort as guns and ammo. My father was a low-key person with a warm, fun personality. He did not take himself too seriously, but his dedication and his stories about the Pacific Theater always impressed me. Like so many of his contemporaries, he was happy that the Allies had triumphed, of course, but what came through so clearly was not chest-thumping pride but pride in serving in the larger cause. I recall my parents talking about people who had actually pulled strings to get their sons *into* the military in World War II, young men who otherwise would have been 4F for nearsightedness or other health issues.

I'm not sure I quite understood how deep these feelings ran in my parents until I saw their dismay at the Vietnam War protests in the 1960s and early 1970s. I recall my dad's utter bewilderment at the idea that people were not rallying around the president at a time when the country was at war. By the end of the war I think my parents, like so many people of every generation, were confused and uncertain about our nation's experience in that devastating conflict. But it was clear to me that it saddened and upset my father not to see the sense of shared national purpose that had been his experience of war.

ANOTHER IMPORTANT POWER of Many force I have witnessed firsthand is philanthropy. I had a unique window on Americans' extraordinary generosity when I was running eBay, and I remain convinced that philanthropy is an important component of any company's efforts to truly build a community.

One pioneering move we made at eBay followed Jeff and Pierre's desire to have our community share in the benefits of our initial public offering. Initially, we debated different ideas, such as sharing stock with our largest-volume users or returning some share of profits to them. But ultimately, we settled on assigning pre-public stock to the eBay Foundation, which turned an investment we took as a $1 million charge to our earnings into an endowment of more than $30 million once we went public. Many other companies, including Google and Salesforce.com, have followed this model. This is satisfying for so many: the recipients of grants, as well as a company's management and employees, who want to feel engaged with their communities.

The eBay Foundation is only one of several avenues to what eBay came to call "global citizenship." The others are deeply connected to the actual marketplace community, such as World of Good, which helps artisans from around the world—people with limited resources who cannot easily reach a global market—sell their handiwork on eBay. MicroPlace uses eBay's PayPal platform to help people invest in helping the world's poor through micro-loans. But the most extensive, ongoing philanthropic project is eBay's Giving Works program. Giving Works has raised nearly $140 million for 17,000 nonprofits since 2003; it does so one used bike, one celebrity-autographed handbag, one commemorative poster at a time. Warren Buffett, CEO of Berkshire Hathaway, has been eBay's "anchor tenant" on Giving Works for several years; every year he auctions off a lunch date with himself to benefit the Glide Foundation in San Francisco, which offers food, clothing, and other basic services to the city's low-income and homeless residents. In 2009, for example, the winner paid $1.68 million to bring seven friends to lunch with Warren and pick the brain of one of the world's savviest investors (not to mention one of its most decent human beings).

Giving Works "is now one of the largest engines for philanthropy in the world," says Bill Barmeier, who has overseen eBay's global citizenship projects for several years. Instead of a huge endowment, its grubstake is the generosity of millions of people—those who post items for sale and those who seek out items that benefit a charity to buy. The company allows community members to donate all or a portion of the proceeds of a sale to a nonprofit, and eBay waives its listing fees on the portion that goes to charity.

The origins of Giving Works go back to that extraordinary spirit of generosity after September 11, 2001. I was on a business trip in Japan on September 11. Maynard Webb, then our technology chief and COO, later recounted for me the surreal quality of that day. Within hours of the planes hitting the first World Trade Center tower, Maynard got a call from our Trust & Safety division saying that someone had tried to post rubble from the scene on eBay. Maynard immediately vetoed it; by then we had a firm policy that we would not allow items to be listed that would allow sellers to profit from a disaster. But by the end of the day, New York governor George Pataki was on the phone, saying that he had people who wanted to auction items on eBay and send the proceeds to benefit the victims. We quickly realized that was the right thing to do.

On my return, I saw a spirit of can-do sweep through the company. We worked with Governor Pataki and decided to launch something called Auction for America. It involved two parts: Web pages where people could donate directly to any of seven funds set up to aid the families of victims and others impacted by September 11, and a format that allowed people to post items on eBay and earmark the proceeds for charity. The coding required to launch this program on our site was, as we say in the tech world, nontrivial. That is computer programming talk for "hard." These were not our typical auctions; the proceeds were sent not to sellers but to a special account managed by what was then our online payment service. Based on the sheer volume of elements we had to assemble and the time it had taken us to finish similar projects in the past, it should have taken at least six weeks.

It took seventy-two hours.

Within 100 days, we had raised $10 million. More than 230,000 items were listed by individuals ranging from children who created group art projects to Governor Pataki and New York City mayor Rudolph Giuliani, who donated a photo of Joe DiMaggio and a baseball signed by Yogi Berra, respectively. Jay Leno donated a Harley-Davidson decorated with celebrity autographs, and just about every company you can think of donated food and other items, from Taco Bell quesadillas to Levi's jeans.

For me, this was a flashback to what my father had told me about the spirit of the country during World War II. This was the Power of Many. We had been attacked, and it was time to get in line and do whatever it was that we could do. It was our way of helping those whose lives had been irrevocably changed by the events of September 11, and it was our way of standing shoulder to shoulder with the troops about to be shipped off to defend our freedom and safety.

That feeling of having a responsibility to our community to do the right thing continued. When Hurricane Katrina hit in 2005, our technology gave us a unique window on how it was affecting our community members in the region. We could pull up a computer screen that showed transactions by geographical areas, and what we quickly saw was that we had some highly valued partners in New Orleans whose trading and sales had just gone off the radar, either because their computers had been washed away or because they'd had to abandon their homes. We felt a very strong desire to do something for these folks who made their living on eBay and had been so brutally blindsided. We made an instant decision to drop $1,000 into each of their PayPal accounts; it was the best million dollars we ever spent. I know that act was deeply appreciated by the individuals whose lives were impacted, and it brought our company together.

I am not talking about these things to blow eBay's horn. In fact, eBay's leadership rarely talks about these efforts. I believe they speak to the larger point that companies and communities that are organized around shared interests naturally look for ways to put their energy and resources toward positive ends. When they team up, everyone benefits. It is true that these endeavors brought new buyers and sellers to eBay and that in the long run we benefited financially from the new or deeper relationships that emerged from them. But we did not organize these efforts to get publicity or drum up business. These efforts reflected our values: people are basically good, and good people help each other out during difficult times. Not unlike my great-grandfather's company, which so wished to promote the spirit of cooperation, I believe any business or community's best chance to harness the Power of Many begins with this foundational value.

2

*Try something. The price of
inaction is high.*

It was midsummer 1999, and Griff and I and the boys were in
the car, all packed for a long-promised weekend trip to Yosemite, a four-hour drive ahead of us. But I had to do one thing
first. We made a detour to San Jose International Airport, and while
the three of them got something to eat, I dashed to the Admiral's
Club to meet a man and convince him to help me save eBay's life.

It was just a few weeks after that critical, twenty-two-hour
system outage at eBay, and I was scrambling. We had some very
talented engineers, but I could see that we needed to hire someone to fundamentally overhaul the entire computer system so that
we could deliver the service we promised and continue to grow.
The trouble was, I had never worked in the high-tech industry. I
did not know the players or exactly how to evaluate what I needed.
What I knew was that neither our community of users nor our investors was going to put up with these system failures for very
much longer. So not long after the outage, I called a leading technology executive recruiter and said, "You must find me the very
best person in the world to help me."

She identified Maynard Webb, then the chief information
officer at San Diego–based Gateway Computer, a high-flying PC

company with $8 billion in revenues. I quickly learned that Maynard was well known among all the major hardware and software companies, such as Sun and Cisco and Oracle, and that he knew how to design and run big systems. Unfortunately, Maynard had joined Gateway from Bay Networks only months before, and he had just hired a global team to implement his vision there. The Gateway job was a fantastic opportunity for him, and on the phone he told me he was not interested in moving. But he had agreed to meet me at the airport to give me advice about how to solve the problem.

Maynard has a low-key, soft-spoken demeanor, but he is fiercely competitive and loves a challenge. The minute we sat down over coffee and I described not only the problem but also the growth at eBay that was causing it, his eyes narrowed and I realized that his mind had engaged. It was one thing to have a big, ugly system problem to fix, but quite another for the root of it to be such enormous and profitable growth in a company's business. The opportunity instantly captivated him. "I'm such a sick puppy," I've heard him say many times since. "I just love a big problem."

We talked and talked (Griff and the boys kept circling the airport and calling every twenty minutes for an update), and by the time we parted a couple of hours later, I could tell that Maynard wanted to do it. Over the next few weeks, I not only hired Maynard but had to ask him to do the unreasonable, almost the unbelievable, in order to get him to eBay and up to speed in time to face Wall Street analysts at a meeting where we had to convince them that our system problems were under control.

One hurdle was that Gateway's CEO, Jeff Weitzen, was so proud of having Maynard on his team that he refused to accept his resignation! Maynard finally prevailed, but Jeff wanted him to stay for at least one more month to help smooth the transition. When Maynard told me that, I literally gasped. Though it was not at all unreasonable for a high-level position, there was no way we would be able to wait that long and still make enough progress to show the analysts that we were on track.

I then did something really desperate. I called Jeff Weitzen directly and said, "Jeff, this is my problem, not yours, and I know that. But I am in such a world of hurt here, you *must* let Maynard come to eBay by Friday." He was so stunned by my direct appeal, he just sort of said, "Uh, well, okay." I'm still not sure why that worked.

As for Maynard, he jumped his own tall buildings. His children were in grade school, and in order to make a school enrollment deadline in Los Gatos, where Maynard wanted to live, he had to buy a house before August 31, which was just a few weeks after our initial meeting. So he flew up from Southern California, did a quick tour with a real estate agent, put an offer on a house, and bought it without his wife ever seeing it. When she arrived a few days later with the kids and actually liked it, Maynard joked to me, "Turns out the place even has a view. I never noticed that. I just thought it didn't suck."

Maynard arrived and went straight to work. We were scheduled to meet the analysts on a Monday morning, and a group of us gathered to refine our presentation in eBay's offices Sunday afternoon. The stakes were high. We got the presentation done, but as we were walking out the door, the system crashed yet again. The other two technology guys with us had to present in detail the next day, while Maynard was new and was simply going to be introduced as our, well, savior. So I told the other two men to go home and rest and asked Maynard to stay and figure out the problem. He worked with the team, got the system back up, and finally left the building at 4:30 a.m., thus living up to the savior part of things. Eventually he would become our chief operating officer.

Maynard's reputation alone sent a very strong signal to the

analysts that eBay was headed in the right direction. But as you can see, from day one Maynard rolled up his sleeves and jumped in. Every day at eBay, he later said, was like "changing the engines on a jet fighter while flying it." He organized the team to create a backup system that insulated our users' auctions from disruption even as we conducted deeper system upgrades. Before he joined us, Maynard had known us mainly as "the ugly baby on CNN." Eighteen months after he came on board, our system had become so reliable that we hardly ever got questions about it anymore.

Both that I succeeded in convincing Maynard to come to eBay and his success have their roots, I think, in a trait that he and I have in common: what businesspeople call a "bias for action."

eBAY NEVER WOULD HAVE PROSPERED as it did without a team with a strong bias for action. We were born and grew up quickly in a fractious, often unpredictable, fast-changing virtual boomtown. At that time, the dot-coms—a term that simply applied to companies looking to make money online—were all lumped together, and investors were so excited about the seemingly boundless possibilities of the "new economy" that they bid up to dizzying heights the shares of even the most speculative start-ups that went public. The whole country was fixated on this bold new online world taking shape in Silicon Valley. But inside eBay, we had a keen sense that this was a time of transition. This superficial attention was going to fade. The online world was not going to remain separate and distinct from the land-based economy for long. We could not be passive and expect our value to increase simply because investors were entranced with the dot-coms.

We realized early on that the real game was not competing with other Internet companies for Wall Street's attention but rather making eBay a powerhouse in the future of what people were calling e-commerce. E-commerce was going to become a big part of all commerce. We could see that major retailers, consumer products companies, real-world auction companies, car dealers, and all kinds of other established entities would eventually go online in order to do significant shares of their business more efficiently and effectively. To prosper in that transition, we needed, at minimum, a rock-solid technology platform. But that was only the beginning.

As fast as our original U.S. auction business was growing, we knew we could not close our eyes to other opportunities to stake out profitable and sustainable new ways to grow. The best companies are always poised to develop or buy complementary businesses in order to create revenue streams that can reduce their reliance on any single aspect of the business. I tried to lay that foundation early. In 1999 alone, the same year as our major outage and the same year I recruited Maynard, we began to expand overseas, opening country-based eBays in the United Kingdom, Germany, and Australia. We also launched eBay Motors to capture the surprising demand from customers for an online marketplace devoted to trading used cars and car parts. We bought the traditional land-based Butterfield & Butterfield auction company. New opportunities popped up constantly, and new competitors saw specific efficiencies they could bring to online commerce.

After watching eBay's early success, for example, a start-up called Half.com realized that commodity-like goods with a well-known value, such as books and music CDs, did not tend to attract many bidders in eBay auctions. That didn't mean people were uninterested in buying and selling them; they just didn't want to bother joining a low-incremental-bid auction for them. To attract those users, Half.com created a well-designed site where sellers of the same exact item offered, essentially, a "buy it now" set price based on the condition of the item. Instead of bidders competing, in other words, *sellers* competed to offer the item at a price people were willing to pay. For example, a buyer could call up a page on which all available editions of *Alice in Wonderland* were offered, where prices might range from 75¢ to several hundred dollars, depending on the specific edition, the illustrations, the condition of the book, and other variables.

The founders of Half.com were clever: they made a deal with a small town in Oregon to rename itself Half.com, thus grabbing national media headlines and launching with a bang. They began to grow quickly and amass "network effects," or growth momentum related to the Internet's ability to accelerate what we used to call "word of mouth." Once network effects take hold, they can be formidable for a competitor to stop.

Half.com's arrival got our antennae buzzing. I figured that while auctions were the heart and soul of eBay, we needed to expand beyond them because (a) some people just didn't like auctions and (b) there was money to be made selling goods that were, for whatever reason, less well suited to auctions. We were about to start experimenting with our own "buy it now" format, but we didn't want Half.com to steal the momentum and network effects in this hybrid space between eBay and Amazon. So in 2000 we bought Half.com. This is still a good business for eBay, and today it has a large share of the market for used textbooks.

Dozens of opportunities like this appeared every month. Considering so many options at once could have been paralyzing. A flotilla of management consultants could have spent months studying each one. For example, before we started expanding internationally, we were not sure whether the way we organized eBay was something that would have to be radically altered to fit the idiosyncrasies of each country or culture. Would we have to completely redesign the site for each new country? We decided we could not spend too much time studying the question, that we had better just jump in and see what happened. It didn't take long after we moved into the United Kingdom, Germany, France, and Italy for us to realize that eBay's basic marketplace platform worked just about anywhere because we didn't have to predict what would sell—the users populated the site with merchandise that appealed to that country's people. Instead of baseball cards, so popular in the United States, Italians collect elaborately decorated phone cards, for example. In France, merchandise related to the *Tintin* comic strips, featuring the adventures of a reporter and his little white dog, is very popular. In Germany, many people bid up Kinder eggs, chocolate eggs that contain a toy surprise (a product that would be illegal to sell in the United States because the FDA prohibits hiding nonedible items in confections).

The acquisitions we made and the swiftness of our expansion into foreign markets show the advantages of a bias for action. But although a bias for action is necessary, it is not sufficient for success. It has to be paired with other analytical skills and management techniques, such as iteration, which I will talk more about later. It has to be rooted in such bedrock values as focus and listening and a relentless fixation on delivering results. And before you take a big risk, you have to be sure to ask not only "What is the worst thing that can happen?" but also "What is the *best* thing that can happen?" By asking both questions, you make sure that the potential value of what you're about to do corresponds to the risk so that you're not just making a change for change's sake or taking a big risk for a modest payoff.

There will be times, of course, when you do all that and still blunder. But I believe that a bias for action is essential in conveying a sense of urgency that focuses the company and its community's energy.

Sometimes that sense of urgency is supplied by an outside

force. The Power of Many efforts I described in the last chapter are good examples of that. A military campaign might be spurred by an attack; philanthropy might spring from a natural disaster or the pain and suffering of an unmet medical need. In business, however, a bias for action is about a leader moving an organization quickly to capture opportunities, knowing full well that mistakes will be made but that the organization can adjust and fix mistakes and ultimately be more successful than it could have been by waiting for conditions to be perfect. The way I usually put it is, the price of inaction is far greater than the cost of making a mistake.

You do not have to be perfect to be an effective leader, but you cannot be timid. I took on some daunting challenges in my career, and not all of them were successful. As I'll explain, however, I usually learned lessons from the failures that would become invaluable later in my successes. My decision to leave Hasbro and join eBay in the first place was a leap of faith that plenty of my colleagues thought was startling. But those who knew me well knew that a bias for action is part of my personality, even my upbringing. In fact, the person who first taught me the value of such a bias for action is my mother, Margaret Whitman.

WHEN JOURNALISTS who have written about me refer to my "Boston Brahmin" background, it always brings a smile to my face. I know the image such a term suggests: formal, perhaps uptight, society people, and a mother whose days are spent figuring out her outfit for either lunch or a charity ball. And in my family tree there *are* some characters who resemble those stereotypes. For example, my great-grandfather William Whitman—the textile entrepreneur I talked about earlier—had transformed himself into a wealthy Bostonian by the turn of the twentieth century.

My mother, now eighty-nine years old, grew up in Boston, the daughter of a successful attorney. But the image I most cherish is a photograph of her in coveralls, hands dirty, leaning under a hood and greasing a huge truck engine. It was taken during World War II, during which she spent four years in New Guinea, fixing trucks and airplanes.

Both my parents served in the South Pacific. My father, Hal, as I've explained, served in Guam. My mother volunteered for the Red Cross and they sent her to New Guinea, where the plan was that the women would wind bandages and dab wounds in the infirmary. "I wanted to help, be part of the war effort," Mom explains today. "I put down on the form that I wanted to be in the South Pacific, but they first sent me to Washington, where I thought I was going to have to spend at least a year in training. Then all of a sudden, a few weeks later, I was on a troop ship headed for New Guinea."

When she arrived in New Guinea, the local base was desperately short of mechanics. Mom volunteered to learn. By the end of her four-and-a-half-year tour she was a fully certified truck and airplane mechanic (and ever since she has always been the first to lift the hood of the family car or van).

When she returned from New Guinea, my mother discovered that her mother—my grandmother—had gone into a deep depression. My mother's brother Cushing had died in the war. He was a mariner in the U.S. Merchant Marine and he had contracted a tropical disease that eventually took his life. My grandmother had retreated to her bedroom and closed the blinds. So my mother grabbed her mother's address book and began making telephone calls. She decided to hold a series of dinner parties to try to pull my grandmother out of her slump. And one of the guests, as it turned out, was the man who would become her husband.

My parents already knew each other before the party. My mother had known my father growing up; their families were friends. As children, "I don't think he liked me and I didn't much like him," she claims. But she knew he was a fun dinner guest and a great storyteller, so she called him and explained the situation, adding, "Hal, this may be one of the worst dinner parties you've ever attended, but Mother's in a bad way and I've got to have people who can keep the conversation going."

Mission accomplished. In fact, missions accomplished. The gatherings gradually drew my grandmother back to life. And my mother started dating my father. The wedding was six months later. (It's probably good that my mother had some time to readjust to civilian life before the wedding. It seems that four and a half years of working on truck and airplane engines had enlivened her vocabulary. She still tells the story of one of the first luncheons she attended upon her return, where she turned to the proper Boston lady next to her and blurted out, "Pass the [expletive] butter.")

My father had expected to run the William Whitman & Co. family business when he got back from the war, but he returned to learn it had been sold. Instead, he ended up in a branch of financial services called factoring. In an echo of his vital but unglamorous wartime service, factoring is a vital but unglamorous cog in the engine of commerce. Factoring companies buy the receivables of a manufacturer so that the manufacturer can continue to afford making products while retailers are selling them. The factoring company then takes over the task of collecting the payment. A factoring company's success lies in buying the right receivables from creditworthy retailers.

Mother and Dad lived in Boston for several years, but he was transferred to his firm's New York City office before I was born, so by then we'd moved to Cold Spring Harbor, a former whaling village on Long Island's North Shore. We led a very happy, comfortable, normal, unfancy life. The party of the year for us was the

Fourth of July, when my very tall dad would dress up like Uncle Sam in full topcoat and striped red pants and march in our community's little parade. He was so tall and lanky, in fact, little children often assumed he was on stilts and kicked his shins!

My father didn't talk much about his work, but I think he was good at it and enjoyed it. He commuted an hour each way every day so that we could live in the country, and he spent a lot of time on the weekends with us, practicing all the sports we played, beating us at tennis. I would go bodysurfing with him on the south shore of Long Island at Jones Beach. He took great pride in his lawn, and I would help him pull weeds and mow and fertilize it. My dad, who died in 1991, was a wonderfully supportive, kind, fun man and an extraordinarily good sport. But he was not the member of our family with the bias for action.

When I was six years old, my mother and her best friend, Judy Gardiner, convinced their husbands to buy them each a Ford Econoline camping van. And off our families went—five Gardiner children and three Whitman children (my older brother, Hal, my older sister, Anne, and I)—on a two-van, three-month camping trip around the United States. We left June 1 and arrived back home September 1. No cell phones, no GPS, no movies in the back of the SUV, no reservations, only the outlines of an itinerary. No men (except for a two-week stretch where the two dads flew out to San Francisco, drove to Yosemite, and spent their vacations with us). We were eight kids, two women, a bag of maps, board games, playing cards, fishing gear, sleeping bags, tents, ice chests, bags of food, and a stack of mystery novels.

We had the time of our lives. We went to Yellowstone, the Grand Tetons, Glacier National Park, and Mesa Verde, Arizona. And we spent a huge chunk of the trip in California, visiting Disneyland (I *loved* the spinning teacups), the La Brea tar pits, the redwoods, and Monterey. We woke up one morning in Yosemite, realizing we had slept under the majestic watch of El Capitan. We waded into the Pacific Ocean. We read like fiends.

In the back of our van, Anne and Hal played a game starring me as a little pig being prepared for the county fair. Hal was the farmer and Anne was the farmer's wife, and they'd fuss and prepare me—braiding my hair and telling me how pretty I was. I would always win first prize. That was the good part. But then . . . well, we all know what happens to prize pigs. Anne would hold me down and Hal would whip out the souvenir Daniel Boone rubber bowie knife he had picked up at a roadside stand. My wail would go up: "Mooooooooom!"

Mom, pretending to be surprised at this turn in the story, would pull over. "Hal and Anne, how many times have I told you that you are not to slaughter your younger sister?" She would make us get out of the van and run alongside it while she drove slowly on, until we got tired. My brother would complain the loudest and have to run the longest. She said, "Every time you do this, you will have to run." That did not deter us for one minute, and tiring us out served her purposes as well.

My mother's bravery in setting out like this astonishes me to this day—as does the sheer amount of hard work and tolerance for dirty laundry that such a trip demanded. This is the kind of trip that probably sounds like it tells better than it lived. Well, don't say that to my mother.

The next summer, we did it again. Same families. Only this time my mother and Judy decided to make the three-thousand-mile trip from the East Coast to Alaska on the Alcan Highway (many miles of it unpaved). And just to make it a little more interesting, we set off just three weeks after my mother had a hysterectomy, after doctors found a tumor in her uterus. We kayaked and we saw the Mendenhall Glacier, Nome, Kotzebue, and Ketchikan. This time the dads met us in Juneau for two weeks. Again, we had the time of our lives. And ever since, my brother, Hal, has brought me all sorts of little pigs—glass, ceramic, metal—to remind me of our great cross-country adventures.

But my mother wasn't done with adventure yet.

A few years later, after Anne and Hal went off to college and with my departure looming, I think my mother was feeling a little uncertain about her own future. She was not the sort to play bridge or lunch or garden. She had kept herself busy raising us and supporting us in our endeavors, and she served our community, but she had a restless spirit.

The opportunity arrived out of the blue. A friend of my mother's was supposed to accompany the actress Shirley MacLaine on a trip to China. Shirley had been invited to bring an all-women delegation of "regular" Americans to see all the changes taking place there, especially since President Richard Nixon's visit to China the year before had led to a thaw in relations between the countries. Shirley was going to make a documentary, and she wanted to assemble a variety of American women—young, middle-aged, liberal, conservative, professional, artistic—and explore China with them, learning about what was then a largely closed society. Shirley had been preparing for months and had a diverse group of women assembled, among them a Texas housewife, an African American woman from Mississippi who'd been active in voter registration drives, a twelve-year-old girl, a psychologist, and a Navajo social worker. My mother's friend was supposed to be "the Republican."

Well, something happened, and suddenly Mom's friend couldn't go. She called my mother and said, "They need a rock-ribbed Republican who can wear a Peck & Peck suit"—a classic, tailored look for conservative women of the day. "Would you be interested?"

"I'd love to go," my mother immediately said, consulting no one. "When are they leaving?"

"Ten days. If you want to go, you need to go into the city and meet with Shirley MacLaine."

"Okay," my mother replied. "Who is Shirley MacLaine?"

A day or two later, she picked up my best friend, Hilary, and me at school and announced that we were going into the city. It fell on us, the sophisticated and worldly duo that we were, to tell Mother about *The Apartment*, *Irma la Douce*, and Shirley's other wonderful films. We parked in front of Shirley's building and Hilary and I waited in the car. Up she went. For an hour or so, Shirley and the woman who would direct the film with her, Claudia Weill, interviewed my mother. In Shirley's book about the trip, *You Can Get There from Here*, she writes:

> Margaret Whitman . . . was the last to be chosen, but certainly not the least. . . . Margaret, arriving from Long Island, swept into my New York apartment as if she were about to ride to the hounds. "You're taking me with you," she said firmly. "My name is Whitman and I'm just what you're looking for. I'm conservative, tweedy, self-sufficient, and way over thirty." I liked her—after all, she *insisted* on it.

My mother was very excited when she got back in the car but she did confess one thing: she still wasn't sure which of the two women was Shirley MacLaine.

Shortly afterward, my mother, at age fifty-four, left for four weeks in China. They covered two thousand miles, mostly by train. They visited schools and farms. They met Chou En-Lai's wife and they even saw a Caesarian section, performed with acupuncture as the only anesthetic, seemingly without pain. Their trip became the basis for *The Other Half of the Sky: A China Memoir*, a documentary film that was nominated for an Academy Award in

1975. It was fun to see my mother on the big screen: good-natured and energetic, albeit skeptical about some of the "programmed" aspects of the trip, designed by their Chinese hosts to impress the group.

The experience changed her life and, indirectly, mine as well. In the years that followed, my mother would learn basic Mandarin and return eighty more times to China, leading tours and delegations. Imagine how tempting it might have been in the first place to say: "Ten days! Why, that's not enough time to get ready. I've never met these people; what if I don't like them? China under Mao—is it safe?" Instead, my mother headed off on a bold adventure, perceiving that the price of inaction would be far greater than the cost of making a mistake.

EVERY LITTLE COMPANY dreams of growing up and becoming a big company, but that transition always comes with a cost. The hard part is to get big while also holding on to the best parts of being small. In other words, you need to retain a bias for action and keep looking for new ways to innovate. Cisco's CEO, John Chambers, sometimes says that a company must be willing to "eat its own young" and quickly abandon investments or strategies when conditions change. There are many examples of companies or even entire industries that have become big and slow and stuck. The U.S. automobile industry is one. In my own career, I worked for several companies that battled inertia.

In the 1990s, I was a senior executive at Disney, which before my arrival had nearly collapsed from paralysis. Founder Walt Disney had died in 1966. However, for more than *two decades* the management of the company ran things by looking in the rearview mirror and asking each other, "What would Walt do?" Walt Disney was a creative genius and a risk taker, and when Disneyland opened in 1955, it was incredibly novel and exciting. The term "an E-ticket ride," born in the early days at Disneyland when rides were graded and priced by their excitement factor, even became part of the vernacular, meaning thrilling and top-notch. But over time, even though many people went back to the parks and there was always a new crop of children who loved the characters and the cartoons and movies, Disney parks became stale. That relentless "It's a Small World" song and its faint background beat of animatronic clicks became a sort of joke about how tedious aspects of the park had become. Disney's movie business had stalled out as well.

Enter the dynamic duo of Frank Wells and Michael Eisner in 1984. What they did so brilliantly was hold on to the core of creativity and magic that meant Disney, while also investing in new ideas, technology, and people with a bias toward action in order to reawaken the brand. One of the first things they did was "open the vault" and start more aggressively marketing the classic movies that children loved. They put them back in theaters and released them on videocassettes. The company had tried to protect the value of many of these properties by keeping them scarce, showing certain movies only every few years. Why? Children loved those movies. They loved watching them over and over, in fact.

Wells and Eisner overhauled the Disney theme parks, improving rides, brightening up the parks, improving the food, upgrading the merchandise, and even opening new parks overseas. They also increased admission prices. They recognized that people felt a deep emotional connection to the parks and were willing to pay more to go there so long as the experience was a good one. They invested in new animated movies with amazing musical scores that really captured the Disney magic, such as *The Little Mermaid* and *The Lion King*, and in turn created rides, shows, and merchandise based on those products. Eventually they invested in all kinds of computer technology to make the animation experience even more thrilling and realistic.

And, by the way, they did all this in a business culture I have often described as a nonstop rugby match. I don't think the most obstreperous guest at a Disney park has ever been treated as roughly as executives at Disney treated one another. When I worked there it often seemed like pure testosterone flowed in the drinking fountains. The simplest disagreement in a meeting would escalate to a shouting, arm-waving confrontation in which nobody would ever back down.

The truth is, the company needed the jolts of energy and aggressiveness that Frank and Michael made happen. Frank in particular became a real mentor to me—a man with high standards and great integrity who drilled deeply into every idea and proposal to make sure it was solid. Frank would pull me aside and tell me, "You are just as smart as these guys. Speak up. Take them on. Don't let them intimidate you."

When Griff took a job in Boston in 1992, we moved and I left Disney. Tragically, Frank died in a helicopter crash in 1994. Years later, after I had joined eBay and the company was doing well, Frank's widow, Luanne, called one day out of the blue. She said, "I just wanted you to know that Frank would have been proud of you." That meant a lot to me.

Another paralyzing development for many companies is when some kind of competitive or external shift changes the rules of the game and they are unable to adjust swiftly. It might be a competitor's innovation or just a change in consumer desires or habits. That is what happened at the company that I joined after I left Disney—Stride Rite. It was actually a very interesting business problem.

When I was a child in the late 1950s and 1960s, there was a

strong feeling, promoted by pediatricians and by the shoemakers of the day, that children's shoes needed to provide stiff support to growing feet. It was considered almost a medical intervention, something on the order of vaccinations. Shoe stores sometimes even had X-ray machines designed to show a mother the architecture of her child's feet through a screen, and the clerk presumably would then recommend a particular arch or some kind of shoe custom-designed for that child.

The upshot was that Stride Rite became a leader in selling hard-soled school shoes. Often called bucks, they could be white or two-toned saddle shoes made of leather or suede. They were stiff, and they had a hard composite rubber sole. They were de rigueur for most schoolkids. As I recall, they were actually quite comfortable. When it was time for gym class, children and teens would put on their Keds, simple sneakers also made by Stride Rite, or perhaps Converse basketball shoes.

By the 1970s, however, the sneaker manufacturers became more aggressive in their marketing and advertising, and children grew more and more attached to their sneakers. Despite some early protests from companies such as Stride Rite, pediatricians gradually backed away from the idea that hard-soled shoes made a difference to the proper development of a child's feet. The notion evolved that we had all been overthinking the importance of hard-soled shoes. Sneakers were fine.

The upshot was that Stride Rite's business began to shrink. Nike, Adidas, Reebok, and other athletic-shoe companies created new styles and poured money into promoting and advertising them. Young people wanted those shoes, and as their parents began to get more involved in organized fitness, so did they. In the early 1980s, Reebok built a huge business selling soft glove-leather sneakers for aerobics to millions of women.

Stride Rite was caught flat-footed. It had positioned itself as the shoe mothers trusted, a brand image that led in part to it becoming the shoe children wore grudgingly. The brand began a long, slow decline that we had to scramble to try to reverse when I joined the company in the early 1990s. The company had not reacted quickly enough to the surging popularity of sneakers.

Finally, I want to mention Procter & Gamble, which offers an example of how a committed leader can reignite a spirit of innovation and energy in a company that has grown huge and slow. I have always had so much respect for Procter & Gamble, beginning when I was a brand assistant fresh out of business school and extending most recently to my term as a director from 2003 to 2009. P&G owns brands that an overwhelming percentage of people trust for the most basic activities of their lives—brushing their teeth, washing their hands, doing their laundry, cleaning their countertops. The company estimates that people around the world use their products *3 billion* times a day. Obviously, the company achieved that size and that huge portfolio of familiar brands by doing something right, and when I joined the company in the early 1980s, there was no better place in the United States to learn consumer products marketing.

As time went on, however, the momentum slowed down. P&G became bureaucratic and known for having a "not invented here" mentality. When A. G. Lafley took over as CEO in 2000, he vowed to make the company a leader in innovation again. "We were trying to do too much, too fast, and nothing was being done well," he wrote in his 2008 book, *The Game Changer.*

As I observed firsthand as a board member, A.G. insisted that "new and improved" become a mind-set, not just a slogan. He began looking outside the company for exciting new products and ideas to buy, and he began preaching that every employee throughout the company should think about new ways to innovate, not only with products but also with processes. His central message was to keep the customer's desires at the forefront of product development rather than inventing things and then trying to convince people to buy them.

I think so much of his success was setting the right tone at the top. P&G executives pay attention, stay alert, keep listening. In my experience, they are not smug. P&G today has a wonderfully active product development group that is constantly talking to customers about their lives and looking for ways to use interesting technologies to make people's lives better.

One of my favorite recent examples involves their diaper business. In the 1960s, P&G revolutionized the homes of parents when it introduced Pampers to the United States. It grew to be one of the company's most successful product categories, and the company kept creating what are called "line extensions." One newer P&G product is the Underjam brand: pull-up diaper pants with a flat profile that protect older children who may be struggling with bed-wetting or just the occasional accident as they mature. An estimated 5 million school-age children wet the bed, a situation often beyond their control because of issues such as how deeply they sleep.

In marketing this brand, P&G took another important step as well. The company created a website where parents can get support and information about bed-wetting. P&G helped create a community whose interactions go beyond the product the company sells, a community that takes on a greater power to help its members deal with this challenge than any of its members could possibly wield alone. This is Power of Many thinking from a company founded in 1837. It brings together an important need, a product with clear functionality, a trustworthy brand, network effects, and support for families dealing with the challenge this product addresses.

Unfortunately, embracing new ideas and being on the lookout

for new ways to relate to customers grinds to a halt in many large companies. The tendency as bureaucracy balloons ever bigger is that you create layer upon layer of management that is always afraid to say yes. Even when individuals don't say no, they say, "Well, let's wait awhile. Let's study this more." Or "Let me wait until I figure out what my boss wants to do." As a leader, you have to fight this mind-set twenty-four hours a day. You have to create a culture where yes isn't a scary answer.

How do you do that? Well, the first tool is hiring the right people. I often think about the huge contributions Mike Jacobson, eBay's general counsel, made to the success of eBay. He was there from the beginning and is there still. As most CEOs can attest, the measure of a great general counsel is not his or her ability to make a list of potentially disastrous consequences every time you want to do something. That is not so hard to do. Lawyers are uniquely equipped to scare people to death, CEOs included. The great general counsel, on the other hand, deeply understands what you want and need to do, and finds a way to make that happen legally and efficiently while still protecting the company from as much risk as possible. Time and again in a world where the rule book had not been written and where the law was trying to catch up to the action on the Internet, Mike would figure out how to keep eBay on the right side of the law and our own values, but still innovating in exciting ways. When we bought companies overseas there were so many elements that could have prevented us from getting the deals done—nothing nefarious, just the complexity of foreign laws, communication gaps, misunderstandings. So often, Mike zeroed in on the key issues and showed a great knack for bringing the parties together for mutual benefit. He had a bias for action.

THE SECOND incredibly powerful tool a leader can use to inspire people to say yes and develop a bias toward action is understanding when and how to emphasize iteration. Iteration is a business tool that is very common in the engineering and design world. It is the process of developing by improving. We used iteration all the time at Hasbro, where our toy designers would mock up new ideas for the Potato Heads or Star Wars toys. They might start with a wide variety of options, and then in subsequent steps we would zero in on the ones that offered the best combination of fun and acceptable production cost. Iteration acknowledges that we will not invest the time or money to take an initial idea out to the fifth decimal point of polishing. The prototypes in the early stages were not perfect, just polished enough to convey the essential ideas the designers were playing with. The message from management was clear: do the best you can within a time frame, try it out, see what happens, then improve it. But iteration is tricky. As I will explain, it exists in something of a creative tension with strategy and vision.

When it comes to new product development or certain kinds of marketing where the parameters are fluid, I very deliberately do not ask people to be perfect. In fact, I'm more inclined to say that in these realms perfect is the enemy of good enough. For example, when we were experimenting with launching city-specific listing sites at eBay, I would repeatedly find my teams arguing over fine points and stalled out trying to make it perfect. I would listen to the challenges they perceived, but there was always a point where I would say, "Okay, I hear you, I get it, it's hard. Now, I want this up in two weeks. Do the best you can. We'll see how it goes and fix whatever isn't working. If we wait to try to anticipate all the problems in advance, the cost of that delay will be too high. We will learn much faster from trying it out."

Iteration makes sense when you talk about it, but it can be

hard to manage it in practice. It requires, in fact, a very specific management style, and it is important to develop an entire culture that understands and supports iteration. The danger is, if you convince people to iterate but you then attack them or allow others to take potshots at their first efforts, the exercise can fall apart. People go back to holding out for the perfect solution, and you lose time and the ability to craft a solution with the input of more stakeholders.

When you are inventing something from the ground up, a bias toward action and an understanding of how to use iteration to learn more, faster, is crucial. It's important to sketch out a logical plan and to articulate for employees where you think the company is going and how they fit into it. But at the same time, you have to keep one eye on what your customers and partners are telling you and how they are reacting to what you are doing. Don't wait too long to roll things out; don't perfect every idea to the nth degree. You may take some criticism for changing your mind, but you will get where you want to go and be more successful by acting, iterating, and improving than by sitting back trying to predict and perfect everything in advance.

The limits implicit in iterating sometimes unleash other forms of creativity. Giving any team unlimited time or resources to do anything rarely produces the desired results. I learned this at Disney. It takes a strong stomach to manage the production of feature films, in part because they are notoriously vulnerable to unexpected glitches that can cause delays and budget overruns. A film demands the high-paid services of all sorts of professionals, from actors to sound engineers to special-effects technicians. A large crew shooting on location can end up twiddling its expensive thumbs when inclement weather cancels shooting, a key actor is injured, or there is some kind of equipment problem. Sometimes a budget overrun is just unavoidable. If a typhoon wipes out a set you've built in Thailand for a big-budget film and you have shot only half the scenes, well, you have to rebuild it. But other issues can cause delays and run up the tab, including a director's desire to add new, expensive sets or effects in midstream.

Michael Eisner was very tough in the face of requests for new funds. He not only was determined to manage costs but also believed that forcing directors to rely on simpler moviemaking techniques rather than expensive locations and special effects sometimes made the product better. The gist of it is, you have this much money and this much time, and you'll have to figure out how to do the best job you can.

Capable, creative, passionate people have a tendency to seek a perfect or near-perfect outcome. At eBay I found this to be a particular issue with software programmers and systems engineers. They hate to let go of something when they know it is not 100 percent what they want it to be. Unfortunately, that path is just too expensive, and sometimes it undermines the larger goals of a project. A new set of features on a website is not graven in stone; you can launch the site and keep improving the features. Forcing the members of a team to do the best they can within limits can lead to something of very high quality that moves an enterprise forward and can be continually updated and improved. Limits focus us. A bias toward action paired with iteration can get you much farther than a fixation on perfection from the get-go.

THERE ARE TIMES when you cannot rely on your own internal resources to develop a capability or product that your company needs to grow. The most successful acquisition we made during my tenure at eBay was the purchase of PayPal, an online payment company that brings secure, efficient payment capabilities to most e-commerce businesses by arranging for the transfer of funds from a buyer's bank account or credit card account to a seller's PayPal account virtually instantaneously.

The situation with PayPal was interesting, because early in its life it claimed what businesspeople sometimes call a "first-mover advantage" over eBay. One could argue that eBay did not move quickly or sure-footedly enough in this area to avoid paying a hefty price to buy PayPal; I would argue, however, that the situation was far more complicated than that. Not only did this deal eventually work out spectacularly well for eBay, it showed the importance of using a bias for action to make proactive moves and to fix situations quickly when they are not playing out as you hoped.

There is a presumption of competence and innovation that comes with establishing a reputation as the leader. Investors, potential partners, and even customers pay attention to pioneering companies. For an online business, this situation can unleash what I already have referred to as network effects. Network effects occur when a critical mass of users of a site or a business begin to actively recruit other users, in part because the value of the experience grows as it gets bigger. In other words, the more people join the network, the faster even more people join the network. Decades ago, network effects fueled the growth of the telephone. But online it can happen so much faster. Today, network effects fuel the rapid growth of social sites such as Facebook and Twitter; the more people you know who use those services, the more valuable those services are to you, and so you help recruit more people to join. It's a virtuous cycle. Network effects fueled eBay's popularity in the collector community early on. The more buyers and sellers of a certain category of goods were on eBay, the easier and more efficient it was to trade those goods, and so the early adopters recruited friends and associates, which in turn increased the value of the site to everyone using it.

Back to how we ended up buying PayPal. Around 1999, we

realized there was a point of friction in eBay transactions: the moment when users paid for goods. Once the bidding on an item was over, the buyer had to send a check or money order to the seller. People had to go through the cumbersome process of getting a money order at a bank, or they had to write a check and put it in the mail. The seller had to wait for the payment to arrive and then wait for the check to clear before shipping the item.

We knew we wanted to offer our community a more efficient payment system. Our initial solution was to buy a credit card processing company called Billpoint, with the idea of integrating a payment system into eBay auction pages. Billpoint had developed some technology we could incorporate into the site, and we struck up a joint venture with Wells Fargo Bank, one of the more innovative banks of the day, to handle the back-office transfers of money. We were deliberately cautious, however. We were wary of trying to become a financial services company on top of everything else we were doing. Also, we had to deal carefully with the security and fraud issues.

Soon after we bought Billpoint, however, we were struck by the growth we saw exploding in our new eBay Germany operation. We had acquired a small German online auction company called Alando. Germany has long stymied the overtures of American retailers. Walmart, Staples—the list of American companies who have established overseas stores in many other places but could never penetrate Germany is long. There was a number of intriguing reasons why. Until fairly recently, for example, German stores could not stay open at night or on Sunday afternoons. They also could not hold sales or discount products. That was why, when we started eBay Germany, it took off like an absolute rocket. Suddenly people could trade anytime they wanted, 24/7. And for consumers not exposed to discounts, it was possible to actually win an auction and feel like they'd gotten a good deal. Germany was the fastest-growing of all eBay sites.

We also realized that a key driver of our growth was the German payment system. It was the only country in the world where electronic funds transfer was in wide use. People were comfortable transferring funds not only from a bank account to a retailer's account at the point of sale but also to other individuals' accounts. If you bought your neighbor's car, for example, you did not need a certified check; you could simply transfer funds from your account to his. For German users of eBay, that meant that a transaction could be financially completed soon after the auction's end and the seller could ship the product immediately. That motivated people to bid and buy more frequently.

However, around the same time, a very smart pair of entrepreneurs, Peter Thiel, who ran a small investment firm, and a computer scientist named Max Levchin, launched a company based on technology that let people actually "beam" each other money using their then very hot Palm handheld devices. Their idea was that this system, dubbed PayPal, would literally help you pay your pal. If you went out to dinner and split the bill, one person could pay and the other could "beam over" his share. They imagined that the currency exchanged would exist in a PayPal account and you would leave a balance in there to cover various expenses.

PayPal was a company of extremely aggressive people with a real bias for action. Its inventors soon realized the big opportunity was not in miscellaneous person-to-person transfers but in becoming a payment currency for online transactions. It didn't take long for them to figure out that the biggest and fastest-growing group of people doing online transactions was at eBay, and that PayPal could ease the payment friction I mentioned above.

Beginning in 2000, PayPal moved very aggressively to recruit eBay users, even paying a cash bounty to new users: $5 to anyone who signed up and another $5 if the person referred someone else who signed up. The company added users in our community with phenomenal speed. Meanwhile, it was taking longer than we had wanted to get Billpoint ready for prime time. One irony was that PayPal moved forward with the eBay philosophy that most people were likely to be basically good, so they didn't focus on fraud and bad debt. At this stage, however, we knew that while most people were good, sophisticated fraud networks and even organized crime were moving into cyberspace, and a small group of bad actors could wreak havoc if they penetrated a financial payment system. We hired executives from the banking industry to run Billpoint, and they took a bank's typical posture, namely, that you qualify everyone coming in the front door before you give them an account. But that more cumbersome process was off-putting to customers, including eBay sellers, whom PayPal welcomed with open arms, just a few clicks, and a little cash spiff to boot.

We tried some strategic marketing efforts to woo more customers to eBay's payment system, but I could see that our users liked PayPal better. It had a great brand name; not surprisingly, consumers liked a name with *pal* in it a lot more than a word with *bill* in it. What's more, we were trying to integrate our acquisitions and expand internationally; our marketing battles with PayPal were becoming distracting and expensive, and we weren't sufficiently closing the gap.

I suspected we were going to need to buy PayPal. I started making overtures to Peter Thiel and to PayPal's primary venture investor, Michael Moritz of Sequoia Capital. Eventually we got together three or four times, sometimes at my kitchen table.

I knew PayPal was pulling away from Billpoint in terms of the percentage of transactions it handled. The trouble was that PayPal was still a very early-stage company and a very high-risk play. This was a form of extreme iterating on their part. I didn't want to overpay, especially since I knew PayPal was going to require considerably more investment to make it more secure and to fix its notoriously poor customer service. First they wanted $500 million. I said I'd go no higher than $300 million. They walked. We watched.

A few months went by, during which they kept adding customers at an impressive rate. They came back to the table and said, "Okay, $800 million." Again, however, I had concerns about the fraud situation and I worried about the distraction that buying PayPal could pose for eBay. I said, "How about $500 million?" No deal. We kept watching. One benefit of PayPal doing business on eBay auction pages was that it created transparency for us: we could keep close tabs on exactly what was going on.

A few more months went by and PayPal announced it was going to go public in the very uncertain climate after the September 11 tragedy. On the eve of that offering, we went back to the table. They now wanted $1 billion. I offered $800 million. We came close this time, but ultimately, they decided to take their chances in the public market.

I knew what I wanted, but this was a very high-risk decision. Despite their exploding customer base, PayPal, unlike eBay, had never been profitable. Worse, we had deep concerns about their ability to safeguard their system. We knew PayPal had lost tens of millions of dollars to fraud and bad credit when various foreign mafias and other hackers exploited gaps in their system. In fact, PayPal had come very close to running out of money, but they engineered a key private financing before it went public. I was still worried that PayPal could become a huge management distraction during an already challenging time.

Almost miraculously, given the larger economic climate, PayPal did go public, but the stock started bouncing up and down very erratically. The PayPal brand had terrific traction, but as a stand-alone company it had to confront a lot of complex regulatory exposures, plus the uncertainty of being so dependent on a third party—namely, eBay. Although the price kept going up, that did not put us off because our confidence in the value of the company was growing. They had fixed many of their fraud vulnerabilities, for example. What we'd done was let PayPal investors foot the risk and the investment that we otherwise would have had to make in fraud protection and better systems, and which might have distracted us from other projects more critical to eBay at the time.

Finally, in July 2002, Peter proposed $1.5 billion (a modest premium over where the stock was selling) and I said, "Sold." At the time, that number represented roughly 8 percent of eBay's value. It turned out to be a spectacular deal for us.

We would have liked to make Billpoint work, and we tried. However, having a bias for action means that when it becomes clear that your first inclination is not working, you cannot stubbornly cling to the original plan. You have to be willing to change course and move, to fight inertia. You cannot let a spirit of "not invented here" dominate your thinking or you will be left behind. We backed Billpoint when it was a close horse race, but when PayPal's lead lengthened and it finally appeared they were conquering some of their security problems, we had to change our thinking.

Today, PayPal is a global leader in online payment solutions: as of the third quarter of 2009, it had 78 million active accounts in 190 markets and 19 currencies around the world. PayPal logged more than $17 billion in total payment volume in that quarter and now is handling about 10 percent of all online commerce. In fact, PayPal is growing so rapidly in off-eBay transactions that it might someday be even bigger than eBay in terms of total revenues.

WHEN YOU HAVE A BIAS for action, you sometimes will try things that don't work out. I believe that if you're a CEO and some of your ideas and bold moves don't come up short, you're probably not the right person to lead the company. In a competitive environment, you have to take risks. You have to place bets before you have all the information you might need to make the best possible decision. The trick is to be bold but not stubborn. Don't put on blinders or discourage realistic feedback about what is happening, and if you've made a mistake, fix it fast.

I have said publicly many times that one of my great disappointments was eBay's inability to export our model as effectively in Asia as we had in other global markets. Yahoo trumped us soundly in Japan, and eBay continues to struggle in China, although it is true that, partly thanks to what we learned in China, we enjoyed success with eBay in Korea.

We had planned to move into Japan in the fall of 1999. We were poised to commit management attention and resources to launching a country-specific site, but after the eBay system's instability became untenable, I had to make a choice. I realized that we could not simultaneously overhaul our system architecture and make an aggressive move in Japan at the same time. The system demanded my full attention and many of the resources we would have needed in Japan. To move forward would have put the entire company at risk. That was a failure due to limited resources, not inaction, but it was a failure nonetheless. Yahoo launched its service in Japan and today controls the online auction market there. We made some smaller efforts but eventually pulled out of Japan entirely in 2002.

We made a different kind of mistake when we tried to storm China. The same year that we pulled out of Japan, we bought one-third of a company in Shanghai called EachNet, run by a fascinating young entrepreneur named Bo Shao. Bo was a math genius who had won a number of China's nationwide high school math examinations, come to the United States and studied at Harvard, and gotten his MBA from Harvard Business School. He worked in the United States for a few years, then returned to China to start EachNet, which he envisioned as the eBay of China.

China was important to me. The e-commerce market in China was projected to grow rapidly, and I knew this would be a competitive situation. In general, eBay's international expansion had followed a particular process that had worked well. We would go into a local market and buy one of the local online auction companies. After a period of making sure we understood the business and the local issues, we would then migrate the company over to eBay's site and take control. This had worked beautifully in Europe (with one intriguing exception in the Netherlands that I'll explain later), and our plan was to do the same in China. In 2003, we paid $150 million for the rest of EachNet, which then had commanding market share in online auctions, and we began plans to move the site onto our U.S. platform and run it from here.

The migration took some time, and almost immediately after we migrated EachNet to the eBay platform, we watched transaction volumes fall. At the same time, a competitor called Taobao, run by Chinese entrepreneur Jack Ma, became more aggressive in recruiting sellers. By early 2005, it was clear that we were rapidly losing market share and were in real trouble in China. I traveled to Shanghai to see what was going on and I brought along John Donahoe, the former CEO of Bain & Co., whom I had recruited to be president of our core business unit, eBay Marketplaces. It was obvious that the existing team in China did not know how to reverse the slide. I was very confident in John's abilities and in those of the team I had in place back in San Jose, so after seeing for myself what was going on in China, I did something most CEOs would never even consider: I decided to move to China for a few months to try to fix our situation there. I brought Maynard and a large team of smart people to China to help me, and we completely reworked the site, trying to give it a good hard kick in the right direction. I stayed for about three months.

But here's what I discovered, and it was something I never would have deeply understood if I hadn't moved there: we had made a fatal mistake when we bought out the rest of EachNet. By buying out Bo, we had taken him off the hook for figuring out how to make the site work. We had imposed a lot of our own design sensibility and page features when we migrated EachNet into eBay China, and it turned off the Chinese community. Users said it just "didn't look Chinese." We came to realize that some of the issue lay in the physical patterns of how Chinese read, right to left and vertically, while most websites are designed to be viewed left to right and horizontally. We had assumed, incorrectly, that our success in Europe could be transported to Asia, but there were inherent differences in the cultures that worked against us. When I finally realized this, we closed down eBay China and started all over again.

We realized we were going to have to be patient. If eBay was going to have success in China, it would have to be as a partner to a Chinese company, not as an American company operating there. We knew we had to let our Chinese partner manage the company and drive growth, because we were not going to establish a strong presence in China through force of will. We invested in a joint venture with a company called Tom Online, which is still playing catch-up to Taobao. This was an example where I believe the potential of the opportunity was enormous and so it justified taking the risk, even though it didn't work out. And based on that experience, we left the Korean auction site in which we invested, Internet Auction Co., in the hands of the local Koreans rather than migrating it to the U.S. eBay platform. That has proven very successful, and eBay recently moved to acquire a significant share of its Korean partner's main competitor, Gmarket.

REGARDLESS OF WHO you are or what you're doing, success demands action. Action alone does not guarantee success, but as basketball and hockey coaches say, "You miss 100 percent of the shots you don't take."

The difference between a competent executive and a superstar often boils down to the willingness to decide and to move forward, even when the path is not crystal clear. However confusing or hard or even paralyzing your circumstances might feel, the price you'll pay for treading water, dithering, not moving forward, is far higher than the cost of making a mistake. Make your best guess and move forward. Do something. Try something. The situation won't always work out perfectly. But you can always recalibrate and adjust later. I have experienced both failures and success in my career; I learned more from the failures, and what I learned invariably educated and empowered me to make decisions down the road that led to success.

3

Be authentic. You can't buy integrity.

When I graduated from business school at age twenty-three, I decided I needed to be taken more seriously. So I started calling myself Margaret. Okay, not exactly an extreme makeover. But every time I said it out loud, it didn't feel right. The sound of me saying it made Griff wince a little. Thankfully, my "serious" phase lasted all of two weeks. My mother is Margaret, but I had always been Meg. I'm still Meg. If I wanted to be taken seriously, I realized, I needed to focus on my performance, not my name.

I believe all of us have a built-in authenticity detector. It sends a little shiver of connection through us when a person says or does something that seems true to his or her nature. And it buzzes in a negative way when a person says something that comes across as false or forced. So when we are attempting to do something significant and inspire others to help us, our actions must reflect our true desires and values. Most successful people I know have a deeply authentic quality; what they have chosen to do in life aligns with who they are. The most effective executives model and live the same behaviors they demand of their organizations.

As we've discussed, there was no manual for how to organize or run a virtual marketplace such as eBay. We were constantly confronted with situations and dilemmas we had never imagined in our wildest dreams. It's precisely in those circumstances that doing the right thing matters most. That's when we must stop and ask ourselves: "Who am I? What do I stand for? Are my actions aligned with what I say are my values? Am I demonstrating integrity here?"

When I think about the lessons my parents taught me, the importance of integrity is at the top of the list. As I have said as often to my colleagues as to my sons, "If you are about to make a decision and you learn your mother will read about it on the front page of the *New York Times* tomorrow, will she be proud of you? Will your rationale make sense to her? If not, give it some more thought."

There was another dimension to what my parents both taught and modeled for me about integrity—one that was less simple but equally important: You will not always know the answer to every dilemma immediately. Values and choices can evolve. You don't have to take rigid positions and never let go no matter what. Having integrity means, among other things, listening and incorporating new information. This lesson would later be critical to the development of eBay's character as a company.

I mentioned my mother's trip to China and how it changed her life and mine. What came from that experience was her new appreciation for the importance of every individual pursuing his or her own course. Here is how it played out.

From a young age, my brother, Hal, was focused on becoming a doctor, and neither he nor anyone else seemed to question that that was his calling. I remember Hal as a very kind older brother, never dismissive or aloof like some teenage boys could be to their younger siblings, and he did indeed grow up to become a wonderful physician. I get to see him in action these days, as he, I, and our sister have formed a good team to take care of my mother, whose health issues have created a lot of physical challenges for her that we all do our part to help ease. Hal, who is a rheumatologist who practices in the New Jersey area, reminds me of my dad in many ways—he's a patient and good-natured person, deeply empathetic, a wonderful father to his twin sons, a conscientious family man.

There were no particular career aspirations laid out for my sister, Anne, and me, on the other hand. We both were good students (Anne studied at the University of Pennsylvania and later at Harvard), but my mother's attitude was that we'd probably be getting married, and then raising a family would be our primary concern. She did encourage us to get our teaching certificates, though, mainly so that we would have something to fall back on in case marriage didn't work out. Teaching seemed to her a good option that would motivate us to do well in school and provide a decent income.

I have no memory of questioning my mother's advice about that. I was a very strong student; I finished high school in three years and graduated as one of the top ten students in my class, and I planned to spend what would have been my senior year of high school in France, in hopes of becoming fluent in the language. But the idea that I might become a businesswoman or anything in particular was not something I thought much about. By the spring of my last year in high school, my exposure to the working world had been a summer I spent as the snack bar cook at a dude ranch near Cody, Wyoming, where I had gone to summer camp for a couple of years.

Adventurous as my mother was, she did not spend a lot of time challenging the prevailing social mores. She seemed to just accept that a woman's interests and education were likely to give way to her role as a homemaker. My mother once told me that my father did not realize until a couple of years after they married that she had gone to college. "It just never came up," she said—something I find utterly baffling. She was adamant that I get a good education, but her primary expectation was that I would marry and have children, with a teaching career as a sort of backstop.

Until she went to China.

In her book about the trip, *You Can Get There from Here*, Shirley MacLaine wrote this about my mother: "Among all of us, Margaret Whitman had been the most resilient. She had remained cheerful and energetic throughout the trip, revealing very little of the inner confusion she must have felt. The key to her self-control lay in her background. 'To control oneself under any and all circumstances was how I was raised,' [Margaret] said. 'But now I think I'll cut loose and really swing. I've decided I never really was a conservative person. I just thought I should be because everyone around me was.'"

I would not describe my mother's homecoming or post-China life as one of a "swinger," and she remained a rock-ribbed Republican, but I love the thought of my mother discovering her desire to follow her interests and curiosities at middle age. This trip was so exotic, so eye-opening for her. She had encountered women doing so many interesting things—not only the women in China, who were training for the same array of jobs as men, from airplane pilots to physicians, but the women in the delegation, especially the film production crew.

I think the trip prompted her to think about opportunities she had not perceived as existing for her when she was younger. After she returned, my mother sat down with Anne and me and said, "Because of this trip, I've seen women doing all sorts of marvelous things. Be a teacher if that's what you want to do, but realize that you'll have the opportunity to do anything, and you should do what *you want* to do." Because my mother had such a deep sense of integrity and honesty, she could adapt, incorporate new ideas, change her mind about what represented the best advice for us.

My dad once did a similar thing. He had smoked for many years, but when it became clear how harmful smoking was, he quit. And he took each of us kids aside and said, "I made a big mistake smoking for so long. I don't ever want you to smoke, because it will hurt you. If by the time you are eighteen you don't smoke, I will give you $1,000." He didn't try to cover up what he had done; he admitted he had made a mistake, focused on the danger of having set a bad example, and corrected it by setting a long-term goal for us. None of us ever smoked.

Of course there are absolutes. Lying, murder, cruelty, cheating on a partner, or harming others is always wrong. But in more complicated arenas, what represents the right thing to do sometimes evolves over time. Determining the right thing to do and adhering to values is not a stubborn undertaking. My mother had the confidence and sincerity to come to us and say, essentially, "Before I went on this trip, I thought I was giving you the absolute best, most helpful advice. Now I have new perspectives and I've revised my thinking, so I need to share that with you."

Bolstered by Mom's newfound enthusiasm for a world of possibilities, I set out to figure out just what my authentic passions would be. I started out in premed at Princeton. But I soon discovered that organic chemistry and I were not destined to make each other happy. Over time, instead, I found that I enjoyed economics, with its blend of math and its ability to describe real trends and human behaviors. And then I took a job selling ads for an undergraduate magazine at Princeton called *Business Today*. It was started by Steve Forbes, the son of Malcolm Forbes, founder of, yes, *Forbes*. I heard they were hiring advertising sales reps, so my great friend Meg Osius and I (our friends dubbed us "Meg-squared") signed up. From the beginning, selling ads flipped some kind of switch inside me. It appealed to my gregarious personality; I loved meeting and talking with businesspeople. And I liked that your success was generally a direct consequence of how hard you worked. You might be smart, creative, personable, and forward-looking, but what you needed most was an intense determination to cross that goal line and make the sale. I found that invigorating.

Meg and I once took a trip to Milwaukee to sell ads, and I came down with the flu. We had four or five meetings a day scheduled and there I was with a 104-degree temperature. In between meetings, I would lie down flat in the backseat of the little car we rented. Meg was determined not to go in alone, so at each stop I managed to crawl out of the back, comb my hair, focus on the sale, and do the meeting. Invariably, I felt better once I got in there. Then, as now, I found that doing business and achieving specific goals energizes me. It resonates with my personality, my curiosity, and my competitive nature.

Before long, I couldn't imagine pursuing a career in anything but business. One of my grandmothers used to throw "come as you wish you were" parties, and during my senior year, my roommates and I decided to throw one of our own. My roommate Carol Wallace came as the queen of England. Carol later cowrote the best-selling *The Preppy Handbook*, a tongue-in-cheek jab at the upper classes. Another friend, Nancy Broadbent, came in a kimono; she would later go to Japan and teach English. And my dear friend Linda Francis, whom to this day I have labeled in my mind as "the best mother in America," came as—what else—a mom.

I borrowed a male friend's three-piece suit, tie, and glasses and came as a business executive. I guess that sealed my fate.

SOMETIMES MY FRIENDS and I had trouble figuring out what it meant to be our authentic selves in a culture that was changing so rapidly for women. I was a member of the fourth coed class at Princeton, and women made up only a small fraction of the student body. The administration, the faculty, and the male students seemed to have no problem having us there. Yet odd resentments cropped up. During my years there, the Princeton alumni magazine ran letters from alumni who were still seething that the trustees had "ruined" the traditions of Princeton by allowing women to enroll. What an outrage that women were siphoning off resources intended to fully educate young men! It seems absurd today that such letters were taken seriously. I almost cannot imagine the thinking of the letter writers, some of whom surely had daughters of their own, in expressing such an old-fashioned position.

As my Princeton graduation approached, I applied to business schools. Many years later I gave a speech at Stanford University's Graduate School of Business, where the dean introduced me in glowing terms and said that his only disappointment was that I had not chosen to go to Stanford's GSB. "Well, I didn't get in here," I shot back; the dean blanched and the room erupted with laughter. But I did get into Harvard Business School, where again I was in a small minority of women. Even more daunting, I was younger than everybody else, having graduated early from high school and applied right out of Princeton. My first year of business school I lost twenty pounds that I did not need to lose from the sheer effort of working to compete.

At my first job after Harvard, at Procter & Gamble, I believe there were four women out of more than 100 people in the brand assistant class. And then three years later, when I joined Bain & Co., I was one of just a couple of women in my office.

I mention all this because I am often asked about my experiences as a woman in business, and I must admit that I always find the question a little difficult to answer. To begin with, having never been a man, I don't have a good point of comparison about how I was treated. I was never conscious of any overt discrimination that held me back in business. However, early in my time at Bain, I worked with a group of ambitious young men who seemed to be part of a club, and I did have some sense of not really belonging. They were bonded by their families' expectations for them and by their own expectations of a traditional businessman's life. I felt like a valued member of the office, but I was married to a surgeon and it undoubtedly irked some of my compatriots that they were competing for the best assignments with someone who might well drop out to have children or who did not "need" to work, as people used to say. As the odd one out, I guess I faced a dilemma many other women have faced: To what degree do you bend your life to fit the culture of an office that doesn't necessarily suit you? And to what degree do you stay true to what you really value and who you are and what you want to do? This wasn't a grave burden for me, but it was a dilemma nonetheless.

When Griff and I married, he was twenty-six and I was twenty-three. Throughout the early years of our marriage, he worked the brutal hours of surgical internship and neurosurgical residency. During the first six years, there were months when he was on call every other night—forty hours on and eight hours off—and during the one weekend in three he was off, what he needed most was to catch up on his sleep. We had very little time together, and so when he had some rare time off, the last thing I wanted to do was be on the golf course or socializing with colleagues from work. However, I could see that those times often provide opportunities to get to know team leaders or other colleagues better, and that can be crucial for being in the information flow of an office. I didn't want to be "one of the boys"; I just wanted to be in on the good deals, get the information I needed, or get the boys to work with me instead of at cross-purposes.

What I decided was that I would not make being one of the in crowd my goal. I would just try to be "in with" the in crowd. There's a difference. I didn't try to be like them; I just tried to be likeable and fun and very good at what I did. I believe that it's important to be fun to work with and easy to manage, but you can't just be likeable. You also need to produce. You have to excel at the tasks you're given and you have to add value to every single project, every conversation where someone seeks your input. I had to be true to my authentic self—not try to be something I wasn't, but figure out a way to work with people who weren't like me for whatever reason, whether they were men, or highly technical, or from another company that saw a consultant as threatening and not to be trusted. Learning that early in my career made all the difference. I prospered at Bain and I was proud that I was able to do that without being something other than what I wanted and needed to be.

I can't remember if the phrase "work-life balance" was in use in those days; certainly early in my career nobody ever gave much thought to helping fathers balance the demand of work and family. It seems to me there still was some expectation that many women were going to leave the workforce once they had children. But as busy as we were with our careers, as much as we loved our work, both Griff and I deeply wanted to have a family. And as it does for many energetic young couples, the decision to have children launched us down one of life's most unpredictable paths. One of the first steps was one of the scariest episodes of my young life.

In early 1984, Griff and I had flown to Birmingham for the weekend to see his parents. Sunday night he'd flown back to San Francisco, while I flew to Shreveport, Louisiana, to meet up with my Bain case team member, Dave McCarthy. Our assignment was a project for a Shreveport, Louisiana–based hospital. What nobody but Griff knew was that I was seven or eight weeks pregnant. We got to the hospital and Dave needed to make a call (this was before the cell phone era), so we walked to a bank of pay phones. As I stood there, a sort of fluttery wave suddenly washed over me.

I then passed out cold.

Dave tells me that one minute he glanced over and I was fine, and thirty seconds later I was sprawled on the floor. He quickly got help for me, and when the nurses revived me, the first thing I said was, "I'm pregnant." I recall the nurses looking at each other and calling for a blood pressure cuff. My blood pressure had completely collapsed. Minutes later I was in the ER and the doctor was explaining that I had an ectopic pregnancy and that my fallopian tube had burst. I was bleeding internally and needed emergency surgery. I asked Dave to call Griff, as well as my in-laws in Birmingham. I remember waving to Dave as they rolled me off to surgery and knowing that he would take care of what needed to be done.

When I emerged from surgery a few hours later, there were my in-laws. A few hours later Griff was there, too, thanks to Dave, who had booked him a flight before even talking to him.

An ectopic pregnancy is a frightening experience, but fortunately I healed quickly, and before long, I was pregnant again. Naturally I was a little nervous, but everything went fine this time around. Little Griff was born in San Francisco in February 1985. I had a wonderful maternity leave of three months, learning to care for my son and pushing him around the Bay Area in his stroller on lots of sightseeing outings with other young mothers. As the end of my leave approached, we hired a wonderful woman to care for him and I prepared to go back to work. I cycled through a lot of the emotions a young mother has when she has been thunderstruck by an adorable baby but also feels the pull of a job and a career she loves. I was fortunate that we were able to find a loving, mature woman who shared our family's values to take care of little Griff.

I remember on my first day back from my three-month maternity leave, the managing director of Bain handed me an assignment and my mind went blank. I simply could not remember how to do the analysis he had asked for. It was like parts of my left brain had fallen out and been replaced with pale blue flannel and fuzzy teddy bears. After my initial panic subsided, my analytical muscles firmed up. My husband and I gradually figured out the math of two working parents and a baby, and we achieved equilibrium— for a while.

Then I became pregnant with Will. The pregnancy was going along fine until about six months along, when I started leaking amniotic fluid. I was ordered to full bed rest (lying flat, not even sitting up; I could go to the bathroom but not take more than one shower per week). At first I actually tried to have some Bain team meetings in my bedroom, my colleagues gathering awkwardly around the bed. That didn't last, as two-and-a-half-year-old Griff would keep popping up and crawling into bed with me, demanding to watch *Lady and the Tramp*. I finally surrendered to meeting-free full bed rest; I learned the dialogue of *Lady and the Tramp* pretty much by heart, and Will arrived in good shape to join his big brother.

Now, here is some math that every mom understands: two kids are more than twice the work of one, especially when one is a toddler. I will not try to pretend that there weren't moments that made me wonder if I really could make it all work. It's never easy to find balance in life. Some women who have children and who have succeeded in business or public life say, "It's fine. Not a problem. I have help and it all works." I was fortunate to have the resources to have help, and I can promise you, it still doesn't always work.

When little Griff started preschool, I got a call from a woman who lived near us in San Francisco and wanted to set up a carpool. She was very friendly and said, "Well, I can drive Monday and then maybe you could take Tuesday, and this other woman near us could take Wednesday." I was a consultant at Bain and still traveling occasionally. I said the arrangement sounded good and would work most of the time but that I traveled once in a while for work and that my husband had a very early start on his surgeries. "There may be times when the woman who takes care of little Griff drives the carpool," I told her. "Is that okay?"

"No," she said in an icy voice. "I did not quit my job as a banker to stay home and take care of my children so that I could hand them over to someone else's nanny."

Wow. Had I really asked her for such a terrible concession? Did she honestly believe I was putting her child at risk? She seemed to take this as some kind of rebuke of her choice, though that's not at all where I was coming from. I think every mother can understand how and why this conversation ate at me for a very long time. We have to follow our own instincts in these situations; what works for me may not at all be the right solution for someone else, but we get nowhere by attacking each other. There are days when a working mom is miserable to have to leave her children; there are days when a full-time mom desperately craves adult conversation and challenges outside the home. The needle rarely settles on the "perfect" setting for more than a day at a time. Flexibility and a sense of humor are the only salvation.

Like many of my friends who look back on the days when they worked and had young children, I sometimes marvel at the energy it required for us to keep everything in balance. But team Whitman-Harsh pressed on, and over time we got back to a manageable equilibrium. My Bain colleagues were generally supportive and understanding—as long as I figured out how to get the work done. I, in turn, became more efficient—less watercooler chatter, laser focus on the day's agenda and deliverables. I still managed to laugh and have fun with my team, but barring full-blown emergencies there was a five-thirty hard stop at the end of my workdays; I had to get that work done, and I did. Sometimes being extremely busy and motivated to finish your work and get out that door makes you more productive and intensifies your concentration. Ultimately, the Bain culture was organized around results and full of smart, reasonable, fun people, and it fit me perfectly. I was promoted to vice president.

I have been asked so many times about being a woman in a man's world, and about how I dealt with sexism in the workplace. My short answer is that mostly I just focused on delivering results. I think that attitude was not uncommon for my generation of working women. My women friends and I had a sense that we were getting opportunities that previous generations of women had not, and we were determined to prove ourselves. It was not at all that we didn't care about equal treatment for women; it was more that we had a sense of not wanting to show weakness. We did not want to appear vulnerable to rivals who might say, "See, they aren't tough enough. They can't handle the heat." Many of us chose to focus on the work, on outperforming those who seemed intent on making our lives more difficult, rather than talking about sexism or fighting back directly. We had a sense of needing to prove our competence. Within a few years the numbers of women in the professional workplace increased, and of course we demonstrated ourselves to be just as competent as our male colleagues. Many women became more aggressive about identifying and trying to root out behaviors in the workplace that were inappropriate, which I think was a natural evolution.

Eleanor Roosevelt once said that no one can make you feel inferior without your consent. Be who you are, but don't be too quick
to take offense. One of the most helpful tools I used whenever I
faced any kind of put-down or thoughtless remark in this arena
was a sense of humor. Nothing better disarms a person who is trying
to attack you or make your life difficult (or even just being thought-
lessly rude) than the ability to smile and the refusal to get ruffled.

One of the funniest experiences I have ever had was in 2000,
the first time I attended what has become a very famous meeting
of CEOs, politicians, philanthropists, and investors in Sun Valley,
Idaho. It's called the Allen & Co. conference. There are a lot of
very interesting individuals from business and other fields who at-
tend: Warren Buffett, Bill Gates, Rupert Murdoch, host Herbert
Allen. It's a remarkable group and I always learn a lot from both
private conversations and the various panel discussions, but just
like at every other conference on the planet, whether with florists
or toy executives or statesmen, you get the same awkward moments
and social faux pas, occasionally born of one too many cocktails at
the mixer.

The very first year I attended, I did not arrive in time for the
opening-night events, so my first event was the second-day cocktail party. Spouses are invited to the conference, but Griff could
not join me until later in the week. I entered the room and didn't
see anyone I knew, so I did what you do in these situations: I
walked up to the first group I saw and said hello. I said my name
and the three or four men standing there said theirs. Most of them
were businesspeople.

The man to my right, however, was a prominent California
politician at the time. He smiled and introduced himself, then
asked me, "And who are you married to?" I could see that the other
men knew who I was, and they winced slightly.

"His name is Griff Harsh," I replied, smiling.

"And what does he do?" was the politician's reply.

"He's a neurosurgeon," I answered, still smiling.

He turned to the other men he had been talking to and demanded, "Since when are doctors invited to this thing?" I watched the other guys try to signal him with raised eyebrows that he should stop.

"Actually, he's not here," I said, watching him slowly become aware that he had put his foot in it. I finally bailed him out. "Oh, there's no reason you should have known," I said. "I'm the president and CEO of eBay."

He then emitted a strange sound, sort of like those underwater recordings of whales singing to each other. Then he threw his head back and searched the heavens for a tractor beam to take him away. I still laugh at this memory. People are always amazed I didn't get mad and set him straight. But it was so much more fun to watch this play out. As Mrs. Roosevelt said, carry on in the face of an insult and you'll usually triumph.

I realize that not everyone has the advantage I had in this situation. But this kind of archaic sexism seems pretty rare these days, at least in the higher echelons of business. There aren't enough women at the highest levels of corporate America, but most of us who have made it over time have come to be judged on the results we deliver, not how well we've done as women. The only other time at eBay when I ever experienced anything remotely similar was when Prince Alwaleed Bin Talal Bin Abdulaziz Alsaud of the Saudi royal family, who had become a significant investor in eBay, had a contact of his at Citicorp call me. The contact said the prince was on a tour around the United States and wanted to meet with me. I was happy to do it but sent word back that I would like to know what he would be most interested in—a presentation on the company's strategy, a visit to the tech center, perhaps a meeting with some users?

The word came back: "The prince would like to take the measure of the woman."

No problem. We had a great meeting, and I must have measured up, because he bought more stock. And my executive team had a good laugh and a go-to phrase for years to follow.

I DO NOT BELIEVE that a CEO can craft a culture that is fundamentally different from his or her own authentic values. If you talk about being open and listening but you bite employees' heads off when they don't agree with you, well, you are training them to only tell you good news and conspire to hide problems.

In many different companies where I have worked or consulted, I have found that a company's executives take on the personality and style of their CEOs. If the CEO yells, everybody yells. Years ago, if the CEO smoked, everybody smoked. If the CEO makes people wait all the time, it becomes a show of power down the chain of command to make underlings wait. If a CEO is secretive, a paranoid culture develops, with everyone constantly reading between the lines of memos and announcements for the "real" story. If a successful CEO is honest and straightforward, the company will evolve in that direction because people who prefer to operate in the shadows and manipulate information will leave.

Over time, the accumulation of these habits and styles, passed down from one CEO to the next, becomes deeply embedded in the DNA of the company. You cannot simply order them out of existence or issue a memo to change them.

As eBay grew in size and prominence, I found myself invited to be on the boards of a number of companies. This is very flattering for a chief executive, but you need to look at this, like everything else, as a strategic choice. Your time is limited. Board seats are an opportunity to learn as well as to serve. In 2001, I agreed to take a board seat at the newly public Goldman Sachs. Goldman Sachs, founded in 1869, was what the business press always calls a "venerable" Wall Street investment bank. For most of its history it had been a partnership, but CEO Henry Paulson and his partners had decided to take the company public. Some partners had fought this for decades, and the company remained 48 percent owned by the partnership pool and a small number of major investors. Nonetheless, they did sell shares to the public in 1999 and needed to build an outside board with credentials that complemented the existing financial services industry expertise already there. I have a lot of respect for Hank Paulson and for the bankers and analysts at Goldman Sachs and I was happy to join the board; I could contribute my background in running a fast-growing, technology-savvy company.

The way boards work is that the agenda for a meeting, which typically goes all day and sometimes part of a second day, is distributed in advance. At our first meeting there were a number of interesting items on the agenda, including one that was slated to take up our time for two hours. I had read the materials thoroughly in advance of the meeting and had some questions. After about one hour and fifty-five minutes of the time allotted for this topic, Hank Paulson finally asked us if we had any questions.

"Yes, I do," I said, and raised my concerns. That took up five minutes.

Hank looked at me and said, "Thank you for your comments. Now, our next agenda item is . . ."

I was furious. I got up, stood behind my chair, and put my hands on the sides of it, toward the top. "Hank, in the future, if you intend to put items on our agenda that are FYI only, that's fine, but please note that on the agenda. I really do not appreciate flying three thousand miles and putting the time into reading and analyzing these materials if you are just going to tell us what you intend to do and are not seeking our input. And by the way, if you do that and most of the items on the agenda are FYI only, I'm really not interested in being on this board."

Poor Hank was startled, to put it mildly, but he graciously apologized and devoted a few extra minutes to discussing my questions. But it was clear to me that going public had not changed the management culture at Goldman Sachs; they wanted to keep acting like a group of partners who did much of their discussion and decision making in private and then expected to get the board's rubber stamp. I lasted only a few more meetings before I resigned. It was going to take a long time for this culture to change, so I decided to move on.

I RAN MY BOARD MEETINGS at eBay very differently, and I considered the eBay board one of the company's most powerful assets. Not because it rubber-stamped my decisions—far from it. It was because I had put together incredibly smart, honest, individuals with integrity whom I trusted to help me figure out how to do the right thing in a brand-new world where there was no rule book. One of the things I always did with any weighty matter before us was to go around the table, asking every board member's opinion one by one. As in any group of people, some are more assertive and some are more comfortable speaking one-on-one with the CEO. I would withhold my opinion and make sure every board member stated his or hers so that we developed a tone of openness and responsibility on the board. Every person would be respected for what he or she had to say, but I also made it clear that opinions needed to be shared.

The other technique I used with the board was what I call my "parade of horribles." At some companies, board meetings are mainly a mind-numbing series of "happy PowerPoints." From the agenda and the demeanor of the CEO, you would think that all is sweetness, light, and ice cream. Invariably, though, board members get a tense, sometimes even panicked, call from the CEO on a Sunday or in the wee hours of the morning when a situation suddenly explodes. At eBay, I would keep the happy talk to a minimum. I didn't need my board's input on the happy stuff—I needed their help on the hard stuff. At the board level and throughout the company, I would always say: "Let's talk about problems when there is still time to fix them, not cover them up and hope they go away."

One of our first outside board members was Howard Schultz, the force behind Starbucks. Howard grew up in a housing project in Brooklyn, New York, and later became one of the world's most successful entrepreneurs. Howard joined the board in 1998 and brought a rare and very valuable quality to eBay. Howard is a person who thinks deeply about the relationship of a brand to the customer, the emotional connections and values shared. Starbucks' success was about much more than the coffee and food—it was about that "third place," as he called it. There was home, there was work, and now there was Starbucks, where you could relax, do personal business, do work business, duck in quickly, or linger all day. Atmosphere was important. When Howard joined our board, I think he was most intrigued by the community aspects of what we were doing and the trust and energy that our users showed every day. One of his most important contributions to eBay was in the category of helping us to develop our own sense of integrity, what he called the "character of the company." That turned out to be a far more complicated challenge for eBay than any of us anticipated.

Almost from the beginning, people put all sorts of quirky and unusual items up for bid on eBay that attracted attention and made us an easily accessible window on popular culture. When we went public, the vast majority of items were collectibles, but later there also was a jet that sold for $4.9 million and a jar purporting to hold a ghost. It is pretty innocent fun to have an auction for a "UFO detector" or a cornflake that inarguably appeared to be shaped like the state of Illinois. It was quite another when we realized that people were selling items on eBay of a much more serious nature: Guns. Tobacco products. Alcohol. Pornography. Drugs. Hate literature and items bearing swastikas. Counterfeit luxury goods. Items related to criminal acts, including murders. In one memorable case, a man listed his own kidney for sale; in another, a sixteen-year-old boy put his virginity on the block.

Some of these things were clearly illegal to sell under any circumstance—narcotics, explosives, sexual services, body parts, stolen merchandise. Our first vice president of marketing, Brian Swette, tells a great story of picking up the phone one day soon after he joined eBay in 1998, only to have a gentleman who sounded like a cast member from *The Sopranos* say, "Uh, my people have been taking a look at your operation and we'd like to set up a meetin' with you and our boss, Tony. Looks like we might be able to move some merchandise." After Brian told him eBay didn't meet with sellers to discuss things like that, the man replied, "Well, ya ought to think about that. Everyone takes a meetin' with Tony."

Some items were legal in some contexts and illegal in others. For example, there is a crazy quilt of regulations about shipping wine. In some cases it's legal to ship wine from state A to state B but not from state B to state A. Or consider event tickets. In most states, once you buy an event ticket, you can do anything you want with it. But in some states there are very specific laws about scalping that apply. Some outlaw resale of certain kinds of tickets completely. Others regulate them, allowing sellers to charge, for example, no more than a set percentage above the face value.

Then there were items that were not necessarily illegal but were bizarre or offensive. After a while, eBay became many reporters' first stop after some historic event or tragedy, because invariably some miscreant determined to prove that all people are *not* good would rush to post an item such as debris purporting to be from the space shuttle *Columbia* accident (handling such material was dangerous and actually did violate federal law). Certain items that had been traded only in the shadows suddenly debuted in the eBay pages—and shortly afterward in the media. Who knew there were people who traded used and unlaundered (what they called "custom") undergarments? Before eBay, I never had a clue there was a collecting fetish called "murderabilia" in which people collect the artwork of convicted murderers, as well as evidence or items purportedly connected to the crime. I will never forget receiving a call one day from the distraught mother of a girl who had been murdered. She told me, "My daughter's autopsy photos are for sale on eBay."

In Chapter 2, I spoke about iterating, and how sometimes you just have to move forward and then you adjust, alter, improve, refine. At eBay this happened with what Howard called our "character as a company." Not because there ever was a point where we didn't care about our integrity, but because we had no way of anticipating the sheer variety of ways it would or could be tested in this marketplace. Therefore, it took a while before we could figure out what we would and would not do in a consistent way. This was a function of scale. When millions of people start posting items for sale, if even a tiny percentage of them post weird or offensive objects, well, that can be a very long list of things. Someone once asked me if eBay put people up to posting sensational items in order to get publicity for the site. Never! When tens of millions of people are involved in anything where they are operating this independently, there is always going to be somebody doing something bizarre.

So, especially in the beginning, it was kind of a free-for-all. Remember, the site was automated. Nobody reviewed the items before they went up for bid. We would take down listings for obviously illegal things when people brought them to our attention, but eBay was not set up to screen items in advance.

For a while, our lawyers told us that we actually wanted it that way. Their position had to do with the Digital Millennium Copyright Act (DMCA), passed by Congress in 1998. The main goal of the act was to stop people from circumventing antipiracy software, but it had another important provision as well. The act said that a platform such as Yahoo chat rooms, where users could post protected content, or a site such as eBay, where someone might try to sell counterfeit or illegal goods, would not be liable for any of that content *as long as the company did not make it its business to selectively police the site.* The legitimate concern was that companies could not afford to get into the policing business—that it would be prohibitively expensive. And so Congress said, "Okay, we understand. If you want to be treated like the U.S. Postal Service or private transportation carriers, who simply provide a service without screening content, you will be shielded from liability—as long as you do not selectively put content up or take it down based on particular criteria." Congress was trying to sort out a messy collision of First Amendment rights, privacy rights, property rights, and criminal issues, not to mention potentially crippling costs for still nascent e-commerce companies.

Because of the DMCA, our lawyers felt that if we selectively policed eBay, we might become liable for illegal or fraudulent activity. For example, if we used software to detect and prevent the listing of fake Prada bags but we also knew there were counterfeit Rolex watches listed and did nothing unless Rolex specifically found those listings and complained, we might be liable.

From the beginning, Pierre wanted eBay to be an honorable, lawful place to do business, but he also believed in a simple premise: if it's legal to sell on land, it should be legal to sell on eBay. He explains, "I didn't see the Internet as some kind of separate place outside the boundaries of the physical world or beyond the reach of law. We needed the protection of existing laws. When certain kinds of behavior took place, I would remind people, you should file a police report, you should make a complaint. If the system somehow can't help you with that, we will work to change the system. . . . I would also say to people that if you don't like something being legal for sale online, then you should work to make it illegal for sale offline."

Remember, we were still a young company trying to build a stable system and to serve the 99.9 percent of our customers whose transactions had nothing to do with serial killers, body parts, or counterfeit Rolexes. But after the DMCA passed, the message from our legal counsel was: "We can't risk losing the whole company for that tiny fraction of items." This concerned me, but frankly I was not yet sure how to proceed.

Two separate situations eventually erupted and challenged us to demonstrate our values in more specific and proactive ways.

Several of the companies that made video games discovered that illegal, bootleg copies of their games were being sold on eBay. I understood their frustration with that and we tried to respond promptly to their complaints about specific listings. But they wanted us to try to screen for and even block the listing of the items in advance, and that was a problem. It was not clear how we could develop a screening mechanism that would distinguish between a bootleg copy of a video game and a bona fide copy that the owner had every right to sell. It was not as if a bootleg copy was described in the listing as "illegally copied version of Grand Theft Auto."

In early 1999, I went to a meeting with the CEOs of several of these companies. At that meeting, Larry Probst, the CEO of Electronic Arts, shared some disturbing information with me. A group of rogue game developers inside Electronic Arts had created a violent video game called Cop Killer. When Larry heard about it, he was offended; he canceled the project and ordered the code destroyed. However, he had learned that stolen copies of this game were appearing on eBay. Larry wanted my help in preventing the bootleg copies from being listed to begin with. He said, "Meg, you need to be proactive about taking these things down."

I explained my dilemma. I said, "Larry, this is terrible and I'm completely sympathetic. But according to our attorneys, because of the DMCA, if we start proactively policing items like this on the site, we could lose the whole company."

Larry looked me in the eye and said, "Meg, what is the right thing to do?"

I swallowed hard. I realized the first answer I had given him did not feel right.

I went back to eBay, and it happened that I had a board meeting soon after. I said, "Guys"—at the time they were all guys— "we've been operating with a particular interpretation of the DMCA, but I believe we have to change our minds about this."

I remember clearly that the first reaction was from Howard Schultz, then the CEO of Starbucks. He looked at me and said: "Meg, it's all about the kind of company you want to run. What do you want the character of the company to be?"

We decided to change our attitude about the DMCA and not use it as a shield. There were maybe 150 people working at eBay then, and I announced to them that we had shifted our position because we could not sit by and become the kind of company that didn't care if it was facilitating the sale of a game called Cop Killer. We began a much more concerted and aggressive effort to remove counterfeit and other problematic items from the site, even if we didn't have a legal obligation to do that.

Later, Howard Schultz played a critical role in another important milestone in eBay's development. Howard Schultz is Jewish, and a few months after the video game issue arose he visited Auschwitz. We were aware that items were beginning to appear on the site that carried swastikas and other Nazi symbols. There was nothing illegal about these items. Some—although not all—were marketed by neo-Nazi groups that clearly were advocating hate and bigotry. This had come up previously in our meetings and was of concern to all of us. But after he returned from Auschwitz, Howard called me and told me he simply could not rest unless he personally did something about the marketing of pro-Nazi material, and he said he was going to bring it up at the next eBay board meeting. He felt so strongly about this, he warned me, that if we did not act on this matter, he would consider leaving the board.

When we convened our next meeting, Howard presented his thoughts. When it came to board meetings, I did something else a bit unusual for CEOs: I always had the senior members of my executive team sit in on them so that the board could ask them questions. Howard's presentation led to an extensive debate that remained very respectful and professional. Everyone saw how deeply affected Howard had been by what he had seen in Poland. But what he was proposing ran against Pierre's original position that if something was legal for sale in the land-based world, it should be legal on eBay. Jeff Skoll, who also is Jewish, took the opposite view from Howard, arguing that eBay was a marketplace, not a retail store. Henry Gomez, our senior communications chief, warned us that if we started banning items, the list was going to become very long. He pointed out that virtually everyone has relatives who were killed or exploited by someone somewhere at some point in history. What about material related to other despots or repressive regimes? What about Ku Klux Klan material? We had legitimate collectors and historians who traded war memorabilia and books such as *Mein Kampf* for their historical value and even for the purpose of illuminating the horror of these ideas. Not a person in the room wanted to be in the business of banning books. The question was never whether we agreed with or supported these groups. What we struggled with was the classic dilemma of censorship: once we started doing this, where would we draw the line?

Recalls Jeff: "Pierre and I were concerned that it was straightforward to follow the law, but whose morality is the right morality?"

Howard listened intently, and then he said something that went right to everyone's heart. He said: "I don't know where you stop. It might be a slippery slope. But I can only deal with this matter right here, right now, on this board. And we should not be allowing this kind of hate-based material on eBay."

I think that was the moment when we decided that we were not, and did not want to be, just an unregulated swap meet. Pierre explains, "This was very difficult for me from an ideological point of view." But Pierre supported me in the decision I ultimately made to prohibit hate-based and other offensive items from the site, and pretty soon after he said that he realized that it was the right decision. "We realized that we wanted eBay to be cleaner and safer than the swap meet. The items might be legal, but they were borderline. Meg was exactly right, and I think over time our approach made eBay stand out," he says.

Eventually, all these kinds of issues came under the purview of our Trust & Safety department, which was charged with making sure eBay was what we called a "clean, well-lit place to do business." The staff of Trust & Safety set policy, monitored and policed the site, investigated complaints, and made sometimes difficult judgment calls. Trust & Safety also created sophisticated software, which continues to evolve, to screen for problematic material, and prevent fraud or illegal activities. Today, there are roughly 2,000 individuals working in Trust & Safety and in other capacities at eBay to protect our users.

Ultimately the character of a company, like the character of a person, is an accumulation of many, many moments when the choices are not necessarily clear and we make the best decisions we can. But over time the logic and reasoning that we use to make those decisions, the moral compass we choose to follow in making those decisions, is the essence of our authentic self, our character. If we hope to engage the Power of Many, because people are basically good, I believe that we must demonstrate that we care about doing the right thing. I don't believe that we need to prove that we are the ultimate authority on the right thing to do. Often our sense of what is right will evolve as we get more information. But we do need to be transparent in our attempts to understand the issues and the consequences.

At eBay we became very comfortable with the position that we were not going to hide behind the idea of free speech every time we faced something we knew was just plain wrong. I remember the day when the serial killer Jeffrey Dahmer's refrigerator showed up on eBay—the refrigerator in which body parts of his victims supposedly had been stored. I thought, "There may be no law against this, whatever this is, but as the CEO, I need to step up and declare that we are not in the business of prolonging the suffering of families whose loved ones were victims of this or other killers." The call from the mother of a murdered girl whose autopsy photos had appeared on eBay still resonated in my memory. We studied the matter and ultimately decided that out of respect for the families of victims, we would not allow the sale of items closely associated with notorious murderers within the last hundred years. To this day, eBay does allow items associated with, say, Jack the Ripper or Billy the Kid, because they are of historical value. However, eBay doesn't allow listings of evidence from a crime scene or memorabilia linked to modern serial killers. eBay also doesn't allow the listing of items that might allow the perpetrator of a crime to benefit financially from contemporary criminal notoriety, such as an autobiography.

I HAVE A SAYING that everyone who has worked for me over the last two decades probably recites in his or her sleep: "Right person, right job, right time." As we grappled with these difficult issues in the early years of eBay, there was no better example of right person, right job, right time than the former federal prosecutor we hired to take on the policing of our site, a talented attorney named Robert Chesnut, who was educated at Harvard Law School.

Rob had spent eleven years in Virginia prosecuting some of the U.S. government's biggest spy cases, including the case of CIA agent Aldrich Ames, in addition to other federal crimes such as bank robbery and drug dealing. On the side, Rob had an unusual hobby: he was a devotee of Polaroid instant cameras, the ones that spit out the picture right after you take it. Polaroid's business was a casualty of the digital photography age, and many models of cameras had been discontinued. Rob was always prowling garage sales and combing classified ads to beef up his supply of cameras and the special film stock. He read an article in a hobby magazine about how eBay was becoming a great place to find camera gear, so he came to the site and was stunned to find dozens of listings for Polaroid cameras, accessories, and film stock. He admits he was a little wary at first. "As a federal prosecutor, you don't always have a trusting impression of your fellow man," he laughs today. But sure enough, he sent his $50, and a week later his first camera purchased on eBay arrived as promised.

Rob became an active eBay user. Separately, he had been thinking about leaving government service for business. On something of a lark, in early 1999 he sent us his résumé with a cover letter making the case that he imagined a site like ours might need the services of someone with his experience as we grew. This was right at the time we were deciding to become more proactive in how we policed the site. The chance of finding the perfect employee for a specialized job from a letter that arrives over the transom is minuscule; however, I think we dialed Rob's number before we finished reading the letter. We flew him out immediately, along with his wife, Angela, and I took them out to dinner. There I learned that Angela was literally a gun-toting federal agent from the Department of Justice with a deep background in investigations.

In addition to some of the very public philosophical and policy dilemmas we faced, we were starting to find ourselves interacting with the law and lawyers in other ways you might not immediately imagine. For example, we were getting subpoenas by the binful: from manufacturers going after counterfeiters, from divorce lawyers trying to find records of what a party had bought and sold and for how much, and from individual sellers or buyers who had filed a complaint with eBay after they felt they'd been defrauded. I could see that both Rob and Angela not only had the kind of experience in law enforcement that we needed but were good people who cared about doing the right thing. I hired both of them.

Rob became our point man for the task of developing specific rules and technology to screen for illegal or inappropriate items being listed on eBay. This was completely uncharted territory. It was almost like dropping him into the middle of Manhattan with Peter Stuyvesant and asking him to write a penal code from scratch. The issues reached into almost every aspect of life and trade you could imagine.

For example, a huge category of concern was counterfeit items. It was easy to prohibit them as a matter of policy, but it was not easy to identify fake items or prevent them from being listed to begin with. Ultimately, we had to create software tools that analyzed the source and volume of certain kinds of items, comparing it to the distribution channels we knew were authorized by a given manufacturer. But in virtually every case a person would have to get involved in the investigation.

Another troubling category was the subject of one of the very first e-mails Rob received when he joined eBay. "I got an e-mail from a user I did not know that said, 'You are selling Jarts and you are all going to go to jail,'" Rob recalls. "I responded, 'First, I appreciate your e-mail because I am here in part to make sure nobody goes to jail. Second, what are Jarts?'"

Turns out Jarts are one of the toy world's dumbest ideas— those giant lawn darts from the 1970s that you were supposed to throw at rings on the lawn but which had a tendency to end up stuck in little brothers and tipsy partygoers. They were incredibly dangerous, and the Consumer Products Safety Commission had recalled them and banned their sale. The e-mailer was correct: it was illegal to sell them new or used. But what Rob instantly realized was that eBay often was a place where people listed items they found in their garages or attics. There were hundreds and hundreds of products that had been recalled through the years, so selling Jarts was likely the tip of the iceberg for all kinds of banned and recalled items that were dangerous but which the sellers might not even realize had been outlawed.

What Rob did next was not the easy thing but the right thing to do. "At the time, a lot of companies took a distrustful and defensive posture toward law enforcement. I thought that really didn't serve businesses' interests well. In general, because of my background, I knew that it was always better to contact a federal agency than to have them find you. I felt we should be open and proactive." With my blessing, he went to the Consumer Products Safety Commission and said, "We have a great business, but we have just discovered this is going on and we are concerned about it. eBay has no desire to sell banned or recalled goods. How can we work together to solve this?"

The commission was so pleased at Rob's attitude and his appreciation for their mission that we worked together to create a special website about the issue of banned items and what consumers should do with them. We agreed to take down any recalled goods the commission found on the site, and to invest in educating consumers about the problems that might be sitting in their attics. The head of the CPSC repeatedly used eBay as an example of a great public/private partnership, and Rob used the same approach with other government agencies, such as the FDA, when we discovered medical devices and prescription drugs being listed on the site.

Making eBay a lawful, safe, positive, global marketplace where all people were treated with respect sometimes meant turning away from product categories that could have represented very large revenues for us. For example, we decided that we would not sell tobacco, guns, or alcohol on eBay. Again, overlapping laws and jurisdictions made overseeing a legal marketplace in these items complex, but we also realized that it was impossible to control how those items would be shipped and by whom they would be received. We decided to put adult content in a special area that was clearly separate from the rest of eBay, and we put controls in place to ensure that it did not appear in searches users performed on the main part of the site.

I would like to think eBay set an example for how to handle these difficult issues the right way. Rob has become an expert in this field, and he tells me that there are a number of companies who have modeled their collaborative posture with law enforcement and government agencies after eBay's. eBay found a way to stay in business and be true to its own values and character. That wasn't the easy route, and it was not an inexpensive route. Today, under the larger umbrella of Trust & Safety, eBay employs fifty people whose full-time job is to work with law enforcement agencies on various issues from fraud to counterfeit merchandise investigations to answering subpoenas.

I'm sorry to say this is not a route that all companies in a similar position have chosen to take. To me, a most unfortunate example of one that didn't is Craigslist, the online classified site in which eBay bought a minority stake in 2004.

We had always been intrigued with the potential for online classifieds. As Jeff Skoll explained, his realization that online commerce could introduce powerful new efficiencies into the marketplace previously served by classified ads was one reason he joined eBay. We realized early on that for certain types of goods and services, some people simply prefer an online classified format to an online auction. Sellers can just describe the item and suggest a price. Buyers can scan the prices and see what they can afford, but they also can contact the seller to bargain if they choose. Unlike an eBay transaction, the parties usually end up meeting to complete the deal.

We had tried to set up special eBay Web pages based on re-
gional auctions where we imagined sellers and buyers might end
up meeting, but that did not catch on. In fact, it actually took a
number of years for Craigslist to become successful in U.S. urban
markets, too. But eventually Craigslist achieved network effects
and began to take off. The real wake-up call for us came when we
realized that in many cities, Craigslist was starting to getting more
listings for used cars than eBay Motors was getting.

We had purchased Mobile.de, a German automobile classified
website, in early 2004, and eventually we also bought several other
overseas online classified sites, including Marktplaats, Gumtree,
and LoQUo. Around the time we were looking to broaden our efforts in classifieds, a Craigslist shareholder wanted to sell his stake,
so we purchased roughly 25 percent of the company. Pierre agreed
to take a seat on the board.

But from day one, our cultures clashed. Craigslist's founders
insisted that they had modeled the company on newspaper classified ads that had very few rules or restrictions, and they resisted
attempts by us, or even law enforcement, to try to make sure the
listings were legal and conformed to some kind of safe and ethical
standard.

I appreciate how complicated it can be to develop rules to
manage this kind of a business. But from the earliest stages of our
relationship with Craigslist, we tried to tell them that they must
pay attention to the integrity of their brand. Pierre tried to tell
them that. We sent Rob Chesnut up to work with them. I tried repeatedly to get them to appreciate the importance of protecting
their brand image. When we purchased other online classified sites,
and when we launched our own classified ads business in many cities around the world, called Kijiji, we integrated Trust & Safety
policies.

Subsequently, it has been well covered in the media that many state attorneys general have put pressure on Craigslist to change its policies, and my understanding is that they finally have changed their minds on this and moved to try to monitor listings and prevent some of the illegal behavior that the site was enabling. But for me, this is a very unfortunate lesson in what happens when a company pays no heed to safeguarding its brand. I have watched with great sadness the case of the medical student in Massachusetts who is accused of murdering two women he allegedly found through Craigslist's notorious "erotic services" category. He now is routinely called the "Craigslist Killer."

I have come to appreciate that the character of a company is one of its most vital assets.

4

Be frugal. Conserve resources.

I really hate waste.

I'm one of those people who reaches to flip light switches off when I leave a room, whether I happen to be paying the light bill or not. I was thrilled when our facilities people at eBay installed a system that could do that automatically.

Conservation is a value that many years of relative prosperity in the United States had pushed out of fashion. The good news is that we crossed a tipping point not long ago where conservation aligned with being green and pro-environment, and that is bringing people of all different generations, regions of the country, and socioeconomic classes together in a classic example of the Power of Many.

My younger son, Will, for example, is deeply concerned with environmental issues, and he and many of his friends consider recycling one of those must-dos. He would no more toss a can or bottle in the regular garbage than into the middle of the street. More and more you see people bring their own grocery bags to the store, or turn off their car engines if they are waiting to pick up their children from school. A former Bain colleague who lives near me has bought a bicycle built for two, and he and his wife ride to dinner and around town on it. I think people are embracing the notion that waste creates a psychic burden. Plenty of people fully capable of living a disposable lifestyle are choosing to be frugal because it makes them feel responsible and proud to be a good steward of precious resources.

In business, conservation of resources is also self-rewarding: conserve today so you can fund more exciting opportunities for tomorrow. As eBay grew, I was always looking to make what we already knew how to do more efficient so that we could invest those resources in the next leap forward and ensure continued growth. We eventually called it "save to invest." In almost any context today, I believe that a leader who conveys a disregard for waste or a lack of interest in making sure resources are used wisely will never fully engage the Power of Many.

Frugality is another trait I inherited from my mother. In fact, you might say my mother is downright cheap. I admire that about her. Well, I guess I should admit that as an *adult* I understand and admire that. I'm not sure I quite felt that way the day I walked into a toolshed on the Caribbean island of St. John and realized that was where my family would be sleeping for two weeks.

When I was a child, my mother and father would take a week-long trip to the Virgin Islands every October, just the two of them. They both loved the outdoors and the beach, but the airline tickets and rental car were the end of their extravagance. They went camping. St. John is sometimes called the "Beverly Hills of the Caribbean" and has stunning resorts and beaches, but many people don't realize that the majority of the island is a national park, thanks to a gift by Laurance Rockefeller in 1956. So while many people went to St. John to seek out the pristine beaches of the resort in Caneel Bay and order drinks with little parasols in them, my mother and dad would pack sleeping bags and air mattresses and spend their time swimming, sunbathing, and grilling their own food.

My parents enjoyed it so much that they started bringing Hal, Anne, and me over the Christmas vacation. For several years we flew down with our sleeping bags, air mattresses, and other camping gear and had a fantastic break from the icy Long Island winter. We loved it. Unfortunately, the national park became so popular that park officials informed repeat visitors like us that we could rent a campsite only every other December.

That did not deter my mother. The next Christmas, we landed, rented a car, and drove into a residential neighborhood and up a driveway. We parked next to a small outbuilding. My mother, pleased as punch, explained that since she could not reserve a campsite, she'd convinced a local man to clean out his toolshed and rent it to us for two weeks. In fact, the tools he had removed to prepare for our arrival were sitting in a giant heap right outside the shed, and he had painted the inside of it!

We spent all day at the public beach anyway, Mom reasoned. All we needed was a place to sleep at night. So we inflated the air mattresses and laid out all five of them, side by side, which just about filled up the toolshed. Each morning we'd get up, have a simple breakfast, go to the beach all day long, come back, use a little outdoor kitchen area to make dinner, play cards, and go to bed. Honestly, it was kind of weird. But it was also really fun.

Through the years, we three siblings have laughed endlessly at the notion of flying all the way to the Caribbean to sleep in a toolshed. I've stayed in my share of four-star hotels, and I do appreciate that interesting and funny are not always the point of travel, but don't knock it. In St. John, we'd go to the local grocery, experiment with local foods, play with the hordes of other kids on the beach. It was an adventure. We enjoyed one another's company. The beach was gorgeous.

I may not exactly replicate my mother's trips, but I appreciate my mother's approach to life. Individuals of her generation who lived through the Depression and a war that demanded that every citizen conserve resources gained a new perspective on the value of putting scarce resources to the best possible use. Many of us with relatives in that age group smile at the habits they developed during wartime rationing and the tight economy of the early to midtwentieth century. Even decades later, some of my relatives couldn't bear to throw out a sheet of gently used aluminum foil; they reused tea bags and repaired the holes in socks.

I remember the first time I met Griff's grandfather, an absolutely charming man. He was one of nine children who had grown up in Sweetwater, Tennessee. During the Depression, his family had lost its house and farm. He went on to do quite well, running the local woolen mill and serving as mayor, and through work and thrift he was eventually able to buy back the house and farm. But you never forget losing your house. The day we met, I walked into his kitchen and there was a clothesline on which he had draped individual paper towels so he could reuse them after they had dried.

AS A CONSULTANT AT BAIN, I found it fun to ferret out waste. Whatever a company was paying us for our services, we instantly earned our keep and made the person who had hired us look smart by pointing to a specific and usually fairly straightforward way to save money. In turn, that made the company pay close attention to our more strategic recommendations. Certain wasteful practices are common to many companies and are pretty easy to find when you know where to look. For example, the purchasing of common supplies and equipment frequently becomes undisciplined as a company grows. Individual units or divisions *think* they are buying in quantity, but when a company centralizes the purchasing of items used by multiple divisions, the savings can amount to an additional 10 percent or more of the total cost. This kind of saving is so easy it's like finding money in the pocket of a coat.

Another interesting form of savings can derive from basic time and motion studies—simply watching employees physically move around a space over the course of a workday. For example, I once had a great project at Bain with a company that ran the food service concessions at several colleges. In food service, tremendous efficiencies can be discovered by studying the physical movement of the cooks and waitstaff. In general, a lot of thought is put into the design of industrial kitchens, where a team of chefs and assistants has to prepare, cook, and distribute food as efficiently as possible, with the added pressure of needing to serve it hot. However, on this assignment I learned that the physical storage facilities for the food varied widely. In some locations the refrigerators were very convenient; in others the cooks had to walk some distance to get perishable ingredients. We recommended changes to limit walking back and forth. We also came up with a method to save hours of food preparation time by washing potatoes in the dishwashers! These kinds of simple changes ultimately lead to a more efficient service that gets the same job done in less time.

The thing about these kinds of savings is, you have to look for them. These are not splashy, career-making projects that get you promoted. You must actively instill an awareness of the importance of conserving resources in your company or your organization. What's more, whenever you attack waste, one of the first reactions you get is an outcry from folks who say that you are cutting into muscle, not fat, and that quality will suffer. People generally hate change. It makes them nervous. My response as a manager is that it's important to cut until you get that reaction. By forcing people to justify what they're doing and what they're spending on it, you're instilling a healthy discipline. Some will be able to justify what they spend; others will not, and they deserve to see their budgets trimmed.

I know that I am in good company, by the way, in my attitude about frugality. A friend told me about what came to be known as the "credenza wars" inside Dell Computer. When the company was in a fast-growth stage, they began to recruit new executives, some of them from traditional, large companies that had a certain familiar office design for top executives: the formal desk, the sitting area with a coffee table, and a credenza suitable for displaying awards, family photos, and perhaps a statue or other piece of art. Executive trappings, in other words. All for show. Well, Dell built its business at the margin; it created custom computers via mail order and had to keep costs low. It was not a bank that had to project an image of stability and classic elegance; it was not a maker of high-end goods that had to project images of the good life to customers browsing through its showrooms (which it didn't have). Apparently Michael Dell noticed these credenzas showing up in his executives' offices, so he started opening up the cabinet doors. Invariably they were empty. After a couple of these site inspections, Michael issued an e-mail edict that there would be no more credenzas and that all existing credenzas were to be shipped off to a used-furniture dealer and sold (I don't think eBay existed yet). Office furniture should be functional, he decreed.

At eBay, senior executives have always had cubicles, not private offices. This was also famously true at Intel, where Andy Grove insisted that such an office design not only was sufficient and a better use of funds but also encouraged better communication. Leaders must set the right example if they want to build a frugal culture. If a CEO doesn't wage a constant war on waste and reward those who rally to that cause, companies gradually get used to adding costs that don't have anything to do with the business.

ONE OF THE THINGS I grew to love about eBay was how, by its very nature, it fundamentally attacked waste. It extended the value and life span of so many objects. Somewhere out there on Anyslope USA, I like to imagine some happy children getting enjoyment out of the kid-sized skis that I sold on eBay after my boys outgrew them. In fact, I like to imagine them being resold a couple more times. I can't tell you how many times I meet people at an event who go out of their way to tell me how pleased they were when they went on eBay and sold something that they no longer needed to someone with a use for it. As I write this, I am fresh from an event in California where a gentleman told me he had bought $85 hiking boots for his son, who wore them on one trip and outgrew them; the dad then sold them on eBay and got a note from the person buying the boots for her son, who added, "He'll probably just wear them once and outgrow them." There was nothing zero-sum about this transaction: Both parties felt a sense of connection and pleasure. Both parties got what they needed, reducing clutter and saving resources to boot.

Almost from the moment I hit the ground at eBay, one of my daily challenges as a manager was to instill that same frugal spirit inside the company, despite the increasingly circus-like atmosphere of excess in Silicon Valley. Given the sobering economic climate we face at present, the memories of what life was like in many young start-ups in those days seems like some kind of fantastical dream.

Except that it really happened. A hot IPO market created a stampede to get in on the next Netscape or Yahoo, among the early IPO blockbuster dot-coms that were started by very young computer science whizzes. The competition for talent and ideas became frenzied. There really were companies that were launched on the basis of an idea scratched on the back of a napkin at Starbucks, and when I say "launched" I mean that a relatively inexperienced computer programmer would get hundreds of thousands, if not millions, of dollars to get a company going based on truly flimsy plans. Venture capitalists really did prowl the halls at Stanford and other universities trying to figure out the next "next thing," and start-ups put ads in college newspapers inviting engineering and computer science students to drop out and join them. There really were companies that dangled a brand-new BMW sports car as a signing bonus for engineers they were trying to hire.

Once these high-flying companies got going, there was the challenge of holding on to these employees. There were companies who, before they had enough employees to fill one school bus, had hired a vice president of fun, or, at minimum, hired someone whose job was to stage morale-building events such as getting the whole company to don camouflage and play paintball all day. Many of these dot-coms were lavishing perks, trips, and goodies on employees, all under the assumption that the company was demanding so much of the employees' attention and time that it had better entertain them, feed them, and make them happy. There were companies who had never booked a nickel in revenues from an actual customer throwing Christmas parties featuring famous rock stars. I was truly dismayed to see young employees whose first job was in this climate and who had stock options in a market they were not old enough to have seen go anywhere but up.

It's important to invest in your people—but in a mature, professional way. I admire Google, for example, but there are dangers to creating a perk-filled culture, and I suspect it is now running into them. The free gourmet cafeterias, free haircuts, and other perks it has offered are well known. But as even Google has had to become more frugal, there have been memos reminding employees that they are to bring only two personal guests per month to the cafeteria and that they are not to pick up to-go meals on their way home. It can be difficult to adjust people's expectations once they have gotten used to certain indulgences. One comment posted on a Silicon Valley blog about this development said: "Oh no, Google is acting like a company!"

Google was not alone in blurring these lines. I'm afraid that I don't buy the idea that a company should take on duties for employees such as picking up laundry or feeding them for free. I don't think companies should foot the bill to bring a chiropractor to the parking lot in a Winnebago. Providing perks like that can end up being as divisive as it is expensive. After all, one person needs his laundry done, but someone else needs her pets walked, and someone else wants free pomegranate juice instead of carrot juice. When a company starts making decisions about which of these things it should offer, underwrite, or manage for the employees, it eventually learns that people's needs and desires are infinite.

My feeling is that a company should treat employees like grown-ups: pay them appropriately and let them make their own decisions.

The good news for me at eBay was that from the company's earliest inception, Pierre and Jeff never bought into a culture of perks. Even at a relatively young age, they were fundamentally mature personalities, grounded in reality. That was true both at the start, when they were young entrepreneurs scrimping along with particleboard desks and beach chairs, and later, when their stock holdings made them personally very wealthy. They knew that the point of running a business was to provide some kind of product or service for which people paid more money than it cost to provide the service, thus earning the company a profit. In our case, eBay was profitable from almost the moment it was born.

That revenues should exceed expenses is a concept that does not require advanced math, but remember, there were Ph.D. electrical engineers all over Silicon Valley who did not appear to understand it. Because of a brief and voracious spike in Internet advertising, many companies spent huge amounts of money because they were in "customer acquisition mode," as the saying went. The idea was to build a website that would attract large numbers of people and then do just about anything to keep them engaged and coming back so that they would be an attractive advertising market. I remember a joke from that era: Did you hear about the dot-com where you can go online and pay $19.95 to have a $20 bill delivered to your house?

All this was swirling around eBay, but I was determined not to let eBay be sucked into that vortex, and the exquisite relationship between eBay and its community helped me in that effort. It was impossible to forget the most basic rule of business—namely, that revenues ought to exceed costs—when we heard regularly from users who lived in a small town in the Midwest and had quit their jobs or given up their physical storefronts to use eBay as their sole trading platform. As much as they loved eBay and the friends they made there, these individuals made us aware every day that what we did mattered to their livelihood and that raising our fees or making it more cumbersome for them to do business had consequences. From the earliest days, Pierre and the entire company knew that eBay needed to show its respect for our community by never being ostentatious or frivolous.

One example: After the dot-coms started to crash in 2000, during a period when eBay was expanding, we needed office furniture. Mary Lou Song, who was full-time employee number three at eBay, recalls, "I used to scan the local want ads, because so many little dot-coms had spent their money on incredibly luxurious office furniture—leather desk chairs and art for the office—and now they had to practically give it away. I was excited to pick it up so inexpensively. Well, this one day there was an ad for a number of items from a company, and one of them was an oxygen bar. I was just disgusted. This was a time when we were reinvesting in our systems to make the trading platform work more efficiently. What popped into my mind was, 'If I were to use the revenues from our users to buy something as silly as an oxygen bar, how could I ever look a community member like Judy Williams in the face?'"

Mary Lou maintained a very personal connection to our community, and she was familiar with many of their individual stories. Judy Williams was a single mother from Atlanta, Texas. She had tried to make a go of an antiques business, but between poor health and low demand in her town of 6,000, she couldn't make ends meet. She was on food stamps. Then, in 1997, she heard about eBay. Not one to sit around stuck, she bought a computer on her credit card and started listing items on the site. Soon she was amazed to find that quilts, tobacco tins, and other items that had languished in her shop were getting snapped up on eBay by people all over the world. It was not long before she eBay'd her way off welfare and eventually was featured in *Time* and in other magazines.

Because of the connections we had with the community—through the bulletin boards and through our policy of answering e-mails and listening to customers—these sorts of stories kept us focused on the real-life consequences of what we were doing, rather than thinking up ingenious new ways to celebrate. And because of that, you will not find stories about Silicon Valley's go-go days that include eBay in lists of companies with break-room hot tubs and other silly excesses. Some eBay *buyers* may have spent ungodly amounts of money for oddities such as Britney Spears's chewed gum or—one of my favorites—the grilled cheese sand-wich on which the seller said the outline of the Virgin Mary was visible (that fetched $28,000), but remember, that was not *our* money or our investors' money in play. Rather, eBay was *making* money on those transactions.

Equally important, we fixed our attention not on these out-liers but on the far larger group of bread-and-butter, serious users. As we grew and became a public company and had to earn money for our shareholders, we saw their faces and heard their voices when we made decisions. We never lost sight of the fact that many of our users were making their living off eBay, feeding their chil-dren, trying to improve their basic situation in life. They could not pay their mortgages with page views or eyeballs (although later I will tell you the story of the community member who financed her son's college education by selling glass eyeballs on eBay).

Our entire community was aligned in this principle: *costs should not exceed revenues.* So during those years when free cafe-terias bloomed and the VPs of fun plotted the latest offsite game of laser tag, our pleasures were more modest. "We had bagel Wednes-days," laughs Mary Lou Song, "and we had to plead for those."

And if we needed more oxygen—well, we would just take deeper breaths.

BEYOND VETOING FLUFF AND EXCESS, I was determined to make sure eBay remained a lean, efficient company in other ways, too. The company was growing at phenomenal speed, and we were hiring at a tremendous rate. Nonetheless, I would go through bud-gets and ask, "Why do we need this initiative?" In a fast-growing company, it is a constant fight to keep executives from "empire building"—adding staff, projects, and scope for the sake of power or status.

One of my personal gripes about many MBA programs is that they convey the message to students that long past graduation day they will be judged by their contemporaries on the basis of how many people report to them. In performance reviews, I have had so many employees say to me, "I really feel my next step is to manage people; I need to get more responsibility to run a team." To which I have often replied: "No, you don't! You need to do the absolute best job we're asking you to do right now for the best interests of the company. That may or may not involve managing anyone, and we're not going to create teams we don't need in order to give you management experience." If you give in to that kind of thinking, you soon have a bloated, wasteful organization that is measuring its success on the basis of head count and budget size instead of on its return on investment.

Executive recruiters sometimes joke about "VP of me" syndrome. It was not uncommon in the early days of the Internet to have a start-up with, say, eight employees: a chief executive officer, a chief financial officer, a chief technical officer, a chief marketing officer, and four vice presidents. The company might have been the brainchild of a group of friends or acquaintances who were determined that it remain democratic and nonhierarchical. But as the company grew, the CEO didn't have the backbone to recalibrate and flatten his organization, and so he'd just keep adding real vice presidents who did build real teams, leaving the original VPs in place even though they didn't manage anything.

We were constantly reorganizing and flattening eBay, and I still regret not doing it even more often. You can end up so top-heavy in a fast-growing company, simply adding people for projects or jobs that may or may not remain central to your mission. You need to appropriately staff new ideas that can help your growth or that can help you build loyalty by being able to say yes to community members, but you also need to keep looking at how you can pare back teams and streamline what you already know how to do. Efficient organizations run lean.

OF COURSE, making money also takes spending money—on the right things. And investing in exciting ideas or people who can do great things excites me.

My family may have camped in the Caribbean, but when it was time for college, my mother would not have dreamed of picking the cheapest school she could find. Likewise, when I was in high school, I took a Russian history class and the instructor organized a trip to Moscow, Leningrad, and Kiev for our class. That was 1972 and my mother knew such an experience would be priceless, so she was happy to pay to send me. As a teenager, I recall being amazed at Russian architecture, at the details of the Cold War brought to life, and also at the notion that we could not go anywhere alone. We had to be accompanied by an official tour guide. I never looked at freedom the same way again. As a mother and as a citizen, I'm with my mother. I believe in investing in education above all else. There is no fancy home or car, no possible luxury item that should ever take precedence over getting the very best education one can for one's child. Whether you want to be President of the United States, teach school, build airplanes, negotiate contracts, or bring joy and magic to children at a theme park, it all begins with a good education.

When young people ask me about where they should go to college, I answer: "Go to the very best school you can get into and then figure out a way to pay for it." If it's difficult to afford, then save, work, and borrow. There is no more important investment you can make in your future. My general advice for any young person is, within reason, to conserve resources in the present so that you have the means to make your future brighter.

I have the same philosophy about how to figure out what kind of job to pursue early in life: work with the finest and best people you can, at the best company you can find. When it comes to salary, don't mistake dollars for value. Understand the experience and educational value of learning from the best. Without a doubt, some young people have taken a chance on a start-up and done magnificently, but they are the exception, not the rule. At my first job after business school, I received a truly world-class education in product branding and marketing at P&G. I became an "all-around athlete" at Bain because of the variety of projects and business challenges I worked on. These experiences prepared me to do so many different things for the rest of my life.

The larger point is: don't just know the cost of everything, analyze the value of everything. When I recruited Maynard Webb to overhaul our system, he was by far the most expensive candidate we considered and he became eBay's highest-salaried employee. It was the best money we ever spent. In such a situation, saving the company money by looking for a lower-cost, lower-value person is foolish.

The danger of going too far in conserving resources is that you don't adequately prepare for the inevitability of competition, a changing economy, or new technology. At eBay we used to say, "Plant acorns early for when you need oak trees." For example, I always hire the person whose skills are beyond the capacity of the organization right now, so that the organization can grow into that person's ability to take it even further. When we convinced Mike Jacobson to come to eBay, he was arguably overqualified. But I was hiring ahead of the curve. He had headed up significant practice groups at a prominent Silicon Valley law firm. We knew the future would present an endless series of interesting legal questions, that we would need a flexible, experienced lawyer to guide us through them, and that the person we chose would be absolutely critical to eBay's success.

I also used to say that we needed to "raise baby tigers." Baby tigers are experimental projects—skunkworks you set up to try out a new idea or investigate a new line of business. Now, established line managers often are not amused by rambunctious and mess-making tiger cubs. These managers can be like ferocious male tigers in the wild, always threatening to kill the cubs they don't consider their own. They resent being asked to keep reevaluating their budgets for waste and efficiency when some small team is given what looks like a no-strings-attached budget to explore something vague and undetermined. The trick is to get across how important both functions are.

I sometimes say strategy is the art of exclusion: "What do we not do?" But the real trick is to practice exclusion and be frugal without demotivating employees. We cannot afford to feed only the adult tigers because eventually they will get old and slow. On the other hand, the babies aren't ready. It's hard for the existing organization to have to keep focusing on efficiencies in order to feed the babies, but this must be done.

After we began expanding eBay's operations internationally, we started using that budgeting technique I mentioned earlier— "save to invest." The term was coined by our team in Germany after an operational review during which I explained the concept of using savings in current operations to fund exciting new ideas. What often happens in companies is that managers want to keep increasing their budgets to expand their empires. Being more efficient is not nearly so much fun. As eBay continued its rapid growth, I would demand that managers document savings in their organization, and I would tell them that whatever money they saved would stay in their budget and could be used to launch new projects. In the short run this was designed to motivate savings without triggering a virtual international uprising (imagine if eBay France were to trim costs only to see eBay Germany get the savings for expansion). But my larger rationale was to get a particular kind of thinking into our corporate DNA: "We are not expert yet in what we need to do in the future, but we are expert in what we've done in the past, so we should be able to do it more efficiently."

WHEN WE BOUGHT PAYPAL, one of the advantages we had because of the company's close connection to the growth of eBay was growing confidence in its value and how we could integrate it. As I've said, it's never just about cost; it's about value. In 2005 I made another bold strategic bet, this one in an exploding market that was attracting the attention of most major players in online commerce. We purchased the Luxembourg-based Internet software company Skype for $2.4 billion, which at the time represented about 4 percent of eBay's total value. I saw (and still see) extraordinary potential in Skype to grow in ways that are both obvious and still emerging.

Skype is a software business that enables users to communicate over the Internet instead of phone lines. That means it has exciting potential on a global basis to broaden communication without huge investments in physical infrastructure. Today, the bulk of Skype's revenues come from users who initiate a call on Skype to a landline or cell phone (Skype-to-Skype calls are free), for a very economical per-minute charge. It is growing incredibly quickly; Skype had 100 million users (accumulated in just four years) at the time we bought it. By the end of eBay's third quarter in 2009, Skype had more than 520 million registered users, and for the first nine months of the year it reported total revenues of more than $500 million.

Skype is a classic "disruptive" technology that has the potential to fundamentally change the way millions of people communicate, in the same way that eBay created a whole new kind of marketplace and Google revolutionized the efficiency of search. Neither eBay nor Google has an analog in the land-based world, and neither does Skype. Skype software integrates videoconferencing, file sharing, instant messaging, and other features beyond voice communication that are efficient, easy, and economical. But its voice communication capabilities alone are exciting. I remain convinced, for example, that connecting buyers and sellers by voice in the midst of certain transactions is going to become far more common in the future. Skype is an ideal low-cost technology to enable that. It also is developing new paid services that should be of high value in e-commerce. I believe it has the potential to radically change global communication among individuals and companies.

The competition among companies that wanted to buy Skype had been intense. A number of Internet-savvy players were also looking at doing a deal, and we could imagine scenarios that would represent threats or impediments to eBay's marketplace. We were excited to complete the deal and relieved that the company had not gone to a competitor.

Once we purchased the company, however, we learned that it was a more difficult task to improve the service and integrate Skype into eBay than we had anticipated. For one thing, Skype remained headquartered in Europe. Also, we structured the deal to give the founders and some other stockholders additional compensation based on the performance of the company. As a result, we kept the founders in senior management. This structure turned out to be unworkable for us; it slowed decision making too much.

We ultimately moved to buy out the stockholders who were due additional compensation, and eBay took a write-off of $1.4 billion on the deal.

For all the integration challenges, Skype continues to grow very quickly, and I remain convinced that this tiger is only beginning to growl. Skype is another spectacular example of network effects; the more people register for Skype, the faster they recruit new users and the faster the community comes up with new and more exciting ways to use it. There are countless businesspeople who use Skype today—not just to talk with suppliers but to look at merchandise over Skype video. There are musicians who practice together over Skype when they can't be in the same city, disaster victims who turn to Skype to find loved ones when traditional phone and cell networks go down, and traveling parents who help their children with homework in real time, all thanks to Skype. I believe Skype's best days are ahead of it and that Skype technology will become integral for bringing the Power of Many to lots of exciting and important global endeavors in this century. When you pursue a save-to-invest course, this is exactly the kind of investment you want to make to ensure that you are building for future growth.

Some say we paid too much for Skype. Subsequently, eBay has moved forward with an innovative deal to sell 70 percent of the company to an investor group for $2.75 billion, giving the new investors the freedom to develop Skype in new ways and still allow eBay investors to profit from that in the long term. Not only do I think eBay made a good near-term deal on the sale but I continue to believe that Skype is a good long-term value that is going to bring eBay investors an excellent return.

ALTHOUGH AS A CULTURE eBay tried to discourage self-indulgence on the shareholder's tab, it's also true that there is a time and place for investing in a company's culture and brand in a public way. eBay's advertising was not only fun but important in cementing our brand. Two of the most memorable television ad campaigns were the one featuring nerdy office guys doing cheesy Broadway dance routines among cubicles in their khakis and button-downs, warbling "I did it eBaaaaaaay" and the quirky "It" campaign that showed people holding and exchanging various 3-D versions of the word *it*. The latter commercial spoke to the growing phenomenon of people answering "I got it on eBay" when asked about their newest lawn gnome or bobblehead or even vintage T-bird.

One of the most powerful cultural phenomena that developed was our decision to start hosting events to express our appreciation of our eBay community members, the most notable being the annual eBay Live! conference we launched in 2002. It was a sort of festival meeting akin to Apple's MacWorld, eventually held in different spots around the country. It harkened back in some ways to the annual meetings of the florists I had attended when I was at FTD. The eBay community was exuberant and deeply committed to the eBay marketplace and to the friends they made on it, and we wanted to give them a real-world way to celebrate these otherwise virtual relationships.

In 2003, that good show took on a whole other dimension.

No more than a few weeks before the eBay Live! event, I was sitting in an executive meeting when somebody came in with a laptop and said, "Wait until you hear this." Out of his laptop speakers came comedian "Weird Al" Yankovic's hysterically funny parody of the Backstreet Boys' hit "I Want It That Way." Except Weird Al's version was called "eBay." The lyrics went like this:

Yeah
A used pink bathrobe

A rare mint snowglobe
A Smurf TV tray
I bought on eBay
My house is filled with this crap
Shows up in bubble wrap
Most every day
What I bought on eBay
Tell me why I need another pet rock
Tell me why I got that Alf alarm clock
Tell me why I bid on Shatner's old toupee
They had it on eBay
I'll buy your knickknack
Just check my feedback
"A++!" they all say
They love me on eBay
Gonna buy a slightly damaged golf bag
Gonna buy some Beanie Babies, new with tag
From some guy I've never met in Norway
Found him on eBay
I am the type who is liable to snipe you
With two seconds left to go, whoa
Got PayPal or Visa, whatever'll please ya
As long as I've got the dough
I'll buy your tchotchkes
Sell me your watch, please
I'll buy, I'll buy, I'll buy, I'll buy . . .
I'm highest bidder now—junk keeps arriving in the mail
From that worldwide garage sale
Hey! A Dukes of Hazzard ashtray
Oh yeah . . . I bought it on eBay
Wanna buy a PacMan Fever lunch box
Wanna buy a case of vintage tube socks

Wanna buy a Kleenex used by Dr. Dre, Dr. Dre
Found it on eBay
Wanna buy that Farrah Fawcett poster
Pez dispensers and a toaster
Don't know why . . . the kind of stuff you'd throw away
I'll buy on eBay . . . what I bought on eBay-y-y-y-y-y-y-y-y

I laughed so hard my sides ached. The eBay Live! event was
going to be held in Orlando that year. After the song finished, I
said to the team: "We have got to get him for eBay Live! The community will go nuts."

Henry Gomez, eBay's head of corporate communications, and
the marketing team made it happen. It turned out Weird Al was
booked in a gig in Wisconsin the weekend of eBay Live! and that
Saturday morning was the only time we could fit him into the
show. There were no commercial flights that could get him there
and back in time for the shows he was already scheduled to perform. So we made an expensive decision and chartered a plane to
go get him. Was this a good use of funds? Well, we debated this.
Some said no. I argued that it was, and we ultimately decided to
do it.

It turned out that Weird Al had a whole routine for the song;
he performed it with five young backup singer/dancers behind
him in a Backstreet Boys parody, and that's what he insisted on for
the eBay show. So Henry's team also had to hire five local dancers
and outfit them in white costumes. The performance lives on You-
Tube still and our members just loved it. Meanwhile, Al made
sure all of us backstage knew that he was an avid eBay user!

We could not have invented a better piece of publicity for our
brand; it attracted new users to the site and it made our existing
customers enjoy their relationship to us even more. Weird Al was
poking fun at the whole notion of online auctions, and we said,

"Poke away!" But beneath the humor, what he really hooked into was the emotional connection auctions had for people, the thrill of winning (a *Dukes of Hazzard* ashtray!) overtaking your actual need for the object. The song got airplay all over the country—essentially free commercials that celebrated what we did. And we got lots of great press coverage for inviting him to spoof us in person.

I personally would have passed on buying Shatner's old toupee, but I found getting Weird Al for eBay Live! an irresistible opportunity.

5

Results matter. Be accountable.

I sometimes think that my first few years at eBay should be measured in some corporate version of dog years. We grew so fast, made so many pivotal decisions, and handled so many curveballs that each year was probably equal to about five normal business years. And it was not just eBay where the pace was intense. In the late 1990s, the economy was booming, and the Internet and its new efficiencies made all kinds of businesses reevaluate what they were doing and where they were headed. It was brief, but I'm not sure there ever has been a more dynamic and explosive period in American business history.

But not long after the turn of the century the business world was jolted into a more sober frame of mind. Investors who had giddily poured millions into one dot-com company after another turned off the spigot when they realized how few of these companies would ever make money. Many of those stocks crashed and the companies were shuttered. Then scandals hit one Wall Street highflyer after another—Enron, Adelphia, and WorldCom, just to name a few. Investors learned that in each of these companies, management ran amok while the boards and auditors averted their eyes. Financial reporting was shoddy and even deliberately misleading. It turns out that it wasn't just the dot-com tyros who were unclear on the concept of revenues needing to exceed costs. Eventually, when these houses of cards fell, shareholders lost billions of dollars in value and thousands of people lost their jobs.

What happened next was both inevitable and necessary: regulators stepped in. After all, these were public companies. No company is ever obligated to go public, but when they do, they enter a regulated arena where public shareholders' interests are protected in part by rules making sure that investors have accurate information about what is going on. The oversight function that the boards of those disgraced companies could and should have provided failed, and so Congress took steps to see that it wouldn't happen again. This follows one of business's most predictable rules: if there is a problem you refuse to fix yourself, somebody will fix it for you.

Specifically, Congress passed far-reaching legislation, the Sarbanes-Oxley Act, that demanded stringent new procedures for management and more accountability from boards and auditors. The CEO and CFO of a publicly owned company were expected to actually read financial reports before signing off on them (imagine that). In some cases, companies found it difficult to find individuals willing to serve on the board, as potential directors feared increased exposure to liability. Meanwhile, CEOs across the country howled, complaining that Sarbanes-Oxley rules were expensive and cumbersome for companies to implement.

Well, the new rules *were* cumbersome and expensive. The legislation was not perfect, to be sure. But the changes did shift board meetings at some companies from a rubber-stamp exercise in doing whatever management wanted into a more thoughtful and penetrating analysis of what really was going on. I looked at the Sarbanes-Oxley rules and told the eBay board: "We're already good, but this will make us better. We will upgrade systems, we will be even more diligent, and we will make sure we are consistent around the world." When asked in private or public, I would say: "I think these new rules are a good idea. If you're running a high-integrity company, this is not the worst thing that ever happened to you. If you've been operating in the gray, well, I guess this *is* the worst thing that ever happened to you."

That earned me the reproach and sometimes the sneers of more CEOs than I would like to admit. For a time I think I was one of the few CEOs in the country who was on record saying I thought Sarbanes-Oxley was a good idea.

Results matter. The widespread nature of the problems in the late 1990s showed that our existing system was broken. When existing regulations are either vague or followed with such indifference that we have the magnitude of scandals and failures that led to Sarbanes-Oxley, regulators have to go to work. It is the right thing to do. Public shareholders have the right to expect that public companies are telling the truth and complying with reasonable rules.

My support for Sarbanes-Oxley flows from a point of view I want to be very clear about. As deeply as I believe in eBay's core values and as proud as I am that we built a company based on them, the *existence* of values at eBay was not by itself a guarantee of success. I don't believe that all a company needs to do is declare that it has values and then say, "Trust us, we know what's best." To be a success, you must identify a goal with a measurable outcome, and you must hit that goal—every day, every month, every year. Trying is important. But trying is not the same as achieving success. I diverge from the philosophers and the poets here; to me, success is not about the quality of your experience in striving for your goal. To me, the journey is not the reward. The journey can be fantastic; my journey at eBay was fantastic. But what matters most is whether or not you accomplish your mission.

I do not focus on values in this book because I am a do-gooder or an ethicist or a philosopher. I believe the values I'm talking about in this book are a twenty-first-century tool kit for success that works for both organizations and individuals, and my evidence for that is eBay's bottom-line success. Pierre did not create eBay to *celebrate* that people are basically good; eBay worked *because* people are basically good. We invented an entirely new form of commerce that had not previously existed. We revolutionized the way big sectors of the economy, such as the buying and selling of used cars, worked. (If eBay were a used-car dealership, it would be the largest in the nation based on the volume of used-car sales it now handles.) We created huge numbers of jobs and new ways for our users to make a living. And I am proud that we did these things while demonstrating a sense of responsibility and account-ability that was sometimes lost during that heady era.

CONSULTING FIRMS such as Bain tend to train what we call "best athletes": individuals who can go into virtually any kind of business, analyze the situation, and come up with an effective plan to solve problems and achieve goals. This is distinct from an-other term, "domain knowledge," which refers to individuals who focus on developing deep experience in narrower aspects of busi-ness, such as information technology, customer service, or finance.

One of the advantages of best-athlete training is that you soon learn that whatever the details of the business or the market, there are basic questions that apply to almost any business: What is the cost structure? Who are the customers and what is attract-ing or losing them? What is the competition doing, or about to do, that may impact the business, and how is the company dealing with that? Over and over at Bain, I watched client executives who had become too fixated on certain elements of their business ne-glect warning signs in the company's fundamental measures and get into trouble.

Project management skills are surprisingly rare in business, even though they are possibly the most important skills needed to be a good operating executive. You can't just talk about what should happen and then cross your fingers. Managers have to manage. They need to define targets, and they need to measure progress in reaching those targets. The trouble is, even when you know all this, it is easy to become mesmerized by elements of a business that you enjoy or prefer to work on. Sometimes it can be doing deals and buying other companies. Sometimes it's the fun stuff like marketing and advertising. Sometimes it's R&D. All these activities are important, but they must be done in concert with the other key aspects of the business or the enterprise will not succeed.

My own wake-up call for the importance of this balanced approach to delivering results came when I was a division president at Stride Rite. I've already mentioned that Stride Rite was in a tough spot when I joined it in 1992. My decision to join the company was tough as well.

At the time, I had been head of marketing for Disney's consumer products division for several years. The work was fun and exciting—it included launching Disney stores overseas and working on licensing projects for merchandise. Then Griff was offered the chance to return to Harvard Medical School and Massachusetts General Hospital's brain tumor program, a job that he really wanted. I flat out did not want to leave Disney or move back to the East Coast, but this was very important to Griff, and I subscribe to the philosophy that sacrifice is not such a terrible thing when someone you love really wants something. And Griff had already made a sacrifice for me—agreeing to commute to Los Angeles from San Francisco—when I was offered the Disney job.

In any event, when I joined Stride Rite I still thought and acted like a marketing person. In marketing, you have to get deep inside customers' minds, asking: "What do they want? What do they need? What are we giving them? What is the segment we're going after from a positioning point of view?" That was valuable experience, and I had success launching new kinds of Keds shoes by asking these kinds of questions and responding with new kinds of fun, exciting products, such as little Keds for babies.

But I later got a promotion and started running the entire Stride Rite division of products and retail stores. I now had what is called P&L, or profit-and-loss, responsibility. In that role, you are not just trying to show that you can make and sell products customers love; you are specifically charged with doing that in a cost-effective way that allows the company to make a profit. You have to manage the entire array of costs: manufacturing, sales, receivables, everything.

My very first mistake as division president was to keep thinking primarily as a marketing person. The Stride Rite stores were tired, drab, and old-fashioned. I invested in making them more contemporary and appealing. I gave our designers free rein to be more creative and unique with our shoe designs, in the process creating shoes that really were nifty. Then the first-quarter results on my watch came in. Nothing I had done had sold more shoes.

It wasn't that I had done any one thing wrong. I had focused on the customer experience. The stores *did* need spiffing up and the shoe designs did need updating and modernizing. But I had not paid enough attention to costs and competition. The new shoe designs we brought out cost more to make, but they weren't compelling enough to consumers that they were willing to pay $5 more than for a competitor's shoe. I hadn't considered how price sensitive our customers were when it came to children's shoes. If I couldn't bring the product lines in below a certain price, they didn't care if our store managers rolled out red carpets strewn with rose petals; they weren't going to spend more on the shoes.

Freshening up the stores had not justified what I'd spent doing it. I had to step back and rethink the whole brand.

After I gained a better appreciation of the big picture, I expanded my attention beyond marketing and figured out how to lower the prices on shoes that were more contemporary and popular with children. Ultimately, though, Stride Rite still was in a strategic bind. The sneaker companies were staking out the "cool" high-end kids' shoes, which benefited retailers such as Foot Locker, while at the same time Walmart, Kmart, and Target were eating the company alive at the low price end. What we did made a difference, however, and after my course correction, results in the product lines I managed and at the retail stores did turn up.

ONE ADVANTAGE OF RUNNING an Internet company is that it is possible to measure many more things than in the land-based world. Every transaction, even every click in a user's path, can be tracked almost in real time. Reporters visiting eBay after I arrived used to make note of all the metrics employees could summon at the snap of a finger. For example, we computed "velocity statistics." When *Fortune* magazine profiled us in 2002, our car guy knew that we sold a Corvette every three hours. Our jewelry manager could explain that we were listing a diamond ring every six minutes. I insisted that our people compute these kinds of stats, because it helped dimensionalize progress (or sometimes lack of progress).

Keeping track of data such as these is not just a geeky exercise. It is essential to good management. After all, management is not just a rank or a pay grade; it's a commitment to taking responsibility. When faced with an enormous number of variables, the best managers develop an ability to internalize the big-picture goal and then push the specific levers most likely to affect that goal. This is where one of those truisms of business kicks in—the so-called 80/20 rule. When you analyze a situation, it typically is possible to figure out the 20 percent of the situation that you can focus on in order to make 80 percent of the difference. For example, when you are trying to make your customer service operation more efficient, it's not uncommon that 20 percent of your customers are taking up 80 percent of your resources. If you focus on the problems that 20 percent of customers are having and figure out why, you stand to reduce costs dramatically.

In order to zero in on these targets, however, you first need to collect data and measure. Probably more than many executives, I am very focused on what are called key metrics, or on keeping a running dashboard tally of important statistics about the health of the business, just as gauges on an airplane's dashboard tell the pilot speed, altitude, and fuel levels. For a good manager, every day is about measuring, calibrating, and adjusting to today's reality, as well as plotting tomorrow's course. When I look back at eBay's critical first few years, it's clear that cofounder Jeff Skoll was one of our unsung heroes. It was Jeff who laid the groundwork for the focus on metrics that I believe is so vital to success. Many start-up companies just do not have the discipline and understanding of how important it is to measure what the company is doing, what it costs, and how growth is impacting different functions in the company's activities.

One reason I think eBay employees' understanding of the key numbers in their areas of responsibility impressed the tech reporters was that we were so much more focused on results than many other Internet-based companies. If the same reporter had visited P&G, Hasbro, or another consumer products company, I can assure you that he or she would have found that product managers and other executives knew the key measures of their responsibilities and used them to defend their budget requests, demand resources, and articulate their strategies. Granted, those statistics might not be updated as of yesterday, as at eBay, but being able to produce an up-to-the-minute statistic isn't as important as knowing what to do with it. If you worked for me at eBay and told me you were selling a Corvette every three hours, the next time I saw you I would ask, "How fast are you selling them now?" If your velocity was increasing, I would be tempted to give you more responsibility to grow other lines of business, too. If it didn't go up, I would expect you to know why and exactly how you planned to reverse that course. (By the way, last I heard eBay now sells a Corvette every fifty-eight minutes.)

These are the fundamental principles of accountability. In anything you want to do in life, success involves measuring progress and delivering results. At eBay there were four metrics that I watched like a hawk:

How many unique users were we gaining every month/ year?

What was the gross merchandise value per user, in other words, the average individual's value of transactions?

What is the conversion rate, or the number of items sold versus the number listed?

How many new items are being listed each month and is that going up or down?

At each management level, each executive would have his or her own dashboard tracking what was going on in his or her division or area of responsibility. It's important to create a culture that understands and embraces this technique. It is both an early warning mechanism and a way to ensure that you are measuring the right things.

For example, there was what we called the "wacko factor." Occasionally there were fraudulent transactions where someone deliberately set up a fake account, bid up the price of an item, and then disappeared without paying. These were rare, but they tended to involve particularly novel items for which the bidding reached high values. One very visible wacko transaction occurred in 1998, soon after we went public, when we auctioned a *Today* show jacket signed by Matt Lauer and Katie Couric on eBay as a benefit for Toys for Tots. Unfortunately, that auction, widely promoted on the show, attracted prank bids that boosted the reported price to $200,000, although ultimately the highest legitimate bid was closer to $11,000.

In the United States, when we became aware of these transactions, we removed them from our total merchandise value numbers, but as we expanded internationally, we realized over time that we had not exported that rule to every new country. Now and then we would get mystery spikes where one country's results would jump ahead of other countries'. Usually it meant that fraudulent transactions had not been excluded from that country's report, and in the early days of the expansion, when trading volume was still low, even a couple of wacko transactions could skew the numbers. Finally, we realized what caused that and made sure every country's numbers were de-wackoed.

On the other hand, there were times when growth was so startling, we thought we had a wacko number when we didn't. From October to December 2002, 34,000 new eBay stores were set up, adding to the 51,000 from the previous quarter. That level of growth was so dramatic, we sent a team in to redo the analysis, thinking we had made a mistake, but we had not.

I would caution that when you are metric-driven, one danger is drowning in a sea of statistics—missing statistical inconsistencies, or just not drawing the right conclusions from your numbers. Numbers alone never tell the whole story.

For example, when we launched eBay in the Netherlands, it just never took hold. We were having wonderful success all across Europe, but quarter after quarter the Netherlands lagged behind all the other European operations and we just couldn't figure out what was going on. We did not have an online auction competitor there, so it wasn't that someone else had first-mover advantage. I had two successive country managers who could not articulate for me what was wrong and why we couldn't grow. Why was it that this one country's citizens did not like auctions?

Then I brought in a new country manager named Josh Silverman, who finally figured it out. A company called Marktplaats was essentially the Craigslist of the Netherlands—an online classifieds site. It had started in 1999, well before we launched eBay there. Marktplaats enjoyed network effects, and it handled most consumer-to-consumer transactions. It turned out that because the Netherlands is such a small country—it has only about 1 million inhabitants, and you can drive from its northern to southern borders in a few hours—it made more sense for many purchasers to skip the shipping step and just go meet the seller and pick up what they wanted. It wasn't so much that Netherlanders did not like auctions; it was that they were content to let them work in reverse. There was no auction capability in Marktplaats, but if the price asked for an item was too high, nobody would buy it, and the seller would usually repost the item and drop the price. Eventually he or she would hit the right price and buyers would come forward. Once we understood this, we bought Marktplaats in 2004 and it became eBay's dominant business in the Netherlands.

Of course, metrics are only useful if you are looking at the right ones. During the dot-com explosion, young employees had a tendency to view the company's stock price, rather than its bottom-line results, as a measure of its value and success. Again, *the point of being in business is to generate revenues in excess of your cost so that you are profitable.* When eBay started, we were surrounded by companies who treated profits as some incidental future goal, the timing of which was negotiable. Not okay. For the most part, because I so firmly rejected that idea, eBay was known as a company with "adult supervision." We did not hire immature personalities who cared only about hourly updates to their stock holdings. But it was a bit of a struggle to keep a company of brilliant young developers and project managers focused on fundamentals when any company with a .com in its name would go public and instantly triple in value. The path I offered was harder and more data-driven, and it demanded more accountable performance.

There was an important milestone in eBay's transition to a grown-up company that I remember distinctly. From January to April 1998, the market capitalization of Yahoo, a fellow Internet highflyer, doubled, from $2.8 billion to $5.6 billion. We had a company meeting not long after this occurred and it was all hands on deck. At the time, we probably had no more than a hundred employees. I gave an overview of recent events and noted the Yahoo stock surge. I asked: "Is there anyone in this room who believes that Yahoo actually is twice as valuable today as it was three months ago?"

Nobody raised a hand.

I smiled. "I like Yahoo, but I agree with you. Remember, over time, the market will accurately value the worth of a company. But you must never confuse our stock price day to day, week to week, or even month to month with the fundamental value of our company. External factors influence a stock price on any given day or week. We can't control those. What we can control are the business results we deliver. If we do the very best job possible in meeting customers' needs, increasing revenues, and minimizing costs, we will deliver profits, and that will be reflected in the stock price. So don't worry about the stock price. Heads down, keep executing."

Sounds so simple. But realize that in many companies, employees were hearing a very different message. At many dot-coms, inexperienced CEOs regarded a rising stock price—even absent any fundamental change in performance or strategy—as evidence that the market was discovering the company's "true" value. It was delusional, to put it bluntly. It was an ego trip.

I was determined to keep eBay employees from taking that trip.

KEEPING YOUR SIGHTS on results sounds basic, but over the years I have seen that people are often distracted from that goal. Some confuse good intentions with good results. They forget that the cleverest and most creative ideas must be revised or abandoned if they don't achieve the desired results. Others confuse the *image* of success with actual success. They focus on other people's perception of their efforts, forgetting that positive media coverage, a reputation for being smart, or high self-regard does not guarantee results. A subset of these people expect to advance in their careers regardless of results and are surprised when it doesn't happen. They feel entitled. Their attitude is: "Because I'm here, because I'm me, you owe me."

Now, a lot of people try to hang this attitude on Generation X employees. I'm sure you've heard the criticism, often from baby boomers: the younger generation has unrealistic expectations about the workplace because they were raised in the Barney culture, where "You're special" was the theme. They want medals just for trying. This assessment may be popular, and it's conventional wisdom to attribute it to younger workers, but I think it's unfair.

For one thing, don't blame the purple dinosaur. Psychologists who study generational relationships say that virtually every generation believes the one behind it is less motivated, more self-absorbed, and more entitled. You know the old cliché about the parents telling the kids, "You don't know how good you have it! When I was your age I walked to school barefoot in the snow—uphill both ways!"

I will admit that I have become pretty jaded about some Gen X *parents*. If you can imagine this, at eBay we actually got a few calls from some employees' parents when their son or daughter—who might be twenty-six or twenty-seven—did not get a good performance rating! I think it's fair to assume that these parents had conveyed to their children a sense of entitlement without accountability. We assured those outraged parents that we were not about to set up parent-boss conferences at eBay headquarters.

In general, however, I believe the CEO must take responsibility for the prevailing attitude in a workforce, whatever the age of the employees. You have to ask: "Am I building an accountable, results-oriented culture, or am I confusing a pleasant journey with the arrival? Am I caving in to temperamental individuals, or am I setting an example that I ask everyone to follow?" It's not unlike parenting: when your children are struggling or frustrated, you can try to be their friend, or you can be their parent. In the long run, it's better to be your child's parent. In my teens, when my mother and I butted heads or I experienced some kind of disappointment, her first instinct was to look me in the eye and ask: "Meg, what did *you* do that caused this result? What could *you* have done differently? What have *you* learned from this so you can either fix it or make sure it doesn't happen again?"

In the same way, a CEO must insist that the company deliver results and focus on the right things. To truly succeed, to do great things—well, you have to do more than show up. The recent financial crisis brought this home to many people. The public was appropriately outraged that executives of some financial services firms stood in line for big bonuses paid for by taxpayers after their companies collapsed. These executives were not the raised-on-Barney crowd. This was a painful example of people who should know better forgetting that results matter. These bonuses were the equivalent of the "participation trophies" some sports leagues give to every player, regardless of whether the team ever wins a game or the player ever comes to practice. Bonuses should be tied to good results; they should serve as an incentive to go beyond the minimum requirements of a position.

To unlock the power of an organization, you create a positive, supportive environment, but you don't give anybody participation trophies. You make the path to success clear and you reward results, not just effort, good intentions, or good press. This was part of the eBay culture, and all of the senior executives I hired preached it constantly.

Shortly after Maynard Webb arrived and took on the huge challenge of making over our system architecture, he told me, "What eBay is doing is so neat and cool and cutting-edge that the technical team has sort of given itself a pass. They seem to think that the users don't have the right to expect that a system this complicated is going to function with the reliability of a bank. We're going have to change that attitude starting now. The community *does* have the right to expect that kind of reliability. They have the right to expect that we're going to deliver what we say we're going to deliver 24/7. Look, things are going to break, data are going to get corrupted, but we have to shield our users from feeling the pain of that. We need efficient backup strategies so that our problems and system failures are invisible to our customers." Maynard realized that he needed to impress on this team the importance of staying focused on the actual goal of the work, which was to make sure the system functioned smoothly and consistently, rather than focusing on the sophistication of the technology.

Mary Lou Song has a great story about the need to revise a clever idea in the face of results—in this case the reaction of eBay users. She had not been on the job very long when Jeff Skoll told her to make over the company's rating system. At the time, eBay's feedback system generated a tally of feedback and put a single yellow star next to the names of users who had achieved a feedback rating of at least 10. The rating was calculated by awarding a user one point for a positive rating, and subtracting a point for a negative rating. Jeff wanted a more detailed visual indicator that would quickly convey who were the most active and successful buyers and sellers. So Mary Lou came up with a proposal to use an array of color-coded stars to indicate how many transactions users had completed and how much positive feedback they had generated. The stars were pegged to various milestones, with the highest level—a shooting star—reserved for those with a feedback rating over 10,000. (These days, the highest level is for 1 million or more.) She posted it on the eBay bulletin board with a little bit of "Ta-da, folks, here it is."

Within minutes she was swamped with negative feedback. Each day there would be more e-mails in her queue relating to the stars—first ten, then fifty, then seventy-five. People challenged her premises for the designations. They hated the shade of green she had picked. They challenged her right to propose a system at all without consulting them first. Mary Lou was startled and taken aback by all this negativity. She says she initially got defensive and annoyed.

Pierre had been copied on some of the feedback and eventually he came and sat down with her and said: "Wow."

She told him she was spending up to three hours a day answering the e-mails.

"What are you going to do?" Pierre asked.

Mary Lou realized that this was not a sympathy visit. "Well, I guess I need to apologize, ask them for their ideas, and redo the stars."

Pierre nodded. "That's right."

This was a uniquely eBay version of accountability. When your goal is to engage the Power of Many, these kinds of moments are jarring. In almost any other kind of company, users would never expect management to consult them before introducing a new product or making a change to an existing one. Jack in the Box might do focus groups to figure out what ingredients their customers consider critical in a new burger option, but they don't routinely poll the entire universe of their customers about store design, drive-through procedures, or milkshake straw length. Customers might later object to a change or a new idea or even stop coming to the restaurant, but their posture would likely be "We don't like this," not "How dare you not consult us ahead of time?" But even in those very early days, eBay had set expectations that it would be a transparent operation, not a command-and-control style company. We had to live up to that standard.

Mary Lou listened to the feedback and revised elements of the system, and it became a key measure of reliability and trust among the users. And she chose a more popular shade of green for the green star.

Unlike a lot of dot-com businesses where the whole point seemed to be a cool home page or various gimmicks to drive traffic, our community demanded that we be accountable to them because in many cases their livelihood depended on us. They were investing their time and resources in using our tools, and they were determined to make sure we knew what was helpful to them and what was not. They didn't care if we were enjoying ourselves, revolutionizing programming, or able to brag to our friends that we worked for an innovative Internet company. They demanded bottom-line results. That made us better.

I DON'T WANT to leave this subject without talking about an experience I had while I was CEO of eBay that still serves as an important lesson to me in accountability.

It was the fall of 2002. At the time, eBay was riding high. We had nearly 62 million registered users who had listed more than 638 million items in 2002, a 51 percent increase over the previous year. Gross merchandise sales totaled nearly $15 billion, a 60 percent increase over 2001. For the first time, the company's revenues topped $1 billion, and our net income had increased 176 percent to a record $250 million. Our computer system was now stable and the envy of the online world. We had purchased PayPal and were working to integrate it into eBay. We were busy and thriving.

Then on Wednesday, October 2, I woke up to discover that a congressional committee had issued a scathing, headline-grabbing press release about a report in which my name and those of several other eBay executives and directors, including Pierre Omidyar, Jeff Skoll, and Bob Kagle, were mentioned, in addition to the names of dozens of other executives from Silicon Valley and all over the country.

The subject of the committee's inquiry was an investment practice called "IPO spinning." The committee was investigating the suggestion that a long list of executives at twenty different companies had profited personally by making sure our companies did business with certain investment banks. The assertion was that the banks had given us special access to shares of initial public offerings that we would "spin," or buy and then quickly sell when they went up.

The details varied, but here's what the situation was for me: Goldman Sachs was one of eBay's bankers. After we went public and Griff and I needed professional help handling our investment portfolio, we decided to invest some of our personal funds with a completely separate group at Goldman Sachs, the Private Wealth Management group. As a wealth management client, I was indeed given access to IPO shares of other companies, which my private broker bought and sold for my account for a profit or a loss, depending on whether the stock went up or down (in these arrangements, the client gives the broker the authority to make the transactions without the client's approval). However, the implication that there was a connection between eBay using Goldman Sachs as its banker on an ongoing basis and any benefit to my personal account investments was totally false; I had never let my personal financial benefit influence my input on eBay's banking choices. There was nothing illegal about the IPO transactions my wealth manager made on my behalf. Such investment opportunities were common at the time, and I had never seen anyone in government, the media, or anywhere else raise the idea that this practice was a conflict of interest.

By the time the committee announced it was investigating this practice, the dot-com meltdown had occurred and we were in the climate of finger-pointing and scandal that prompted Sarbanes-Oxley. The investment banks' integrity in taking companies with thin results public had been widely criticized. eBay had sailed through the collapse with its steadily growing revenues and profits and had won high marks for its performance, but in general, even high-tech CEOs who had been treated like visionaries were now seen as suspect.

When I learned that I was on a list of those under scrutiny, I was surprised. The IPO investments made by Goldman Sachs on my behalf were a very small fraction of my personal investment portfolio. Given that I was a major individual eBay shareholder, I had far more to gain by working to make sure eBay used the most competent investment banking we could find. Anything that benefited eBay shareholders benefited me.

Goldman Sachs, where I was a board member, tried to defend its practice and explain that wealth management and its banking business were two very separate things. Our communications chief, Henry Gomez, made many calls to members of the committee, trying to get a meeting with them to walk them through the steps eBay had used to pick bankers for deals and to explain that these choices were not made at the discretion of a CEO; rather, they resulted from board review of the banks' terms and experience in financings. The committee members never returned his calls. Despite the inflammatory language of the investigation, these transactions were legal. No one ever suggested that they were not.

That press release was the last we heard from the committee. They just let it drop. The next step, however, was that independent lawyers filed a shareholder suit suggesting that those of us from eBay mentioned in the report had personally profited at the expense of the company. There was an absurd assertion that the company should have been offered the opportunity to buy the IPO shares, even though it would have violated eBay's bylaws to make speculative investments with its corporate funds. My board stood behind me and urged me to fight these suits, because they knew I had done nothing wrong and was deeply upset at the assault on my personal reputation, and aghast at having eBay dragged into these stories about corporate greed.

To this day, when I think about this episode, I feel very frustrated. There was no conflict of interest, but when I look back I can see why the committee pounced on the appearance of one. As I said earlier, I was not a good fit for the Goldman board, which was the primary reason I resigned from it in December 2002. But combined with the issues raised in this matter, I also was determined to move forward in a way that removed any suggestion whatsoever of a conflict. In 2003, the Securities and Exchange Commission adopted new practices that limited the discretion of banks in offering IPO shares to directors or executives of companies. I supported those changes. The lawsuit remained a distraction, and there was so much to do to run eBay and keep growing the company that eventually I huddled with our lawyers and with Pierre and Jeff, who also were named in the suits, and we three decided to personally settle the suit with our own funds. After the lawyers' fees, half the proceeds went to charities, and the other half went into eBay's treasury. Goldman Sachs also contributed $395,000 to the settlement.

I have put this story in a chapter about accountability and results because the fact is, there was the appearance of a conflict, and it bloodied our noses—mine in particular, but also the company's. As I wrote to every company employee the day this story broke, "Some of you have heard me say that whatever you do in life, you should never under any circumstances compromise your integrity. I live by that rule and know that Pierre, Jeff, and Bob do, too." But results matter. Whatever my personal discomfort, that episode brought distractions and bad publicity to eBay. And that was on me.

When something unanticipated happens that puts you on the defensive, you will likely have a range of very human reactions, including anger and frustration. But the lesson for me is that you need to rein in your emotions and find a way to turn it into a productive situation. You have to ask yourself some very simple questions: "What is my responsibility here? Did I trigger a bad result, even if that was not my intention? If so, what should I have done differently? Now, how can we move forward in a way that makes things right? And how can I make sure this never happens again?"

Those of us fortunate to hold any kind of a leadership position in business must reject *any* appearance of a conflict even when we know that one does not exist. To deserve the trust of our employees, shareholders, and customers, we have to be willing to be held to a higher standard. The result we want is trust. Trust can't directly be measured in page views or dollars, but over time it is essential to create a thriving community that works for everyone.

6

Listen. Everyone has something to contribute.

No person with an MBA ever feels so smart and on top of the world as in that very brief period between graduation and the first day of your first real job. You know the theories. You've read the case studies. You've worked through the accounting problems. You've generated brilliant solutions for hypothetical companies, perhaps even written business plans for new technologies that don't yet exist. You've debated economic theories late into the evening with your study group. You have a brand-new briefcase and some serious professional clothes. You are so ready to impress.

Then that first day comes, and you get your desk, your phone, and a tour . . . and an assignment like the one I got shortly after I arrived at P&G, where I was hired as a brand assistant: "We're developing a new shampoo product. We need you to figure out how big the hole in the bottle should be."

Like many a newly minted hotshot before me, I thought, "You have got to be kidding me. I'm an MBA, not a designer! What is the point of having me do this? Don't you have people who've spent their careers designing shampoo containers who already know this answer? Isn't there a chart someplace? Besides, what possible difference could it make if the hole is four millimeters or six millimeters?"

Of course, I did not say any of that. My next thought was, "Wait a minute. Maybe this is a logic test. The answer might be simple: make the hole bigger and the customer will use more shampoo and then buy more."

But based on all the materials they handed me, I could see it was not a trick question. I started reading. I realized that I was about to start my real marketing education. This project was going to be Consumer Products 101, P&G style. They weren't asking me to figure this out because the guy in design who knew the answer was on vacation and they couldn't find the key to his file cabinet. I had just learned my first and arguably most important lesson in consumer marketing: you do not know what you do not know. Don't forget to listen to the people who have a stake in whatever you are about to do.

Consumer research is the heart and soul of Procter & Gamble. There are many kinds. There are the notorious focus groups held behind two-way mirrors, where you assemble a group of consumers, and a facilitator guides them through a discussion about a product or perhaps an unmet need in their lives that the company might be able to fill—a better-tasting mouthwash, a more environmentally friendly detergent, a citrus-scented room freshener, or a new version of any one of the thousands of products P&G makes and sells. Another technique is called "following the customer home." Over a period of time, the market researcher shadows several consumers as they go about their day, seeing what they buy, then going home and watching them use the product—to clean their counters, moisturize their skin, brush their teeth (yes, that is an odd experience for both parties). And there are one-on-one interviews—intense sessions spent grilling individuals about their needs, desires, pet peeves, dreams, the way a product makes them feel about themselves, the things they wish it did. (In later years, A. G. Lafley created the "living it" process, which required P&G employees to live with customers for several days at a time, resulting in a number of new products.)

I used these techniques to investigate the proposed hole in the shampoo bottle, in addition to reading stacks of past research from other folks who had done these studies and exercises. Here's what I learned: Consumers are very particular about products such as shampoos, not only because of what they want from inside the bottle but because the shower is a very personal place. There is a limited number of objects in there, and you need to use many of them with water or soap in your eyes and slippery hands. Consumers don't want to feel duped by some inexperienced MBA's plan to increase sales with a hole bigger than necessary for them to get the amount of product they want to use. They don't want to accidentally squirt out more shampoo than they intended. The customer wants to be in control of that container. I'd never given any of this a thought until I had this assignment. We used these various listening tools to figure that out and we came up with an answer, the right answer, about how big the hole should be.

The answer is: it should be the size the customers like best. That happens to be the smaller size, which offers the most control.

In almost any situation involving human beings, you can never go wrong by actively listening with an open mind. Consult the people who will potentially be affected by an issue or a decision and pay close attention to what they say. Talk to your colleagues, even those who don't agree with you.

I believe that being willing and able to actively listen is a vital skill for any leader. Not only is listening the right thing to do, an antidote to arrogance, it also leads to all sorts of competitive advantages. Again and again, eBay used listening and appreciating that everyone had something to contribute to develop its business, its brand, and its reputation.

THIS POSTURE AT eBAY began very early. Pierre invented and launched eBay, then called AuctionWeb, over the Labor Day weekend in 1995. The first item he listed was a broken laser pointer that sold for almost $15. He advertised the service only to other techie types who frequented what were then called Usenet bulletin boards with pizzazz-free names like "misc.forsale.noncomputer." Slowly, traffic picked up and other people started listing items for sale. However, it didn't take long before Pierre, who put his own e-mail address on the site, started getting e-mails from people complaining about their transactions. Someone had bought an item but the seller hadn't responded to the buyer's e-mail about it, for example. Or an item had arrived at the buyer's but was not exactly as advertised. Or it had been a couple of weeks since the buyer sent his check, but the item had not shown up.

As Pierre explains it, "In the very early days it was just me, and my background was as a software engineer. My approach to everything was about experimentation—a technologist's approach. In the beginning I spent the most time listening to what the users were saying. People started to have issues and problems and they would e-mail me and want me to personally intervene. In most cases what I would do is suggest that they communicate directly instead of turning to me as the parent to resolve the dispute, and I found that when I did that the problem tended to go away. Most of the problems were not fraud, they were just misunderstandings. I'd say, 'Put yourself in the shoes of the other person and try to figure out what happened.' In those days it was not that common for people to check e-mail or even turn on their computer every day."

By the time I began to analyze the auction site, what struck me was that eBay had already built listening to its customers into the experience. Pierre had listened carefully to what his early users were saying and he had created a tool for them to listen to each other. The company's managers could lurk on the bulletin boards and watch users talk about different elements of the experience they had buying and selling: what worked and what got in their way. eBay employees sometimes responded to individual questions and issues raised on the boards (like Mary Lou Song and the stars issue), but not in a defensive way.

The platform also helped users experiment. There might be a vigorous debate on the bulletin boards about the best way to launch an auction. Was it better to set a low opening-bid price, for example, in hopes of attracting lots of bidders, or should you set a higher price to weed out all but serious bidders? Did it create more excitement and interest to list a "no reserve" auction where the final bid was the final bid, or did a seller need to protect him- or herself with a hidden reserve price so that the item did not sell for too low a price? Sellers who routinely sold a lot of merchandise could test sales and marketing approaches they heard about in a way that would be much more difficult and expensive in a traditional retailing space. They could try, for example, listing similar items with a high minimum bid, a low minimum bid, and no minimum bid, just to see what happened.

Both by personality and training, I am a listener. I do not like to delegate my own education. I want to understand the impact of something I am considering, and I need to consult the stakeholders to feel confident that I do. And one reason why eBay was such a good fit for me was that Pierre and Jeff also held fast to the value that everyone has something to contribute. Over time, I found that we attracted more individuals with not only a bias for action but also a bias for listening and understanding. Some companies' executives are full of swagger and pride themselves on following their gut. But as Rajiv Dutta always liked to say, "Trust your gut— just remember to recalibrate your gut from time to time." You do that by paying attention, not assuming you know all the answers, and listening.

Rajiv is a perfect example of the kind of listening and thoughtful attention that helped make eBay tick. When we met Rajiv, we were looking for a director of finance and operations and he was in the finance department of a semiconductor equipment manufacturer. He came in and met with me and my senior team, and we liked his background and experience and were anxious to have him meet more people and stay in consideration for the job.

I later learned that he liked us after that first meeting, too, but also thought we were a little crazy to think we were going to build a large business on a glorified garage-sale model. But instead of simply trusting his gut, he calibrated. He and his wife, Sumita, had bought a clock at an antiques store. It didn't work. They liked the way it looked and kept thinking they would get it repaired but had not gotten around to it. Rajiv went home from the interview and told Sumita that he wanted to list it on eBay to see what happened. She was very skeptical. "It will probably cost us more to ship it than we will get for it."

He listed the clock for a three-day auction and closely monitored its progress. A day or so went by and a few bids came in, stalling around $40, just about what he'd paid for it, the very price Rajiv thought was the maximum it would fetch. Then, all of a sudden, the bids started jumping up. He got a couple of e-mails asking him exactly what seemed to be wrong with the clock (would it not wind, did it start but then stop, etc.) and he answered them to the best of his ability. When the auction was over, the winning bid was $150.

Rajiv was startled. He could not figure out why anybody would pay that much for a broken clock. So he e-mailed the buyer, who lived in Pennsylvania, and asked him. The buyer responded with a very friendly note that said, "Actually, that clock is worth a lot more than $150. I know exactly what is wrong with it and I can repair it."

"I was blown away on the spot," says Rajiv. He realized that this was what Pierre had been talking about in terms of creating a fair market to arrive at a fair price for goods that were otherwise hard to value. A clock enthusiast or repairer could not profitably scour enough antiques stores and yard sales in person looking for good deals on broken clocks. But by using eBay, he could find those hard-to-find clocks more efficiently. And, happily for the seller, he might even be willing to pay more than a regular browser in an antiques store would be willing to pay. Someone who made a living restoring clocks could reach sellers of broken clocks across a vast geographical area. After buying and repairing them, he could list them on eBay and sell the now-working clocks at a profit. Therefore, he was highly motivated to use eBay and to keep using eBay.

The upshot was that by doing some firsthand consumer research, listening carefully, and calibrating his gut reaction, Rajiv made a career move that changed the course of his life and added considerable value to our company. Over the course of my career, I have come to believe that this is the kind of executive that rises above the pack.

IT HAS TAKEN some companies many years to figure out what to do when their customers try to talk with them. In the early days of the Web, I remember hearing consumer bank executives say things like "We aren't sure that we want to put e-mail contacts on there. We don't know what we'd do if customers wrote to us."

Interestingly, it wasn't just the technology they found intimidating. A number of them had built a culture that depended on listening to their bank managers, not to their customers. They did not want to hear from customers—it was too chaotic to have to respond personally.

Well, pretty soon the more innovative banks realized that the Internet was a great way to forge a connection to customers. If one bank you do business with seems interested in hearing from you and responds effectively when there is a problem and another doesn't, eventually you are likely to switch your accounts to the responsive bank.

Sometimes very technically advanced companies get tripped up by not listening as well. They will adopt an odd arrogance about customer concerns, almost as if to say, "If you have to ask that question, you obviously aren't smart enough to use our product, and we're not going to waste time with you." I have seen investors place expensive bets or even launch new companies without having truly open-minded conversations with those who have tried it before, and without taking time to develop a deep understanding of the concerns that customers or partners might have.

I learned that lesson the hard way as the chief executive officer at FTD, probably the most frustrating and, ultimately, least successful executive experience in my career.

Founded in 1910, FTD had been a member-owned association for eighty-five years, and its initials originally stood for Florists' Telegraph Delivery (later for Florists' Transworld Delivery). FTD enabled a customer to go to a florist in Chicago, for example, and order a Mother's Day bouquet for Grandma in Florida. The customer would look in a catalog or design a custom arrangement, and the florist would take the order and the payment and then send a telegram to a fellow FTD member in Florida, who would make up the bouquet and deliver it. Over time, they switched to the telephone, then ultimately to a proprietary computer terminal system called Mercury. You might remember the golden Mercury figure from the television ads in the 1970s and 1980s, zipping his way around the country, bouquet in hand. In any event, both the florist taking the order and the one fulfilling it made money, and that model was the basis of florists' revenues throughout the association's history. But there was a lot more to FTD than met the eye.

Florists are creative people who love what they do and typically have strong bonds to the communities in which they operate. They know all the ministers and priests; they know the wedding planners, the country clubs, the morticians, and the facilities managers. They interact with their customers during times of great joy but also in times of sorrow. They take these interactions very seriously. And they enjoy one another's company. For many years, FTD sponsored an annual meeting, usually in a family-friendly spot such as Disneyland, where the members would have business meetings as well as seminars on topics such as new arrangement and corsage designs. Their families would socialize. These meetings, serviced by the staff of the association, were extremely important—florists bonded with one another and established trusting relationships that translated into revenues for both the ordering and fulfilling florists. By the 1990s, FTD comprised seventeen thousand independent florists, and its members were often second- and even third-generation florists.

In 1994, a group of investors from Perry Capital and Bain Capital decided to do a leveraged buyout of the association, whose leadership had determined that they needed to modernize and become more competitive with new floral delivery companies entering the industry. Led by Wall Street arbitrageur Richard Perry, that LBO team borrowed a large sum of money to buy the infrastructure and assets of FTD and turn it into a for-profit company. One of the first things they did was put a CEO in place who looked at the management operation for the association and saw enormous opportunities to cut costs. The central headquarters had indeed become very bloated. In short order, he let go 600 people at the headquarters in Detroit and began looking for ways to make the operation more profitable. But then he left to take another job.

Richard Perry heard about me through some Bain connections and contacted me at Stride Rite. He offered me the position of CEO at FTD and the chance to shepherd a dramatic turnaround. He had an ambitious plan to streamline FTD's costs, modernize its operations, and make it more profitable, eventually taking the company public. CEO job offers were not so abundant for women executives. FTD was based in Detroit, but my boys were now in school and it appeared I could set up a reasonable commute schedule back and forth to Boston. It seemed like an exciting opportunity, and I took it.

After I came on board, it became clear that although the investor group and the first CEO had conducted a thorough analysis of what it would take to make FTD profitable, they had not fundamentally understood the human dimension of the undertaking. It was a strong reminder that it isn't enough to ask questions and listen carefully to the answers if you don't ask all the right questions.

I think in part the problem was that they relied on benchmarks. For example, when analyzing a potential acquisition, it's common to look at other companies in roughly the same business and figure out what the revenue per employee tends to be. If the number at a company of interest is much lower than the benchmark, then the company probably has added too many management layers and become inefficient. The acquirer will have some confidence that considerable cost savings can follow by reducing the number of employees and bringing that number back in line with the norm.

Often this approach works well. However, it turned out that FTD was not a typical company. The new investors had not understood the value of the close, trusting relationships that were deeply embedded in the members' DNA—relationships with one another, with the staff of FTD, and with customers. They had moved quickly to pare the staff way back at headquarters, but they had lost more than they bargained for in the process.

Why was FTD so different? I think it was in part the personal nature of the business. When you send your mother flowers, remember, you hear about the transaction. She calls immediately. When you're trying to win your girlfriend's heart back after a falling-out, those roses had better be perfect. If the fulfillment florist used wilted flowers or the bouquet didn't arrive when ordered or there was some other kind of problem, it reflected on the florist *taking* the order in the customer's hometown. The florists depended on one another to maintain high standards, and they were quick to report those who did not provide excellent service—or just never use them again.

Similarly, these multigeneration florist families had interacted with the staff of FTD through the years, from the account managers who sold them the holiday-themed flower containers for mass-marketed bouquet designs to the billing staff and the tech specialists who maintained the Mercury terminals. The florists cared deeply about such things as a new holiday arrangement design in a way that someone from the outside trying to reduce costs would never intuitively appreciate.

From the day I arrived at FTD, I enjoyed learning about this business, and I could see that it was full of lovely people—lovely, angry, unhappy people. When the staff at headquarters was reduced, employees who had been with FTD for years were let go, disrupting long-standing relationships. I think these changes could have been made more gradually and methodically, and in a spirit of cooperation and growth. Instead, everyone was angry and mistrustful. By the time I arrived, morale was terrible, remaining staff were paranoid, and the investors who bought the company had no idea why I couldn't just snap my fingers, cheer everyone up, and get them motivated to help us grow. The problem was that the debt the investors had taken on demanded near-overnight results. Remember, one reason for the LBO was to better meet the competition coming into the business, but the chain-saw approach had actually chased FTD florists away to competitors such as 1-800-Flowers (one of the easiest-to-remember toll-free numbers in history).

We actually performed remarkably well given the disruption and unhappiness, reversing a large, multimillion-dollar deficit and getting to the break-even point. Unfortunately, the plan called for a multimillion-dollar profit at that stage. The chairman and investor group had not quite understood what they were buying, and they weren't too keen on listening to my explanation for the results that disappointed them. I finally quit that job, telling Richard Perry after one exchange where we debated projections versus realistic goals, "This company is not fixable, at least not by me."

However, what I learned at FTD served me extremely well later at eBay in a couple of ways. First, I learned about the dynamism of small businesses and how vital a force small-business owners are in their communities. I had never worked in a small business, except in college selling ads for *Business Today*, so this was an important realization for me.

The other thing I learned had to do with the power of affiliation. Spending time with the florists showed me that they policed their own ranks, anxious to maintain high standards in order to keep everyone's reputation excellent. Later I would realize that the florists of FTD had the Power of Many; it just needed to be updated for the Internet age. That helped me appreciate the relationships and dynamics of the eBay community. After I was hired for eBay, Pierre shared with me that the CEO search had come down to five good candidates, each with strong consumer marketing experience. However, according to Pierre, the other four each brought a particular point of view. "Their attitude was that they understood enough about consumers that they were going to be able to convince people with wallets to step up. You were the only one who understood that at eBay it wasn't us versus them." In fact, I remember telling Pierre and Jeff in our first meeting that the way they described the eBay community reminded me of the floral delivery business because it was not just one retailer selling to one customer, end of story. Rather, there was the ordering customer, the order-taking florist, the florist who made up the arrangement and made sure it was delivered, and finally the recipient. And there were often intense emotions—love, condolences, perhaps even a desperate plea for forgiveness—invested in the transaction. Like I said, you often learn much more from failures than from success.

WebVan was another company that did not adequately investigate all the dimensions of an ambitious venture it launched during the early days of the dot-com explosion. It was a splashy, high-tech grocery delivery service that seemed to me, when I first heard about it, like a dream come true for busy families. You filled out your order online; you could have a recurring order with all your staples and you could supplement with other items; you could easily match it all up with the recipes you wanted to cook; and for a reasonable fee your groceries would be delivered to your front door. In fact, someone from WebVan once shared with me that when they held focus groups with working women, some of the women actually wept at the prospect of being able to order food from their computer at work and have it waiting for them when they got home.

At first, new customers flocked to WebVan. Having goods delivered to your door was so convenient for people like me who were very busy and didn't like to shop, and the prices seemed reasonable—roughly equivalent to those at an upscale grocery store, plus delivery charges. The company in turn bought all kinds of trucks and set up a vast distribution network for the food.

Unfortunately, the founders were mesmerized by technology, overly ambitious in their expansion, and not nearly as focused on the nuts and bolts of the grocery business as they needed to be. Had they spent more time with grocers and supermarket chains who had attempted delivery in the past, they might have learned that grocery delivery is one of those businesses that does not scale up very well. What sinks a business like this is that every order is different, everybody wants their order delivered at the same time of day, and the variables that go into supplying the groceries for those orders can be both unpredictable and formidable—from a shipment of produce not arriving on time to a run on a particular item because of a recipe published in the local newspaper. My understanding is that grocery delivery time and again has proven to be a business where the more customers you have, the more money you lose. Remember the joke about delivering twenty-dollar bills for $19.95? Therein lies the rub. When you lose money on every transaction, you can't make it up on volume. (I actually toured one of WebVan's distribution centers once and thought, "Good grief, this had better work because the capital cost to build all this is staggering.")

In Woodside, California, where a lot of high-tech executives live, there is a beautiful market called Roberts that has been in the Roberts family for generations. The food is fresh and nicely presented and the service is wonderful, and the prices reflect that. It's quite expensive relative to other grocery stores in our area such as Safeway. After WebVan folded I saw an interview with a member of the Roberts family, who pointed out that he knew WebVan was doomed when he saw WebVan drivers in the produce section at Roberts, filling in gaps in an order. On top of everything else, that order carried Roberts' markup costs.

"My father and grandfather used to deliver groceries to people's homes in San Francisco with a horse and buggy," George Roberts told *BusinessWeek*. "I used to make deliveries in a two-tiered truck when I was a teenager. I know how extremely difficult it was to satisfy customers profitably in those days, and it would be way more costly today." Ironically, a conversation with their hometown grocer might have saved some of WebVan's investors quite a bit of money. The company went bankrupt in 2001.

At eBay, the sense of community we built was every bit as important as the technology we created. Feedback was essential. The discussion boards showed us that people wanted to know what was going on. They had ideas for how to improve processes and policies, and they were the keepers of the knowledge about how changes would impact our members. And it wasn't just the discussion boards that exploded with commentary when the community reacted strongly to a new development.

As time went on, we tracked the numbers of e-mails that we received. (These statistics stand for me as an almost mind-boggling measure of our growth). In 1996 the company began getting roughly 100 e-mails per week. By the end of the year, it received 100 per *day*.

By the end of 1997, eBay got 1,200 e-mails per day.

By 1999, we received 4,000 e-mails per day.

By 2001, 17,000 e-mails per day.

By 2002, 23,000 e-mails per day.

By 2003, 44,000 e-mails per day.

By 2004, we logged 130,000 e-mails, chats, and customer calls per day.

Clearly, we had achieved the E-mail of Many! But as you can imagine, the trick was to remain alert and open to this feedback without becoming either defensive or bogged down by it.

Also, as important as e-mail and message boards were to us, I never completely let go of my P&G roots. I knew there was a special kind of value to looking real customers in the eye. So we launched what we called the Voices of the Customer program. We invited members of the community, usually ten or so at a time, to sit down with us at headquarters, and we listened to their ideas, their complaints, and their suggestions. We didn't just use these meetings to cheer ourselves up by inviting eBay users we knew liked us; we often invited members who were very angry and had made that very clear to us.

Invariably, after these meetings, community members would tell us how happy they were to realize that *real* people ran eBay. The eBay site was so highly automated that it was possible sometimes to think of the company like some manifestation of Hal from *2001: A Space Odyssey*, a computer generating responses to all manner of developments with a sort of eerie and toneless machine voice.

What often struck me in those meetings was the extraordinary passion people who depended on eBay felt about what might seem like the most mundane things. For example, in the early years there were particular categories where we allocated a set amount of space to describe an item, perhaps 300 characters. For one reason or another, we might change that number, usually reducing it to try to get pages to look better or to load more quickly. Well, the response from the pottery sellers to losing even fifty characters from the space for their descriptions could be deafening. They would spell out the descriptors that were required to distinguish one make or brand from another and would explain that the change would surely reduce the amount of money those auctions would raise. They were deadly serious about this, and in many cases I'm sure they were right. They made their living selling a specific type of item and had arrived at what they thought was the best way to do that, and one sentence more or less of description made all the difference to them. We always listened. We tried to find a way to make them happy and achieve our goals, too. It was a constant balancing act.

Sometimes, we made a change that prompted such an instant negative reaction that we scrambled to fix it. In early 2001, for example, we came up with an idea to better serve buyers by sending an e-mail to bidders who did not win an auction, referring them to similar products being auctioned by other sellers. The seller community went nuts. They felt that they had done the up-front work of attracting a given buyer to their auctions and that we were interfering in that relationship. Pierre and I actually flew to Salt Lake City and met with one seller who had been particularly vocal in complaining about this new plan, and we listened carefully as he explained his reasoning. We realized that we had made a mistake. We changed course and sent bidders e-mails referring them to the seller's other auctions, unless the seller decided he or she did not want us to do that. Over time, we relied on our community managers' ongoing dialogues with eBay users to make sure we had not inadvertently made more enemies than friends by trying something new. While we became better at predicting that response, it was never 100 percent. Some changes we worried might set off howls did not; others we thought were relatively minor hit a nerve. Whenever we were surprised it was a great reminder that you cannot get complacent and smug; you have to keep listening.

Being open and honest is easy to advocate but harder in practice. An organization can get bogged down by the sheer volume of feedback, or factions can develop inside the company, each marching out kindred spirits from the user community to help make its arguments. But the best companies, organizations, and even community groups today embrace the importance of listening and use technology to help create a culture in which listening is valued.

In fact, three of the original seven eBay values spoke directly to the importance of listening. When we said we believed everyone had something to contribute, the message was that every member of our community can help us understand and improve the experience—sometimes by validating one of our ideas, sometimes by pointing out the flaws in a change, sometimes by suggesting something we haven't thought of.

When we said we encouraged people to treat others the way they want to be treated, part of that message is that everyone wants to feel like those in a position to impact their lives or business are listening to them. The idea is not to just pretend to listen or provide some unmonitored "suggestion box" but to create a feedback mechanism so that real people review and think about the ideas and complaints and observations coming in. Ignoring criticism leads to mounting frustration.

Finally, when we said we believed that an honest, open environment can bring out the best in people, we were talking about listening to and being honest with one another within the company. In other words, we should not become obsessed with a plan and ignore its impacts, or even new opportunities that might emerge from unexpected places.

Used cars are an example of a customer-driven product category that many of us inside eBay never thought would work in our online auction format. But it's a good thing I listened to people who did not share that opinion, as eBay subsequently became the largest seller of used cars in the country.

Here's what happened. Like countless people over the years who have told me, "It's too big and complicated a purchase," I could not imagine buying a car sight unseen, over eBay. I knew that full-sized automobiles had appeared on eBay from the beginning; in fact, one of the very first noncomputer listings back in 1995 was a Rolls-Royce. But these were one-offs. The average selling price of items on eBay for the first several years I was CEO was about $40. We never imagined that selling cars would be a good business for eBay, largely because we thought that the shipping costs and logistics would dissuade all but a few people from doing these transactions.

We knew car auctions were a profitable business in the land-based world, however, and in May 1999 we bought a land-based automobile auction company called Kruse International. We turned that business over to a very bright guy named Simon Rothman, who in addition to being an avid collector of die-cast cars (the tiny little models) realized that people did want to use eBay to buy and sell full-sized cars, and he eventually created a separate site called eBay Motors that was a huge success.

What I and others had underestimated was the sheer misery most people associated with buying a used car, such as the fake performance of the salesman who pretends to consult some mystery manager about the discount he can extend if the buyer drives it off the lot today. The advantage of using eBay was that the buyer had to spell out in writing all the significant details and an honest assessment of the vehicle, warts and all. There would be photographs of the vehicle. Plus, what ordinarily was so inefficient about the used-car market was that you might very well be happy to drive a couple of hundred miles for just the right car, but you didn't have the ability to get the local want ads from every car dealer within your acceptable driving distance. And even if you heard about a car being sold in a nearby town, could you trust the want ads, or even a person on the phone, to describe it accurately? Newspaper classifieds, after all, tend to be written in the cryptic shorthand we now associate with text messaging: "Slvr Chevy Sbrban, 05, low mi, gd cond, air, CD, new tires."

I became a true believer when Griff and I finally bought a car on eBay ourselves. We needed to get a new family car, and young Griff went to work combing eBay. He found a car that had initially been purchased in Canada and had a special paint job that, as I remember, either had a drop of gray in the black or a drop of black in the gray. Either way, the upshot was a shimmer that made no difference to me, but that my son found irresistible. The seller was in Denver, and he provided so much data about the condition and details of the car that we felt very confident about what we were getting. The price for the car, which had very low mileage, was so much better than any comparable car we could find near us in California that it would be a good deal even after we paid $600 to have it shipped to us. So we bought it. The seller could not have been nicer (he knew only that the buyer was an eBay employee, not that it was me), the car arrived as promised and ran for a long time, and when we were done with it a few years later, we sold it on eBay, too.

A FINAL DIMENSION to listening that developed at eBay came after we decided to start policing the site more proactively. We knew we had to proceed very carefully. We had to listen to involved parties and make sure we fully understood the nature and context of the items we thought about either banning or regulating more carefully. Some of the most controversial prohibitions turned out to be the least difficult decisions. Prohibiting the sale of firearms, for example, infuriated many people. But we were not taking a stand about the Second Amendment; we were focused on the incredible complexity of state laws governing firearm sales, and on the grave concern that we simply had no way to control how these transactions were completed or who might take possession of the firearm when it was shipped. It was just too easy to imagine sellers cutting corners and shipping the firearms without precautions, possibly allowing them to fall into the hands of children or individuals with a criminal record who could not legally purchase them. After Columbine, a rumor briefly flew around the Internet that the two young killers had purchased guns on eBay, but it was later shown to be untrue. Still, I was so relieved that we had opted out of this category. For similar reasons, we had opted out of alcohol and tobacco sales.

The path did get slipperier, however. One of the interesting problems that erupted was in perfectly legitimate categories of collectibles, such as stamps. As collectors know, factors such as whether a stamp has actually been used to mail a letter affect its value. In some cases, having glue on the back makes a stamp more valuable, as might a cancellation mark. At one point, Rob Chesnut started getting irate e-mails from stamp collectors alleging that some eBay sellers were doctoring stamps to increase their value. "We had no ability ourselves to judge this in listings," Rob explains, "so we engaged with a very passionate group of stamp collectors and told them, 'If you see an item that looks suspicious or seems like it was altered, send us an e-mail.'" He then reached out to the American Philatelic Society and made a deal with them that in exchange for eBay helping to promote their organization on our site, they would help us evaluate some of the items to determine whether they had been doctored. Thus began what Rob calls a sort of "neighborhood watch" approach that spread to other types of collector communities, where we relied on expert watchdogs to alert us to issues with items.

Rob had his own eye-opening experience in this regard. After his mother passed away in 2006, he opened her safe-deposit box and found what appeared to be Confederate currency, which is widely collected. Rob had no idea how to evaluate it or what it was worth, but he took careful photographs of the banknotes and listed them for sale on eBay, intrigued to discover their value. Immediately he received an e-mail from an expert in currency, who explained that the bills were counterfeit. Apparently the money had been produced in the 1930s and given away as a cereal box promotion. Not knowing that he was talking to eBay's chief police officer, the expert explained that the bills were still collectible but warned Rob not to describe them as authentic, since it is a violation of federal law to trade in counterfeit currency. Rob hurriedly took down the listing. Eventually, eBay developed specific rules for numismatic material (coins and currency) stating that reproductions of paper currency, for example, were only legal to list if they were significantly smaller or larger in size than the original currency.

Ultimately, some people or groups who were either upset about an item listed or upset to have had their own item removed—unfairly, they thought—would contact our customer service department. Eventually, these issues became the stuff of what we called "gray meetings."

If an item was illegal for sale in the land-based world, it was unquestionably illegal on eBay. The task of the gray meeting team was to discuss items where the situation was not so clear. Remember, our basic desire was to have as few rules as possible. The goal was a free marketplace, albeit one aligned with the values of our global community. In gray meetings, customer service would share the pro and con arguments users were making, and sometimes the customer service and gray meeting teams would go off and do more research. Rob's team often would reach out to organizations, law enforcement, or other outside parties he thought would have important insights we might not be considering. Sometimes they would just pick up the phone, call a seller whose trading patterns seemed to indicate categories of goods known to be commonly counterfeited, and ask, "What's going on? Where are you getting all these Gucci bags?"

The issues that cropped up were so often far more complicated than we could have imagined. One day, Rob got a call from the attorney general's office in the state of Florida because someone had listed tickets to a Florida vs. Florida State football game and the bidding had exceeded that state's legal limit for the price at which football tickets could be resold. However, when Rob looked at the item in question, he replied to the attorney who'd called, "Well, I see the seller is in Georgia, the buyer is in Alabama, the game is in Florida, and the website is based in California. Whose law applies here?" They realized they were operating in uncharted legal territory. Eventually, beginning in Florida, Rob worked out a solution involving our creating software that automatically intervened when state laws were flouted. Here's how it worked: If the state where an event was being held set a limit on the upper price a ticket could fetch, a resident of that state could not legally bid above that amount and a resident seller could not legally collect more than that amount. So if the buyer or seller lived in a state with laws of this sort and the bidding went above the legal limit, eBay's software would intervene and either end the auction for the in-state seller or prevent an in-state bidder from bidding any higher. However, buyers or sellers from out of state were not bound by these laws. These often were not the most popular outcomes for involved parties, but it was the only way for us to continue to legally sell tickets in these complex cross-jurisdictional situations.

After that important board meeting where Howard Schultz argued his position about Nazi-related items, I asked our people to not only thoroughly research the specifics of Nazi merchandise but also think about the broader issues of banning what came to be known as "offensive items." For example, I shared Henry Gomez's concern about where a decision to ban this material would ultimately stop. What offends one person may not offend another, but almost anything offends someone somewhere.

If you ban Nazi-related merchandise, must you also immediately ban World War II Japanese military-related items from the site? Some Americans lost relatives when Pearl Harbor was bombed, or their relatives were held in brutal POW camps. What about groups on both sides of the conflict in Northern Ireland—do you ban anything related to either side because the other might object? What about items with some kind of likeness or relationship to countless other brutes and dictators—Idi Amin, Pol Pot, Saddam Hussein?

I think we talked with just about every group you can imagine that had an opinion or an insight into these kinds of merchandise categories. In considering the Nazi memorabilia, for example, we talked with people from the Jewish Defense League and the Simon Wiesenthal Center; with historians and museum curators; with World War II history buffs and memorabilia collectors. We even heard from neo-Nazi groups defending their free speech rights. Ultimately, we decided to put some very specific rules in place that we subsequently extended to other categories.

You can read about them in detail on the eBay site, but generally speaking, we prohibited the listing of items or material that appeared to be marketed for the purposes of promoting hate or violence, or bigotry toward any race, ethnic group, or religion. This included all Nazi replica material and all replica or modern items bearing a swastika. We allowed trading in legitimate historical artifacts, including German uniforms, medals, helmets, books, or other items bearing Nazi insignias. Our reasoning was that there are huge numbers of collectors of World War II memorabilia who have nothing to do with advocating hate or bigotry. In some cases, the veterans who brought helmets, swords, firearms, books, belts, or medals bearing Nazi symbols home from the battlefields were trying to sell all or part of their collections because they needed the money. In other cases, organizations and educational groups would buy and sell the items to create educational displays designed to shine a light on the horrible consequences of the behavior and philosophies of Nazism. Museums are enthusiastic members of the eBay community.

However, even when the items involved were authentic historical artifacts, we did not allow the listings to carry photographs that displayed swastikas. A seller could describe the item and the markings, but we asked that the symbol itself be obscured or digitally removed from the photograph. This was partly in deference to countries where displaying the symbol was a crime. We also created software filters that prevented buyers from Germany, Austria, and Italy from even seeing listings for objects related to Nazism, because trafficking in such items in those countries in many cases is expressly illegal.

If the intent of an item is to ridicule or offend others, it may not be listed. If an authentic item is presented as an historical artifact that gives insights to a set of particular mores and values, we respect its collectibility and historical significance and allow the listing. This is the overriding philosophy we apply to many categories of items in our "offensive items" policy, from materials related to slavery or the KKK to murderabilia.

There is no perfect way to do these things. There are often compelling arguments on both sides of an issue. There sometimes were inconsistencies. And there were times when what might seem like a theoretical or legalistic debate about offensive items would erupt into something much more frightening. One of the most dramatic examples of that involved a young and fairly small online auction company we acquired in India called Baazee. Baazee was founded by a man named Avnish Bajaj, an American citizen of Indian descent. A few months after we purchased it, in December 2004, I got a phone call early in the morning from India: Avnish, whom we had kept on as CEO, had been arrested.

The circumstances were as follows: Two teenagers had created a videotape of themselves of an explicit sexual nature. They attended an elite private school and came from prominent families. Another student had burned the video on CDs and listed them for sale on Baazee. India has extremely strict laws about pornography, and out of respect for that, we did not allow listings of any pornographic materials on the site. In fact, there were never any pornographic images or video on eBay, just a listing saying that the CD that featured this material was for sale. Unfortunately, before the listing could be removed from the site, it was seen by users.

Police officials in New Delhi contacted Avnish and requested that he collect all the information he had about sellers and buyers of the video and bring it to them. He complied and traveled from Mumbai to New Delhi to turn it over. They then arrested him and charged him with transmission of obscene material through electronic media.

Avnish spent three nights in a prison cell. I conferred with the U.S. ambassador. We sent attorneys from eBay to India, called the State Department, and worked around the clock with Avi's family to ensure they were comfortable with our efforts. We hired the best legal help we could find in India. After a few days, we managed to get Avi released on bail, but, five years later, certain issues in his case remain open. During this period, U.S. and Indian laws on Internet crime and liability have become more similar, but areas of potential misunderstanding remain. In this case, I wish the progress had come earlier, accompanied by a greater spirit of trust and cooperation, so we could have spared Avnish and his family such an ordeal.

AFTER I HAD BEEN CEO of eBay for several years, in 2003, I was invited to join the board of directors of Procter & Gamble. Given my high regard for the company and the fact that I had started my business career at P&G, it was an honor and a pleasure to be involved with steering a company of this size and quality. I was strongly impressed by how, even at the board level, listening is so deeply embedded in P&G's DNA. Once a year, each director went out to talk to customers and watch them talk to a P&G representative about the products, often in a foreign country. One year I went to China to participate in this effort and I attended one of these meetings in a customer's home.

We were there to talk about personal beauty products. The family clearly did not have a lot of money. The P&G person asked a woman to bring out her beauty care products, and she produced an amazingly large box of makeup and lotions and potions. A translator relayed her answers to the questions we asked.

This is where you get into that dimension of consumer marketing that charts and graphs just don't capture. You quickly realize as you're sitting in this family's home that this beauty product is not just part of a woman's routine. It is transporting her beyond her perhaps difficult circumstances to a hope, a dream, a wish. It was clear from speaking with this woman that for her, putting on makeup was almost like going to the movies. The features and functionality were a lot more than the red in the lipstick. When she used these products, she clearly felt special, better than she had before she put them on. This feeling is as common to an impoverished Chinese woman in Beijing as to a wealthy woman on

Park Avenue. When she buys these products, she is saying: "I have dreams, my life can be better, I can feel better about myself."

When you listen carefully, you realize that it is these emotional components in any enterprise that can mean the difference between success and failure. Connecting with people's hopes and dreams is a dynamic I perceived in the eBay community. Both buyers and sellers so often loved eBay because it connected them to their aspirations—perhaps the desire of amassing a great collection, or the dream of financial stability from successfully building an online business. At FTD, on the other hand, when management underestimated the bonds between the staff and members of a family-like association, it drove some florists away. An emotional connection is central to any great relationship in business and in life.

7

Focus. Prune distractions.

Try to imagine what the following things have in common: $5 bills, soda cans, ceramic, paper, beads, wood, glass, metal, and twigs.

The answer is that all these materials have been used to make teapots.

I know this because Sonny Kamm, the owner of a remarkable collection of more than ten thousand teapots, once proudly gave me a book about his and his wife's collection. Sonny told me theirs is the world's largest and most comprehensive teapot collection, and, looking through his book, I was amazed at the creativity artists have shown in crafting these pieces. Sonny is retired now, but he had a very successful career as an attorney in Los Angeles. From a young age, he was drawn to collecting—coins, modern art. But then he and his wife, Gloria, became entranced with teapots, particularly unique art pieces. Several years ago he attended an event where he knew I would be, and he very kindly introduced himself and handed me the book, thanking me because he had bought more than a thousand of his teapots on eBay.

Wherever I go, even now that I have left eBay, people love to tell me their own personal eBay stories. Strangers at the airport will point to the watch on their wrist, wink, and say, "eBay." In boardrooms, in the grocery store, in hotel lobbies, in taxi lines, both men and women will tell me about some unusual item they tracked down on eBay, or confide to me how proud they are to be married to a "titanium power seller." Cisco Systems CEO John Chambers and I once met with President Bill Clinton before we spoke to legislators in Washington about technology policy; President Clinton greeted me by saying: "You know, I go on eBay to buy my gubernatorial campaign memorabilia."

But I think eBay's most devoted fans are collectors such as Sonny Kamm who feel a deep connection to the objects of their desire. They are passionate. They are driven. They are self-motivated and strive constantly to know everything they can about whatever they collect. Their faces light up when they talk about what they love, be it teapots, flagpole eagles, antique rocking chairs, or Elvis memorabilia, and what they always stress is how eBay has changed their lives by helping them pursue their passions more efficiently.

We once made a series of videos about some of our passionate collectors in the eBay community. For twenty-five years, for example, an eBay user who went by "Tiptie," from Highlands Ranch, Colorado, would get up at four o'clock on weekend mornings, grab a flashlight, and go to flea markets looking for radios. Tiptie was interested in every kind of radio: World War I and World War II military radios, cheap plastic novelty radios, classic radios, crystal radios. At the point where we met him, he owned more than 2,000 radios. Thanks to eBay, however, he was able to sleep in a little later on cold Colorado mornings. Instead of combing flea markets where a good day produced only one or two items he'd consider buying, Tiptie was delighted to find that several hundred new radios appeared for sale every evening on eBay. He explained that his motivation was not just the radios, but the stories and images of the eras attached to those radios. I get that. You look at this kind of collection and you imagine a soldier leaning close to the speaker on an old World War I field radio, hoping to learn when a backup infantry division might arrive. Or you hear in memory those scratchy versions of popular songs that used to bleat from cheap plastic transistor radios. "My passion is what they represent in the history of America," he explained in the video.

And then there is the eBay seller I always think of as the eyeball lady, a cheery, impish entrepreneur who starred in another early eBay video. While walking through a swap meet, she happened on a man selling glass eyeballs—700 of them, to be exact. She instantly was captivated and asked what he would charge for the whole lot. He said he would sell them for $5,000. Apparently he did not know much about eBay, but she did. She hurried home, looked up glass eyeballs on eBay, and noted the prices they fetched. She then withdrew the money she'd set aside for her son's college education, bought the whole stash of eyeballs, and began listing them on eBay. Eventually she made a $10,000 profit. With a twinkle in her (real) eye, she described in the video all the customers she got hooked on collecting glass eyeballs: "Normal people can afford one eye . . . but once you get one, you've got to have more."

Personally, I am not a collector. I have shelves of items I love, mostly because of the thoughtfulness of the giver. I have all those little pigs my brother, Hal, always finds for me to recall our cross-country trips. I have many different Potato Head toys wearing all kinds of different get-ups that friends and colleagues have given me through the years, along with other souvenirs of career stops. I have sports passions such as skiing and fly fishing that require gear, most of which I buy on eBay. But left to my own devices, I have never felt that compulsion to amass every stamp printed in the year of my birth, or Eiffel Tower replicas, or any one of the seemingly millions of specific objects that entrance collectors.

My mother, Margaret Whitman, as a
Red Cross volunteer in the early 1940s.

Mom always jumps in where she is needed.
Here she's fixing a truck engine in New
Guinea during World War II.

The Whitman kids were always
beachcombers. Here, in 1962,
Anne, Hal, and I (left to right) are
at Long Island Sound, where we
enjoyed swimming with our dad.

Here I'm with my mother and my father, Hal, in Florida, 1964. I've always loved fishing; I'm holding a feisty bonefish I caught myself.

My husband, Griff, and I have always enjoyed the outdoors and the mountains. Here we're in Colorado in 1982.

The family fishing tradition continues: Griff and I and the boys, Will (left) and little Griff, on the dock after fishing on vacation in 1991.

Pierre Omidyar, shown here with me in 1998, had the original vision of a perfect marketplace where anyone could buy or sell virtually anything. Here we ham it up with items from a big eBay collectible category—vintage sporting goods. © *James D. Wilson/ Liaison Agency*

When eBay launched Auction for America after September 11, 2001, I was grateful that my mother could share the experience with me.

My great executive team helped me successfully lead eBay. Here in 2003 (standing, left to right): me; Bill Cobb, head of eBay Marketing; our COO, Maynard Webb; and our general counsel, Mike Jacobson. Seated are Matt Bannick, head of eBay International; Jeff Jordan, head of eBay North America; and our CFO, Rajiv Dutta. © *Kim Kulish/Corbis*

I loved to meet our community members at eBay Live! events. Here eBayer Pam Giffin-Brees, with her handmade hat, joins (left to right) Jeff Jordan, then president of PayPal; John Donahoe, then president of eBay Marketplace, now CEO of eBay; and me at the 2005 event in San Jose, California. © *Kim Kulish/Corbis*

Here I'm talking with an energized group of young voters at the California Republican Party Convention in Indian Wells, California, in September 2009.

However, during my first few years as eBay's CEO, I realized that to be successful, what we as a company needed to collect was collectors. We needed to build a core community interested in collectibles; from there, I was confident, we would be able to expand almost infinitely.

The eBay of today is known for having such an eclectic mix of items for sale that people don't realize how much of our success rested on our early and intense focus on collectible merchandise. This is an example of how one secret of good management is the art of exclusion. Choosing to focus on doing a limited set of things well and pruning those efforts that threaten to distract you will help you be more successful in virtually anything you want to do.

FOCUS DEMANDS DISCIPLINE. Choices have consequences. If a child wants to be good at basketball or soccer, he or she has to practice the sport. That's just how it works. A young person cannot go to college and meander through the course catalog, change his or her major six times, drop classes when they become difficult, and four years later be a good candidate for medical school. Cannot be done. We can decry the intense pace of modern life and the pressures we put on our children. But we do the next generation a profound disservice if we don't help them connect the dots between focus, discipline, and the achievement of their goals.

Now, the reality is that when you focus, something's got to give. I look at women with beautifully decorated homes or spectacular wardrobes, women with every hair in place, and I think, "Wow, very impressive." And sometimes I think, "It would be so great to be able to do that." As with any other kind of success, I know that it doesn't happen accidentally, or by luck.

But here is the truth: I am not naturally drawn to fashion and decorating, so I do not focus on those things. I have made peace with that. My priorities have always been family and work. And thanks to the pressures and time commitment of my job, I have tried to spend my nonwork hours with Griff and the boys— hiking, skiing, helping with homework, having family dinners. That meant that Griff and I hardly ever socialized or went to charity events. We went to the boys' sports competitions, we took trips, we saw movies, we attended dinners with parents of the boys' friends. I never set aside much time to go shopping for the house or for myself. And when I worked at eBay we all wore casual polo shirts and khakis most of the time. To this day, I walk into a department store and I am slightly baffled about where to begin. Most of the time I take my close and very fashionable friend Diane Forese with me and she tries to steer me to outfits that she thinks will look good on me. My typical response: "Fine. Great. Are we done?"

This attitude works for me but does not always play so well with others. Early in my tenure at FTD I attended a cocktail party at the home of the chairman of the company, and he invited me to stay with him and his wife in their beautiful, art-filled Manhattan apartment. When I arrived and got settled in my room I saw that a gorgeous navy blue Armani suit lay on the bed waiting for me! I guess he didn't think much of my wardrobe. One of my friends was attending the party and I thought she was going to attack him with a butter knife for the insult when I told her what he'd done. I didn't have time to be offended; I found the whole situation easy to laugh about and shrug off. I accepted his gift and I loved wearing it. But would I have taken time away from Griff and the boys to go shopping for a party during that crazy, hectic period? No.

I once said something offhand to a *Fortune* reporter that I know will follow me for the rest of my life. She asked what I thought people thought of me, and I responded: "She's frumpy, but she delivers." They ran the quote in the story in giant type. She didn't misquote me. I would love to look snazzy and stylish every day, but something's got to give. I know that focusing has consequences.

IT WOULD BE EASY to look back on eBay's remarkable trajectory and assume that all we had to do was sit back and watch it grow. We were keenly aware that Pierre had tapped into an unmet desire of consumers to trade more efficiently in used goods—a dynamic so powerful that it put the wind to our back. However, eBay's growth was neither inevitable nor automatic. In fact, my team and I saw that the path branched off in different directions, and along the way we had to make choices.

Not long after I joined eBay, we had an executive retreat during which we made two of those choices. In fact, I don't believe I am exaggerating when I say that they determined the future of the company.

The first had to do with respecting the values of the eBay community. Chief among those values was inclusiveness. Pierre's original concept had been to level the playing field and allow any individual to compete in the marketplace regardless of whether he or she sold a few items from time to time, or thousands of items per year. High-volume sellers already were angling for volume discounts on listing fees and other special accommodations, but we decided we could not offer them those advantages. At the retreat Pierre made clear that our focus should be on developing a broad, democratic marketplace, not on identifying the most potentially profitable item categories we could possibly find to sell, or only supporting high-volume selling partners. I agreed.

We easily could have chosen a different path. In fact, many years later, thanks largely to competitive pressures, we had to go in some new directions. The explosion of social networking on the

Internet—everything from Facebook to online games to blogs—meant that people seeking a social experience or a community had many options beyond eBay. Some users did not want to spend quite as much time hanging out on eBay; rather, they wanted a more streamlined shopping experience. We learned from customer feedback that some had grown tired of the auction format and wanted a way to buy something quickly, without having to monitor an auction. To satisfy those users, we adopted options such as "buy it now" and instituted changes to the search and display formats that tended to favor large and efficient sellers. But for the first decade, we focused on creating a level playing field for all sellers and attracting as broad and committed a user community as we possibly could; that set the stage for the groundswell of support for eBay, and for its unfettered growth.

The other decision I made after a thorough and at times heated debate at that meeting involved how we were going to position ourselves when we went public. What market did we intend to own and how big was it?

The answer to this wasn't obvious, either. The total land-based U.S. auction market was enormous: it included sales of foreclosed homes, manufacturing equipment, repossessed cars, and government surplus items, not to mention high-end antiques, paintings, and jewelry. At various times we had listings for big-ticket items like those on eBay, but we were not trying to compete with government auctions, bank foreclosure sales, or Sotheby's. We also had both new and used electronic equipment, which was a very active category. From time to time people sold real estate and event tickets.

In his excellent book about eBay's early years, *The Perfect Store*, Adam Cohen reprinted a list of items that were for sale on eBay's non-computer-related section on September 12, 1995, just a couple of weeks after Pierre launched the site. There were eighteen items, including autographed underwear from the then-rapper, now-actor "Marky" Mark Wahlberg, a Toyota Tercel, a toy powerboat from the 1950s or 1960s, an Amiga video game console, and a membership in a Chicago health club. Meanwhile, there was another, slightly longer list of computer items up for auction, such as hard drives, software, and a used Sun workstation. Pierre put no restrictions on what could be sold, and he grouped the items into only the loosest of categories.

By the time I joined eBay two and a half years later and we were off on our retreat, eBay's listings had evolved more in the direction of Marky Mark's underwear and the toy boat than in the direction of Tercels or hard drives. In 1998, eBay's listings were dominated by collectibles. I believe, for example, that nearly 10 percent of the items listed on the site in that year were Beanie Babies. We had a very active set of buyers and sellers of camera equipment (like Rob Chesnut), pottery, and specialty antiques (like the clock Rajiv Dutta sold). We had vintage lunchboxes, sports cards, antique prints, stamps and coins, and back issues of an array of magazines from *National Geographic* to *Sports Illustrated*. In total, more than 90 percent of the items could probably be called collectibles.

The point of our executive debate was to answer the question "What is our core market? What are we *focused* on?" We were preparing to take the company public and we had to create a true brand and positioning statement for eBay so that investors would have confidence that we were focused on a solid market with high growth potential. What we found was that the people in the room were split into at least two camps.

Half the members of the retreat thought the goal should be to stress categories that represented huge retail markets, such as apparel, consumer electronics, jewelry, kitchen appliances, and sporting goods, in addition to vintage items. Those were indeed gigantic markets; the trouble was that there were huge competitors in each of them, and it was not clear to me that eBay stood to dominate any of them.

I argued for a different point of view. I felt collectors were eBay's most ardent buyers and sellers. These were people who not only bought and sold their particular flavor of merchandise but *cared deeply about it*. They trudged through the snow to find old radios; they could not resist buying more glass eyeballs! They liked to talk about their collections with other collectors. They subscribed to enthusiast magazines that they read cover to cover. And remember that collectors seek both vintage and new merchandise. Some covet every new kind of high-end Nikon camera; others love Prada bags; still others want to get their hands on items related to a hit movie or a young pop star. This market segment had very specific desires that eBay was unusually well suited to fulfill. Collectors were our Power of Many power alley.

I believed that the deep and abiding passion of these collectors was the beating heart of our nascent marketplace. Our best path, I believed, was to thoroughly embrace the collectibles market, to double down on it. Although in those days we had no idea how big eBay was going to be, I thought we had a very good shot at taking the collectibles market online. Instead of spreading our advertising and marketing dollars across huge categories where we would have to compete with established and well-heeled retailers, I argued that we should focus on collectibles, which we could market more effectively and efficiently than anyone else could. In that arena we could tap into "viral marketing," or the emerging tendency of happy e-commerce customers to recruit others.

So when we went public, we ultimately did so on the claim that we aimed to dominate and expand the $100 million market for collectibles. My vision was actually much grander: in 1998 I knew that only a fraction of collectors were online and that eBay represented such a dramatically more efficient way for them to find the items they wanted that they would soon be streaming to our site. Second, I knew that their enthusiasm for the marketplace would inspire them to sell other things on eBay and that would likely drive the growth of the business organically, which was going to save us the trouble of trying to anticipate what categories beyond collectibles should be the focus of our expansion.

Today, more than $100 million worth of goods is bought and sold on eBay *every day*. But I believe that keeping our focus tight at that stage was critical to how well we executed, and it gave us a lot of room to surprise investors on the upside.

WHAT DID IT MEAN to "focus" on collectibles? To support our general brand awareness and the growing interest in eBay, we did a modest national ad campaign in 1998 called "What Are You Searching For?" that helped people figure out how to use eBay to find anything they wanted. The ads ran in *Parade, Newsweek, People*, and other publications. But at the same time, Acme Idea Company, the boutique advertising agency we hired, created dozens of distinct ads for collector and enthusiast magazines—everything from *Maine Antique Digest* to *Contemporary Doll Collector* and the *Journal of the American Philatelic Society*. The basics of those ads were the same—we tried to demystify the Web and explain how to find us—but we would also include a photograph of an item with appeal to that magazine's readers, such as a rare China doll or a vintage globe. This was a bit of a logistical and trafficking challenge; we had to make sure we didn't accidentally put a photograph of a hand-carved duck decoy in a magazine for bird-watchers. But the strategy proved to be a great one for attracting both buyers and sellers of these vertical-market items to the site. There is an old saying in mass-market advertising that only about half the dollars you spend on it are effective, but you can't tell which half. But what we knew for sure was that readers and subscribers of enthusiast and collectors' magazines tend to read every word of every page, every ad, every chart. Each time we put an ad in one of these publications, traffic in that category on eBay went up.

Despite the eclectic mix, our success came from our focus. Rather than starting with the biggest possible market opportunity and trying to figure out how to compete with more entrenched companies already operating in it, we identified a path that was specific and manageable but that had the potential to scale up. eBay would be a very different place today if we hadn't doubled down on the collectibles market. Over time, collectors grew comfortable with eBay and they began to buy and sell other things on the site. But we aimed right at their sweet spot: they *loved* what they collected and they *loved* that we made that process even more fun and efficient. And we maintained a level playing field that made every individual feel like he or she had a chance.

REMEMBER, there was no precedent for a fast-growing online auction company in 1998. Many times in the early days of eBay I felt like I was driving the company down a Los Angeles freeway and approaching one unfamiliar cloverleaf after another. Should we take that off-ramp? Should we buy other businesses already a mile or two ahead? Should we hitch ourselves to a much bigger vehicle and let ourselves be pulled along? Or should we just keep barreling straight ahead, passing certain opportunities by? Did I mention that we were going about 100 mph? And, by the way, our competitors were racing right alongside us, trying to cut in front of us.

For example, a couple of days into our first road show for our initial public offering, Yahoo announced its own auction business, with one twist over ours: any listing would be free unless the item listed sold. When Pierre started eBay, he did not charge for listings, but over time we began charging a nominal fee because we discovered that it improved the quality of the items for sale. Otherwise people would take a chance and list all sorts of uninspiring things just to see what would happen, and that created a cluttered, uninteresting site. Even if it cost only a dime or a quarter to list an item, that tiny barrier to entry meant people were less likely to list a pair of used tube socks or a broken pencil described in mind-numbing detail. When we launched an eBay site in a new country, we often made listings free at first, and then later instituted the fee. After we began charging for listings, we quickly saw that the metric we called "conversion," or the ratio of listed items to sold items, grew dramatically because the tube socks and other meaningless items disappeared. In fact, conversion zoomed from less than 5 percent to around 50 percent.

We knew this when we set out on the road show. But investors did not know this, and at the time, Yahoo was a much bigger and better-known company. So everywhere we went, we had to field questions about why we weren't answering Yahoo's move by eliminating our own listing fees. Fortunately, we were very good at explaining the conversion issue, and so we held the line and did not react. And fortunately, Yahoo's auction site was very weak and sputtered out before long. About a year later, exactly the same thing happened with Amazon when they tried to launch an auction site: they launched trumpeting free listings, we held the line and explained why, and their site did not succeed, either.

Those two competitors were experimenting, trying to go after us. But they took us on on the wrong playing field. They were dabbling in auctions. Our competitive advantage was that we were focused on online auctions, albeit auctions for a wide variety of goods. Had we chosen the other path my team debated at that pivotal meeting—trying to take on some of the nation's largest retailers in categories such as electronics or apparel—we might very well have been on the wrong side of the focus equation. We might have been just another distribution channel for those goods and we might have been outfoxed by competitors with a deep expertise in selling those kinds of products at large scale.

But the power of focus does not lie in being single-minded, and it cannot become fixation. When I was in business school, reading hundreds of pages of assignments per week, I would sometimes get headaches and blurry vision. I went to the eye doctor, thinking I needed new glasses. Instead, he prescribed a series of exercises: Focus on a pencil in front of your face. Focus on something five feet away. Focus on something far away. Hold the pencil in front of your face and move it toward you and then away, keeping focused on it.

From all that reading, my ability to adjust my focus to different distances had suffered. I was locked in to the space eighteen inches in front me, but I'd short-circuited my ability to move easily from near to middle to long distance. Thanks to those exercises, I got it back.

When you run an organization, as vital as focus is, you cannot focus on just one metric, one point in time, or one context without missing other information you need. Focus exists in a relationship of tension with the need to grow, and growth is essential for any healthy organization. If you become too focused on the immediate needs of your business or on one component of your strategy, you will not be able to see opportunities for growth that demand that you adjust your strategy.

The need to manage this tension is one of the reasons why broad management experience is so vital for CEOs. As Pierre once put it, "Focus seems like a truism. I think it's something that is well understood and hard to pull off. It takes a skilled executive to differentiate between focusing on your core competencies and not adapting to the market as it changes." I also believe that being a leader is a constant exercise in moving your gaze back and forth between different focal lengths—what's right in front of you, what's ahead of you, what's coming at you, what's happening elsewhere that may eventually ensnare you—and making decisions in real time that steadily move the organization forward.

Resolving this tension involves many of the values I'm talking about in this book. They complement one another. You need to respect and listen to the people around you; you need to seek and demand measurements both at the highest level and on the ground so that you can track progress and understand the effect of what your organization is doing; you need to enfranchise all your partners in this quest so that you get early warnings from the people closest to the details. You need to experiment and take chances, but you can't get so attached to those moves that you hold on to them when they turn out not to work. Also, certain tools, or in the case of companies certain business lines, might be valuable at one stage of a company's life but outmoded or counterproductive at another stage.

Pruning can be difficult. When executives muster the courage to take a risk or try an experiment, they often get emotionally attached to the decision. But I have found that letting go of experiments that don't work gets easier when you do it routinely.

A good illustration of how this works in practice is the story of eBay's acquisition of Butterfield & Butterfield. In 1999, our stock had topped $200 per share and we were looking at ways to keep building on the collectibles business. When your stock is highly valued, it gives you a lot of options as a CEO, because you can make an acquisition without depleting cash reserves. We were enjoying very good growth in our core collectibles business, but we were looking at ways to capitalize on our brand by moving into higher-priced items.

Butterfield & Butterfield, based in San Francisco, was one of the world's top three land-based auction houses, along with Christie's and Sotheby's. All of these companies were getting nervous about eBay, and Butterfield had taken some preliminary steps to develop online auction capability and actually had filed for an initial public offering.

Now, this was an interesting opportunity from our point of view. The company had a prestigious brand in higher-value goods. The company also had widely respected appraisal and authentication services, with more than fifty specialists on staff able to authenticate, appraise, and market a wide range of art and fine collectibles, including paintings, furniture, and jewelry. I thought that capability might be of value within eBay itself as we tried to boost listings of more expensive items. The hope was not only that we could help Butterfield & Butterfield expand its business but also that our association might attract more high-end sellers and buyers to eBay. And again, we were playing a little bit of defense. The land-based companies were lining up with Internet companies, and we thought it was important to have a strong brand as we explored where the world of high-end auctions might go.

We agreed to pay $260 million for the company, all in stock. Wall Street liked the deal, and we were excited to try this new avenue that felt like it was the logical next step for collectibles.

As we moved forward, however, the differences in our cultures became starkly clear. When I went to San Francisco to meet with the Butterfield & Butterfield management, it was like going back in time. The average age of employees was at least twenty years older than at eBay. The attitude was sort of, "Oh, technology, shmology." This was a high-end, high-touch client service business. Men were in suits and ties, the women in dresses. Everything was mahogany and Oriental rugs and ornate frames around somber art. If you visited eBay, you would never see any of the items for sale on the site, but since Butterfield & Butterfield actually took physical possession of the items it sold, it had galleries of silver, paintings, and rugs. It even had galleries with full suits of armor! It would dispatch a team to clear out dear Mrs. Gotrock's estate and then spend weeks determining the provenance of a single painting.

At the time, eBay's average item selling price per item was under $50, whereas Butterfield & Butterfield had an average selling price for the artworks, antiques, and other collectibles it handled of about $1,500. Yes, it occasionally would get attention for selling a famous painting for millions of dollars, but that was not the norm. The company's actual revenues at the time were only about $20 million. In fact, the total value of the goods sold at the three best-known traditional auction houses annually today is about $500 million.

We encouraged Butterfield & Butterfield to keep growing and expanding its traditional business. We launched Great Collections, where we featured merchandise from Butterfield and some other auction houses, breaking from our past model of person-to-person trading. We were able to assure buyers in these auctions that the items had been authenticated by professionals.

But after about two years we realized this acquisition just wasn't working for us. We were trying to merge a hundred-year-old, white-glove culture with a four-year-old Internet culture. Their folks were not especially comfortable with e-mail and responding to community questions, and they were not used to having to ship items in a very timely manner. It turned out that while the elite strata of traditional auction buyers were united by shared interests, just like collectors on eBay, in fact they also craved the real-world physical setting and traditions of a live auction. They liked the champagne served from silver trays, the attentive staff, the pleasure of going head-to-head with a known rival collector and emerging triumphant when the hammer came down and the auctioneer shouted, "Sold!"

If we had been fixated on owning every possible corner of the collectibles market, we might have stayed with this foray too long. In my view, the synergies we'd thought were there simply weren't. Plus, it turned out that relative to how big eBay was becoming, it just was not worth it to us to try to expand into what actually was not that big a market. Auction houses get headlines when they sell a blockbuster item like Monet's *Water Lilies* for $71 million, but eBay was on its way to doing that much merchandise volume every afternoon.

In 2002, we called it a day and sold the company to the British auction house Bonham's. We had too many other things to do to keep trying to figure out how to make this work. It was a good idea and worth trying, but I'm glad we didn't keep throwing attention and money at it. We pruned Butterfield & Butterfield.

SOMETIMES PRUNING MEANS ADMITTING that you can have too much of a good thing. One powerful example of too-muchness is a phenomenon peculiar to the high-tech world called "feature creep." One version of it is when the folks who write software programs include little pet tools, extra features, or clever design preferences that turn out to be not all that useful for customers. Most users of Microsoft Word, for example, admit that they only use a tiny fraction of the program's capabilities. In general, that's okay; the program serves a broad market, and the abundance of features allows many different kinds of users to choose from a large menu of tools. However, it's not okay if this abundance of features clutters up in the interface so much that a person who just wants to write a letter and print it out can't figure out how to easily do that. That's feature creep.

At eBay, we found there was a tendency for our Web page designers and marketing people to want to add different cool functions—different ways to search auctions, customizable layouts, new payment options. Users were always suggesting buttons, tabs, or little tools that helped show off their items or sell them more effectively. Over time, we responded to some of these requests, adding capabilities that our marketing people thought would improve customer interactions and transactions.

Well, around 2003 or so, we began to realize that our auction pages were becoming loaded down with a lot of options, buttons, and tabs. We were starting to get feedback that some people found all the options distracting and confusing. We were in the grip of feature creep. The trouble is, every feature has its fans, and when you remove that feature, you make someone—or many someones—unhappy.

The escrow option was one of those features that initially seemed like a great way to create a safer transaction for both parties. Just like the escrow for a house, we designed it so the parties could agree that the buyer would send the money to a trusted, independent escrow account to be held until the item was delivered; the seller would be notified that the funds had arrived and would ship the item, and the escrow service would then send the seller the funds once the item arrived at the buyer's.

Well, we launched the product, but hardly anybody used it except in Korea, where the auction company we bought was designed to rely on escrow and everybody uses it. Neither I nor anyone else could have predicted this, although it does go back to the trust factor in the eBay community. Then, as we were integrating PayPal and trying to clean up the transaction process, we realized that having the escrow option was confusing to users. It wasn't something they expected to find and they didn't really understand how it worked. They would sometimes go read about it, but then they usually wouldn't use it. Worse, we started to see escrow fraud rising, as third parties would contact eBay users, pretending to be legitimate escrow services.

A prominent escrow option was only useful to a few thousand people who, for whatever reason, really liked it and insisted on using it. I said, "Let's get rid of it," and we announced that it was going.

The next day, it felt like every one of those rare users personally sent me an e-mail expressing their fury at the decision.

I called in our customer support staff and made sure that we sent each and every person who had written to us a response. Essentially, it said, "Thank you for your feedback. We hear you, and we understand that for you and a small group of people escrow was a very important and trusted feature. Unfortunately, so few members of the community use it and it takes up space and resources to keep it going, so we have made a decision that we think is in the best interest of the eBay ecosystem as a whole."

This response did not fix the fact that we had unhappy customers. People do appreciate getting a response, but this was not the response they were looking for. Nonetheless, you have to make decisions like this when you're pruning; you need to think through how it is going to impact the community and listen carefully to their feedback, but you have to exercise those pruning muscles from time to time or the clutter and confusion will actually drive users away.

I believe success in any endeavor demands focus when times are good or bad, stagnant or shifting, peaceful or perilous. If you are the leader of an organization or a business, that focus must become part of the DNA of your enterprise. However good times may be, resources and time are always limited, and it is better to do three things well than ten things in a halfhearted way. No matter what you are doing, realigning your efforts with your core mission and strategy and then pruning back extraneous shoots will always help create a more accountable, stable, efficient operation.

8

Enfranchise and validate.
Teamwork works.

I know and have worked for executives who relish few things as much as the fear they see in a subordinate's eyes. Some even have rituals designed to keep those who report to them in a constant state of fear and uncertainty. They purposely interrupt staffers when they are speaking. They keep them waiting to establish superiority. They sift through an otherwise strong report or presentation and play up its weaknesses. They needle, needle, needle. And they always want to make life as hard for a new recruit as they feel it was made for them.

I have two thoughts about this management approach.

First, life is too short to act like this.

Second, I don't think you can create the Power of Many by bullying people into doing what you want and trying to make every day an excruciating mind game to figure out what the boss really wants. For one thing, in this age of transparency, it's too easy for employees to communicate and share information that whittles away a secretive, manipulative, command-and-control structure.

In the very early days of Bain & Co., the partners would spend a lot of time and resources recruiting very smart and talented people from the very best business schools. Then they would throw them into the deep end of the swimming pool, stand along the edge with their arms crossed, and watch to see who could swim. There was virtually zero training and there was an almost deliberately aloof posture toward new hires designed to cull the herd. When one person showed weakness, not only the leadership but the other members of the recruiting class would pounce. It was common in law firms, too. It was the way partnerships tended to operate. The focus was on proving yourself to be tough and smart enough to figure it out, compete, and survive.

When I joined Bain, this practice was in full force. I was in San Francisco, and the first couple of years I spent a lot of time trying to decipher the unspoken, unexplained techniques and tools of management consulting. I loved the work, and I not only survived but thrived. So did another young consultant in the office, a woman named Barbara Goefft. What Barb and I had in common, in addition to staying afloat in the deep end (albeit with a few crocodile teeth marks on our legs), was that we had both come to Bain from Procter & Gamble, which took a completely different approach. As I've said before, P&G was known as one of the finest training organizations in the country.

After we had both been promoted, we learned that a senior partner was visiting the San Francisco office, and he wanted to take us to dinner and talk about how things were going and what Bain could do better. I think Barb and I had a sense that we had a little bit of political capital, and so we devoted much of our dinner to advocating that Bain rethink the way it handled new hires. My argument was simply this: "We spend a lot of money on recruiting, and I understand survival of the fittest, but if we throw some of these new hires a life preserver, we might just raise the retention rate of recruits from three out of ten to five out of ten. If we made even a modest investment in orienting new hires and preparing them better for their first assignments, we might very well

reduce overall costs by offsetting some of our recruiting investment. We also can improve loyalty and morale. And if that's not
enough, if a person still doesn't make the cut but you have at least
extended some help, they will feel better about the experience.
These are highly intelligent, highly educated, often well-connected
individuals. They are not going to leave us and disappear into a
monastery. When you meet them down the road and they need to
hire a consulting firm, wouldn't it be better if you had parted on
cordial and respectful terms?"

To his credit, the partner listened, and Barb and I were
charged with developing a training program in San Francisco.
Bain started paying more attention to training at headquarters in
Boston as well. The results played out just as we had predicted
they would: we improved both individual performance and retention, and boosted morale and loyalty. Extending a hand to help
new recruits assimilate and succeed reduced the Roman spectacle
factor in the office, and the culture really changed. The company
even created a Bain alumni club that maintained ties to consultants who moved on into all sorts of important positions where,
when the situation called for it, they would consider hiring Bain.
Bain began enfranchising its new hires in the larger goals of the
organization.

THERE IS NO MORE central notion to harnessing the Power of
Many than enfranchising. Enfranchising is not about being liked
or being kind. Effective leaders have to make tough decisions,
crack the whip, and sometimes even let people go. They have to
make each and every individual accountable for his or her performance. I have fired young MBAs at eBay and elsewhere when
their ambition outstripped their willingness to listen and do the
task they were asked to do.

However, in my experience, using petty shows of power and intimidation is a sign of fear, not strength. More important, it doesn't yield a team in which every individual assumes responsibility for the team's success. That is what I mean by enfranchising. Enfranchising means convincing every stakeholder—not just employees, but partners, consultants, even customers—that we have a shared mission that we can best achieve by working together rather than attacking and undermining one another.

I can think of a lot of examples in my business career where enlisting the help of other people was invaluable. But no example will ever mean more to me than the system failure that those of us who were there still tend to simply call "the outage." I have referred to some of the steps I took after the outage occurred, but since we are talking here about enfranchising, I want to go into some detail about what exactly happened and how the solutions laid the groundwork for us to become a large and successful company. In fact, I consider it a key reason that eBay never developed the arrogance so many high-flying Silicon Valley companies display. I also believe the approach I took during that crisis validated my management approach and the values of the company.

To appreciate the drama of what happened, imagine for a moment that you run a shipping company. You have just arrived home from the office and the phone rings. It's your assistant, calling with the news that your entire fleet has disappeared into the Bermuda Triangle. For all practical purposes, on June 10, 1999, eBay vaporized for twenty-two hours, and during many of those hours, we did not know if it was going to reappear in a form that would allow us to stay in business.

Pierre wrote the original computer code that launched eBay in 1995. But by early 1997, before I had ever heard of the company, the traffic was outstripping his original system's ability to handle it. So he brought in a talented computer engineer named

Mike Wilson. By the end of 1997, Mike had completely replaced the original system with a new one of his own design.

Around this time, I met Pierre and agreed to come to eBay. What I did not appreciate was that the new system already was groaning under the pressure of the exploding number of transactions. Mike and his team were pretty good at keeping it together and getting it back up to speed when things went wrong, but they went wrong quite frequently. As I will explain, Mike and I had a conversation about this that would prove fateful, but the fact was that by the time I joined the company in early 1998, there was so much to do to organize the management of the company, set strategy, and bring marketing up to speed that I simply had to rely on Pierre and Mike's understanding of the technology. I had not had any experience directly managing technology. Although we launched FTD's website on my watch, it was in the very early days of online commerce, and we were just beginning to experiment with a Web presence. At Hasbro, our computer systems were just an internal tool, not much more of a management issue for me than our heating and air-conditioning systems.

Many websites went down a lot in those early days; people forget that now but it was not uncommon. Both AOL and Amazon, for example, experienced a number of system outages that lasted a dozen hours or more. The trouble at newly public eBay was that the tendency for the system to crash seemed to accelerate through 1998 and early 1999. Especially in the spring of 1999, our system had been very unstable, going down for several hours at a time several times per month. Our most basic problem was that it was not designed to grow as rapidly as the volume of our transactions was growing.

As Maynard Webb later said of that period, "eBay was a one-bedroom house trying to hold eight kids." Actually, I think it was a little worse than that. You can add more rooms to a house, but it is a monstrous task to try to do that while the family is living in the house and a new baby is arriving every few weeks. That is what our engineers were trying to do. I don't want to give the impression that we did not have talented and smart engineers at eBay before Maynard arrived; we truly did and, in hindsight, the fact that Mike Wilson and his team kept the company going as well as they did for as long as they did was something of a miracle.

But there was another aspect of that issue that also was causing us more and more trouble. The system was not designed to recover quickly when things went wrong. Imagine the difference between an air mattress that you buy to sleep on while camping or to float on in a swimming pool and a rubber raft you might take down the Colorado River. Both float, but the latter not only is built more ruggedly but has at least three or four different distinct chambers that are inflated independently. Before Maynard arrived at eBay, our system was like an air mattress. Every time we were punctured by a single failure, the whole thing sank until we could fish it out, patch it, and reinflate it. After it went down, the system often needed four hours to reboot itself. On top of that, since we tried to make up the glitch to our community immediately, we would write a program to extend auctions or refund fees, and running that took an additional forty-five minutes. We did not have what systems people call a "fail-to-backup" plan, like the generators that kick on in a hospital when there is a power outage. Even a relatively simple problem meant at least a five-hour outage, and CNN seemed to enjoy covering every one.

Another complication was that the hardware and software we used to run the system came from multiple vendors. Sun provided the servers; Oracle provided the database software; Veritas provided the storage capacity. Our people coordinated with our vendors' respective engineers to make it all work together. What someone like Maynard Webb later brought to the table was experience in systems integration and a keen understanding of how to deal with multiple vendors in a large systems operation. Neither I nor anyone else at eBay was expert in that. In complex information system designs, the different vendors have competing preferences for how to perform certain tasks and solve problems, as well as their own interests. When you need to make decisions, each vendor is whispering in your ear that his or her solution is the best one and the other guys are just trying to sell you. Like a good general contractor in a home remodel, somebody needs a strong enough grasp of the technology to sort all that out.

By June, the system had been unstable for weeks and had gone down several times. Then on Thursday evening, June 10, a few minutes before eight, it went down again. I had been home for just a few minutes when the phone rang. I had a standing order that someone call me when the site went down, and every hour after that until it came back up. The first three or four hours, I got my hourly call and things sounded (I hate to say it) fairly typical. Engineering was scrambling to determine the problem and what to do.

The patch between 11:00 p.m. and 4:00 a.m., however, was rougher. I could hear the rising panic in the voices of the systems engineers. They were not quite sure what had happened or when the site would come back. I also was not comforted by the cryptic reports I was getting by phone from Bonaire, an island off the coast of Venezuela. That's where Mike Wilson happened to be taking his first vacation in three years, and he was trying to talk our systems engineers through the crisis via e-mail, relying on a dial-up modem. Sometime in the wee hours of the morning, I told Mike he needed to get back home, only to learn that there were just three scheduled flights per week off the island. I immediately authorized chartering a plane to go get him.

As the hourly updates came and went, I could tell that this time was different. We were "hard down." And we later learned that, in addition to our own system design, several different products from different vendors had failed. The most terrifying immediate problem was that our entire database of transactions and buyer and seller information had become corrupted. That typically means that the actual data are in there, but key instructions in the software have gone haywire and made it inaccessible.

As far as our buyers and sellers knew, eBay had sailed into the Bermuda Triangle. Sellers could not access their auctions and buyers could not bid.

I came back into the office very early in the morning, sometime before six. Everyone on the technical team was scrambling, but I could see that only a small group of people seemed to be systematically attacking the problem. Most of them just didn't know enough about the overall system to figure out how to be useful. We had a few technical support reps from our vendors, but the minute their switchboards opened the next morning, I started calling the CEOs of our software and hardware suppliers. I called Scott Mc-Nealy at Sun, Ray Lane at Oracle, and Mark Leslie at Veritas. "We love your sales guys, we love your tech guys," I told them, "but right now we need your absolute best engineers. We are in a world of hurt."

In a time of crisis, I think all leaders have to operate at different functional levels. We had a hornet's nest of a system problem that needed the best brains our vendors could send us. That was priority A. But there were practical needs as well. I dispatched my assistant, Anita, to collect cots, food, and toothbrushes because I could see that this situation was going to take a while to resolve and I wanted to convey to the team that I knew that. I wanted to let them know that I was going to ask each and every person to do what it took to fix this, and that I would remain beside them throughout the ordeal. I don't recall spending much time on those cots over the next twelve or fourteen hours, but I did stay in the office for a couple of days straight as we continued to battle the system's unstable behavior. I also called in members of my executive team who were not systems people and who did not have a clue how to reboot a system. I figured it could only help to have everybody supporting our technical crew regardless of what they normally did.

Partly because eBay had been such a successful stock and the company was in the news so much, by midmorning the media were covering the outage almost the way they sit perched outside the Vatican when the cardinals are voting on a new pope, watching the color of the smoke. Employees and vendors going in and out had to run a gauntlet of reporters.

As I waited for Mike Wilson to return, I secretly battled a frustration that was well over a year old. About three weeks after I joined eBay, I'd had a meeting with our lead venture investor, Bob Kagle, and I remember telling him, "Every bone in my body is telling me that we don't have the right guy in place to lead our technology group."

The reason was that I had gone to Mike Wilson and said, "What is your capacity?"

He'd replied, "I don't know what you mean."

I said, "Well, look, when I was at Stride Rite I could go to the manager of any of our plants and say, 'How many shoes do you produce in a day? How many Keds can you produce in a month?' So I need to know, what is our capacity? How many transactions do we have the capacity to do before we exhaust the processing and storage resources of the system?"

"I don't think that way," he said, shrugging.

Mike Wilson had joined eBay during a critical time in its growth. He brought valuable experience to the table; he had worked at The Well, which was a precursor to the kind of thriving, energetic community that eBay became. He was a rare combination—a systems engineer with a keen sense of community. He even had an alter ego called "Skippy" who cruised the bulletin boards, serving as an often playful voice of reason and upbraiding members who seemed to be doing things against the spirit of eBay.

However, Mike's technical team was created and run with the sort of bachelor's-apartment ethos common among many programmers. They were independent and tended to resent being accountable to anyone. They came in late and left in the wee hours of the morning. On the coldest days, they dressed in T-shirts, shorts, and flip-flops. They built sculptures out of soda cans. They created an office space that looked like an unmade bed. They prided themselves on cheap workarounds, such as hand-splicing cables. When we finally rigorously analyzed our system after the outage, outside experts could not believe some of the particulars of eBay's system. To cool the servers, Mike and the guys had simply run out to some household products store and bought big upright fans.

I think we could have survived all those cultural issues, but from day one Mike saw me as a "suit" imported from a world that didn't and probably never would understand what he did. I generally have good luck figuring out how to get along with people even if we are very different, but I was not able to do so in this situation.

So I had to push all that frustration way down as we struggled through the outage. At one point a young engineer looked at me and said, "We're not sure we can bring it back up." When I shared that with Pierre, he said quietly, "Usually about the time when everything looks the worst, the engineers are about to figure it out."

I intuitively knew that this was no time to get angry at our vendors or blame them for our problems, even though some of the issues were caused by product failures. There were plenty of examples of system failures at other companies that had turned into pie-throwing contests. In talking with our vendors, I made it clear that we desperately needed help, not a scapegoat. And not more than a couple of hours after Pierre made his prediction, thanks to the combined sweat and efforts of both our team and the vendors, the site reappeared. Sun CEO Scott McNealy in particular was a great help to me during not only the early part of this crisis but also the two-to-three-day period afterward and beyond (the initial outage was twenty-two hours, but then it would come up for eight hours and go down for eight hours, and parts of the site would not function properly). Scott would later tell *BusinessWeek*: "Instead of making me angry, she made me want to do just about anything we could to solve her problem. And that's what we did."

Once the system finally recovered, it was like what happens after you have some kind of collision in your car. It may run, and all four wheels may turn, but it's not the same car. Our feedback pages, for example, took five days to come back. Other sections of the website were sort of blinking in and out like a neon sign in an old movie. Mike was meting out minimal information selectively instead of briefing his team so they could attack the problem as a group. I think by the following Thursday, I went to Pierre and said: "This ends now. Mike has to go." Pierre said, "Do what you need to do for the good of the company." And to his credit, Mike stayed around to help us with the transition out of this disaster and into the next phase of the company's life, but then he did leave. These moments are never easy, but there are times when they are necessary.

AS IF THE TECHNICAL ISSUES were not difficult enough to sort out, we had the business issues. As I already explained, we decided to refund the auction fees to all sellers. A number of staffers worried that the earnings hit we would take would crater the stock, but some on Wall Street actually thought this overture to our sellers was a good idea.

"When you have a problem caused by too many people wanting something, that's actually a pretty good kind of problem," Mary Meeker of Morgan Stanley said later. "In a way, the publicity about the outage actually brought even more attention to eBay and I think made more people check it out. It was like there was this really great restaurant that had opened and it was hard to get in, so you just kept trying."

Our investor relations team of course fielded calls from shareholders; we had suffered a terrible hit to our reputation. But the most devastating thing was having let down the eBay community. We had not delivered results. At this point, many people were making their entire living from running eBay businesses, and when we were down, they were down. They were losing money every minute that bidders could not access their items.

With that in mind, my management team took the list of eBay's thousand or so top sellers and divided it among us. We went down the list and personally called our sellers to apologize, and I can tell you firsthand that some of the sellers were shocked that we were willing to do that. Our CFO was charged with managing our financial position and making sure our investors were informed about what was going on, but he picked up the phone to call customers, too. Our head of Europe, Michael van Swaiij, was Dutch and spoke several languages, and so we had him personally call many of our high-volume sellers all over Europe.

Ultimately, the eBay fleet escaped the Bermuda Triangle. We had sprung plenty of leaks and were not at full strength, but the importance of this crisis was that it strengthened our relationship with both our technology partners and our community. Our partners became even more invested in keeping us up and running. All of us were tired of being embarrassed and appearing on CNN to explain yet another outage. We were honest with our community and apologized with humility. And we learned many lessons that made us so much better. Eventually Maynard even convinced eBay's major systems vendors—Veritas, Oracle, and Sun—to make part of the compensation of the teams that serviced our account dependent on eBay being up and running at full strength. Nobody else had ever thought of doing something like that.

In terms of customer relationships, we did not try to hide behind "technical difficulties" or avoid taking responsibility. As we apologized, we listened to our community's point of view. We refunded their auction fees. We gained new knowledge about ways to make the system even better. The connections we forged deepened the trust between us. I think the message that came through was that we were there not to exploit them but to empower them. "We let you down," we said, "but we vow to fix this problem; we understand how vital it is to you that we do everything we can." And we did.

The heart of what we did, in hindsight, was validate how important all our partners were to us, and how we respected and needed their involvement so that we all could move forward. I think you can see that in Scott McNealy's comment. The outage was truly the defining moment in eBay's first decade of existence.

TO BUILD A GOOD TEAM and enfranchise your partners, you need to learn to validate their efforts. When we do something right and somebody notices, it pleases us and motivates us. When we express an opinion that others find insightful or useful, it pleases us. The success of eBay and other sites that build community is due at least in part to the satisfaction and sense of validation that people get from sharing useful knowledge with one another and being recognized for doing so.

What more evidence of this do we need than the social networking sites where people post their stray thoughts on everything from the weather to their favorite singer to the political events of the day? Among the options for those reading Facebook status updates, for example, is a simple button marked "like" that starts a tally. I think people of my generation sometimes react to sites such as Twitter and Facebook by saying, "Who could possibly care about or be interested in every stray thought I have?" But we're overthinking it. That "like" button is just the electronic version of the smile and nod that we might get at a cocktail party in response to a funny little remark. It's no different from the thank-you we might get for giving someone advice on the best place to get a sandwich.

When people care about anything—parenting, collecting teapots, their career, a local sports team, being positive members of a community—they are motivated and energized by feedback. My older son, Griff, is almost a savant when it comes to cars. He has devoured car magazines since he was a young boy and can tell you the manufacturer, model, and sometimes even the model year of a car by headlights he sees in the dark. It is a source of pride to him that he can rattle off these details, and it makes him happy to be able to answer someone's car question. When our friends and family treat him as our go-to car guy, he feels validated for the effort he has made to learn that information.

If you think about it, few of us experience a lot of validation in our daily lives. That brief article in the local paper featuring a photo of your child's soccer team matters because it doesn't appear very often. In fact, before social networking sites existed, most people went through their days collecting mostly neutral to negative feedback, or no feedback at all. Even the most famous, award-winning actress and the most powerful political leader are constantly barraged with criticism and advice about what they could do better.

Trust me, CEOs are in constant contact with shareholders, customers, and partners who are dissatisfied, even angry. Even when we might appear to be riding high, there is almost always plenty of behind-the-scenes friction. One evening when my son Griff was in middle school, I drove him to the local bookstore so he could buy one of his car magazines. When he came out, he handed me four or five other magazines he had bought—I was on the cover of every one. "Geez, Mom, it was a good week," he said. But these little bright spots rarely last for long. During the period when I was on those magazine covers, it's also true that I would make a decision two or three times a week and within hours have hundreds of angry e-mails from the eBay community in my inbox. Occasionally some would accuse me of all sorts of nefarious motives, call me names, even predict my imminent demise. When I was on CNN during our outages I ran out of ways to say, "We're on it, we hope to be up soon, and I'm so sorry this happened."

As parents, we are proud of our children, but when we come home after a stressful day, their shortcomings can elicit all kinds of criticism and annoyance from us. "Hey, your room's a mess!" "What do you mean, you didn't turn your paper in on time?" "Don't tell me you wore your cleats in the house again—look at this mud!" "Go to a concert on a school night? Uh, no, that's not going to happen. Why would you even ask?" Sometimes the subtext to those remarks is really: "What am I doing wrong here? Why aren't you figuring these things out on your own?" Both of you end up in a bad mood.

In short, modern life is not one big warm hug after another for anybody, and we can't do much to change that. But I must confess that the business strategist and marketer in me knows that validation is in short supply and sees it as an incredibly powerful tool to grow a business.

Look at the whole concept of auctions. Many people have written about the frenzy that comes over some auction bidders in real life and online. Winning an item is thrilling, but so is jumping into the lead every time you increase your bid. When this happens on eBay, your screen says, "You are the high bidder and currently in the lead." Where else do we have a small action validated so swiftly and reliably? As I mentioned in Chapter 7, the success of live, land-based auctions for fine art is intensely related to the validation art collectors experience when they gather to bid on their passions. Nobody *needs* to spend millions of dollars on a piece of fine art. Nobody *needs* a suit of armor or a Paul Revere silver pitcher. But these customers know they will be tended to, they will be seen, they will mingle with other collectors, their purchase will be covered in art magazines, their taste will be validated, their investments and commitment to the arts will be noted.

Or let's consider the star ratings on eBay. The rating system is the heart and soul of eBay; it motivates people to behave properly, so as to build and protect their reputations, and it is a real source of pride. Once at eBay I was at my desk when my assistant said Arthur Levitt, then the chairman of the Securities and Exchange Commission, was on the line. I was not expecting his call and it was one of those moments where your heart skips a beat. At the time, there had been plenty of corporate scandals and accusations of insider trading. What in the world did he want? I actually called our general counsel, Mike Jacobson, and asked him to join me for the call.

I picked up the phone. Chairman Levitt said that he had been reviewing all of eBay's documents for a stock offering and it all looked fine, but that he wanted to ask me a few questions to collect "customer feedback." He wanted to know how well the SEC staff had performed in our dealings with them. I could finally breathe again. We had a nice, brief chat, and it soon became obvious that what Levitt was most anxious to tell me was that he was an avid trader of Depression glass on eBay and he had just received a yellow star rating for receiving ten positive feedbacks.

Here was a powerful government official who could make the CEOs of every public company in the nation quake with just a phone call, but he took tremendous pride in the fact that people he had never met considered him a trusted and capable trading partner on eBay. Realize that people didn't know who Levitt was on eBay. He had bought into our community, followed our rules, and prospered. In this arena, people respected what he'd delivered without caring who he was. This pleased him thoroughly. That's the power of validation.

PROCTER & GAMBLE was great at teaching how to use validation as a business tool. As a brand manager at P&G, you were the center of the wheel; the spokes were sales, packaging, product development, finance, and human resources. The challenge was, you had no authority over the spokes but you had to influence them to do what you needed them to do. You had to go to them and say, "Here's my objective for my brand." I learned that you get people to do what you want not because you tell them to but rather because you listen and enlist them in your vision. This goes back to enfranchising. You get their input so that your vision can be better, and when they see that you are listening and you are incorporating their input, they feel validated.

For example, I once worked on a display for a consumer shampoo product for drugstores. The sales force manager took one look and said: "It needs to take one minute to set up. Our guy will make fifty stops that day and he can't spend ten minutes at each store just setting up this display." It would never have occurred to me—and it made perfect sense. We redesigned the display.

By listening and implementing a colleague's advice, you enfranchise him. You validate his expertise. He now is part of this team and wants this program to work. The next time he might suggest something you never thought of that makes it work even better. Or he might notice something a competitor is doing and let you know about it when he returns from the field; armed with that information, you might change your approach. You are teammates now. He is invested in your success. He knows that you're listening to him, and he has an opportunity to contribute. Ideally, he knows you will give him credit for those contributions.

PERHAPS COUNTERINTUITIVELY, providing validation sometimes requires getting employees or other stakeholders—or even yourself—to back away from the notion of being perfect. We talked about the danger of perfectionism in the context of getting stuck, but I think we need to watch out for it in a lot of different areas of life.

Personally, I wonder whether trying to be the "perfect" wife, mother, and executive undermines a woman's ability to be effective in a balanced way in those pursuits. It's always triage in life. At any given moment something is more important than something else. Priorities have to be set—but not permanently and not in stone. It helps to be open and honest and acknowledge that. If you don't, you can create unbearable stress for yourself and your family.

If your child is ill and you're asked to take on an impossible list of tasks in the office, is it better to agree to do it and then fall short and offer up the child's illness as an excuse? Or is it better to say, "Ordinarily, I would be able to do this, but today is not an ordinary day. Can we discuss what is most important so that I don't commit to anything I'm not sure I can deliver?" My preference is obvious. People are basically good and reasonable. They respond to honesty. A manager deserves an honest answer and should respect you for it. Don't cling unrealistically to the idea that if you aim for perfection, you can do everything. That manager, in turn, needs to acknowledge that an employee concerned about doing the most important tasks first is showing good judgment.

Would you rather have an imperfect Thanksgiving with burned sweet potatoes where you nonetheless are welcoming and everyone is happy to be together, or be in the kitchen fuming and obsessing because you got held up at work and a few things didn't get done quite right? I always say that I think my house is lovely but Martha Stewart would not be impressed. You have to make compromises in life. When you do, focus on the elements that are positive, not on what you lose in the compromise.

My husband is a world-class neurosurgeon. Most of our career moves during our nearly thirty-year marriage have involved a trade-off for either his career or mine. That was always okay; when the other person really, really wants something, making sure that he or she gets it is deeply satisfying and clearly the right thing to do. However, there is never a "perfect" solution. As I said, when I was at Disney and Griff's dream job was offered to him in Boston, I was sorry to leave Disney and sorry to leave California. But I later had some very valuable experiences at FTD, Stride Rite, and Hasbro because we moved. It was fun to reconnect with family. When the eBay opportunity came along a few years later, I was so excited that this time Griff agreed to move west. He now is very happy at Stanford. Holding out for perfect can be the enemy of a great opportunity to do something new.

In business, as we've discussed, iteration is the process of trying something new but accepting that we won't get everything perfect the first time. Iteration is a critical technique when you are designing products or launching new initiatives, and I return to it in this chapter because to iterate successfully you must understand how to validate interim steps. When you buy into the idea of iterating, what you're saying is: "We're probably not going to get it perfect on the first or second try. Therefore, let's say up front that we're not going to treat the people taking on this challenge as if a trapdoor is going to open under them if they come up with something that isn't perfect. We're going to look at what they did right, validate that, and then tinker."

VALIDATION IS AT THE HEART of another underused set of management and problem-solving tools. Never be afraid to borrow a good idea. Pay for it by giving credit. In fact, share credit as liberally as you can.

If you had said that to me when I was a Bain freshman, I would have blanched and responded, "Are you kidding me? Credit is everything!" I spent a lot of time watching my Bain colleagues jockey for credit and thinking, "Okay, my future is going to depend on learning how to do this." There was even a wry expression I heard Bain managers repeat when the jockeying started to interfere with the work: "Imagine what we could accomplish if we didn't care who got the credit."

The person who gave me the best advice about how to think about credit was former Massachusetts governor Mitt Romney. Mitt was the partner at Bain who hired me into the company in 1980, and over the next eight years I was often a member of his case teams. Mitt and I have now been friends for twenty-five years. When I was very new to the organization I was talking to him about some project and how I wasn't sure I was going to get credit for what I had done. He said, "Do the work. Make sure you have contributed everything you can to every project you work on. Borrow good ideas when you hear them and give credit to whoever thought of them. If you focus on that instead of on trying to or-chestrate getting credit for yourself, it will be obvious that you are always in the neighborhood of good things happening and you eventually will get all the credit you deserve."

In any given instance you may indeed be outfoxed by some schemer. But your career is not a single project, it is a long-term play, and Mitt was right.

Too many businesspeople have an unquenchable thirst for credit, or an ego problem that prevents them from reaching out in a sincere and effective way to people who can help them. Once you establish a track record for giving credit to those who help you, I guarantee you will get even more help. The fact that you ask someone for help or advice or the benefit of their experience val-idates them. The appreciation you show when they provide their help and you use it validates them. Later, when you mention where an effective idea came from, it validates them again. Validation motivates and energizes.

In business we call borrowing certain kinds of ideas "seeking best-demonstrated practices." Every student in business school reads cases that show how real-life companies handled particular situations and what lessons can be learned from their experiences. And yet, borrowing ideas often is not well understood as a business tool or even as a life tool. A preoccupation with being singular and uniquely able to solve a given problem can be deadly. Sometimes it springs from arrogance, sometimes from ignorance. This is very common in start-ups and small businesses, where entrepreneurs become so focused on their own dreams they can't imagine anyone else has anything to share that could be helpful.

Even for companies that are pioneering entirely new kinds of products and inventing all sorts of exciting new technologies, much of what it takes to run the business is similar to what it takes to run other businesses. Payroll systems, personnel policies, procedures for handling product returns, or designs for physically shipping your products typically are not trade secrets that set you apart from the competition; they simply need to work. Whether you are a biotechnology company, a gas station, or a small real estate office, your people need to get paid. If you are a business of a certain size, there are 401(k) plans that someone else likely has determined are the most cost-effective way to meet your need for a retirement plan. There are people who've come before you and invested time and money in figuring out what works best. They've analyzed the options and often published papers or reports that spell out the details.

Sometimes taking advantage of best demonstrated practices means abandoning your own stab at a problem. For example, when at eBay we found ourselves in a horse race with PayPal as we tried to develop Billpoint, the tendency was for some of our people to look for flaws in PayPal and decide it was inferior, an enemy eBay inevitably would roll over. I do like to see that competitive spirit, but the land mine in that sentence is "inevitably." If you start thinking like that, you are headed for trouble.

In 2007, we bought another neat business that was competing with us, the ticket seller StubHub. We had a very popular and successful ticket category on eBay, but StubHub was aimed at a different audience: buyers who were not only willing to spend a premium to purchase high-priced event tickets for Super Bowls and other special events but were also willing to pay to have those tickets shipped overnight with a guarantee. The ticket business is a complex one, with a full range of participants from pretty shady characters to completely professional authorized resellers. We liked that StubHub had partnered with a number of professional sports teams and that it brought legitimacy, integrity, and transparency to these kinds of transactions. It complements eBay's ticket business on the main eBay site.

WHEN I WAS AT HASBRO and running the Preschool Division, we needed some new energy in our product mix. We were facing a collision between the kind of simple, classic toys that had been a very good business for Hasbro and the fact that children were, to use a strange but apt phrase, "getting older younger." Exposed to more media and technology at a younger age, they were getting bored sooner with more basic toys. It was not unlike the plot of the movie in which our Potato Heads played a supporting role, Disney's *Toy Story*. The little boy, Andy, gets a fancy, bells-and-whistles Star Commander toy, and his simple, low-tech classic cowboy doll gets shoved behind the bed.

We had some great classic toys, but we needed to reenergize the category, and to do that we chose to look around for ways to partner instead of trying to invent everything in-house. Some people might not think of licensing as an example of borrowing best-demonstrated practices, but for certain kinds of companies, like Hasbro, it is a great tool for moving quickly and with more confidence in what tends to be a hit-driven industry.

This was the situation we faced: children were getting older younger partly because of their increased exposure to characters that starred in television shows, movies, and even video games. When you license the right to use a character on a product, you are leveraging the other company's investment in the brand. A toy company could sit down and try to invent a character like Barney, for example, or it can work with Barney's "people," so to speak, and take advantage of the brand's momentum and hard-won exposure So we did that. We also signed a blockbuster deal with the creators of Teletubbies to create toys based on those odd little blobby creatures that made young children positively coo with delight. Marrying a great toy company with a great character brand creates that wonderful math equation every businessperson seeks—the $1+1=3$ or even 4. It would be nice to invent everything from scratch, but remember, businesses exist to sell products and services for more than it costs to provide those products and services. License a great idea, marry it with a quality toy, sell it effectively, and everybody wins.

Similarly, we revived the Mr. Potato Head brand with the same technique. I remember the day our designers called a meeting and brought some unexpected guests. Hasbro already had the license for the Star Wars merchandise, and our Potato Head product team unveiled our leading man—Mr. Potato Head—wearing a Darth Vader helmet and wielding a light saber, along with various other accessories.

"This is perfect!" I remember saying at first sight. It was just hilarious. The accessory packs flew off toy-store shelves. It was a terrific way to revitalize a brand that several generations of people loved, without starting from scratch. It became something we did in small quantities for the Potato Heads all the time—sell just the components based on seasonal merchandise, a new movie, or other designs we could license.

Toys, after all, are about fun. If the Potato Head team had fussed and worried about going "outside" for the extra creative juice that delighted our customers, we would have missed an excellent opportunity. Similarly, business is more fun, and surprisingly productive and successful, when you create a team that works together, learns to iterate and respect that process, and worries about the result rather than about who gets credit for inventing something.

When you make people accountable and create mechanisms to validate their success, it's another way to fuel the Power of Many. Everybody—every employee, every customer, every colleague, and every partner—will thrive when their work and things they care about are validated. This is one of the most underappreciated notions in marketing, in management, in marriage, in life. You can build a culture of fear, which I do not believe works in the long run, or you can build a culture in which you validate what someone has done and then ask him or her for more. That's the trick: validate but make sure every interaction ends with the idea that this is just the beginning of where we can go.

9

Be brave. Most things worth doing are hard.

his is the stupidest thing I've ever seen a CEO do. It's reckless and irresponsible. If you miss, you're a dead woman."

I still remember the look on the face of my friend Mary Meeker when she said these words to me. It was September 2000, and eBay was hosting its yearly Analyst Day, where we typically laid out our plans for the coming year.

All around us, the dot-com world was crashing. Since March, the dot-com stocks had been in free fall. Hundreds of little companies had hit their inevitable dead end, when their lack of a sound business plan or accountability resulted in an inevitable lack of revenues and profits. But things were going well for eBay. We had made a number of acquisitions we were integrating, and growth continued to be spectacular. But we were doing so many things that threatened to pull us in different directions, I felt we needed a rallying cry—a shared goal that would get people pulling together, and pulling for one another.

My executive team and I sat down and discussed the upcoming analysts' meeting and what we would say. This was an annual exercise where we would determine the content to be covered with the analysts, who would then probe about the strength of certain parts of the business. In these kinds of meetings, most executives try to give as few hard numbers as they possibly can. You can be upbeat, confident, and all that, but when you get into forecasting and give specific numbers, you will end up living with those numbers appended to your name until you either make or miss the goal.

CFO Gary Bengier, Rajiv Dutta, and I looked at the growth curves, and I told them I wanted to announce a big, hairy, audacious goal. Gary and Rajiv were not ones to flinch in the face of a challenge, but we did spend some time figuring out exactly what the goal should be. Gary, like me, is a fly fisherman, and he used an analogy that resonated with me. When you are fly fishing in a still lake, it's common to see trout cruise the lake in a pattern, slurping bugs just under the surface, or sometimes even jumping out of the water to snatch flies in midair. When you are trying to catch them, it's important to place the fly right in front of their path. Not too far in front, not to the left or right, not right on top of them, but directly in that feeding path, motivating them to speed up and take it. That's what we agreed we wanted to do for eBay. We wanted that goal right along our growth path, but not so far out that people were discouraged or put off at the sound of it. We wanted the goal to be achievable if we just sped up and focused our resources on hitting it.

Finally we agreed. We were in the middle of an aggressive expansion in international markets that was going better than expected. "Our revenues are $430 million. I think we can hit $3 billion by 2005. Let's say that," I said.

So I walked out in front of the analysts—two banks of them, BlackBerrys at the ready—and announced, essentially, a five-year goal: I predicted that eBay would be a $3 billion company by 2005.

People about keeled over when I put a number to it. Many

analysts expressed surprise in the press reports that followed (even though the stock did go up). A few investors even so mistrusted my prediction that they announced they were selling their holdings.

Mary Meeker was in the front row, and when I looked at her face after I finished, she was not smiling. Mary is a superstar analyst for Morgan Stanley, widely considered one of the most savvy when it comes to Internet companies and e-commerce. When we finally had a chance to talk, she was truly upset with me, not only as the Morgan Stanley analyst who followed us but as a friend. Since CEOs are never obliged to give long-term forecasts, Mary reasoned, it was reckless to put a specific number out there, both personally and because that goal could splash back negatively on the whole company. The assumption would be that we had a specific plan, and coming up short of that plan would suggest weaknesses of leadership, planning, and execution that could make shareholders uneasy. To put a specific number up this far in advance to her just didn't make sense.

The truth is, I wasn't the first person to lay out a "stretch goal." In the mid-1990s, John Chambers, a CEO for whom I have great regard and respect, told Wall Street he expected 30 to 50 percent annual growth for Cisco for the next several years. The press attached that to every story about Chambers and Cisco. Wall Street was uneasy with that prediction, too, although Cisco did make those numbers. Another prominent example of a CEO attaching his name to a stretch goal was the late Robert Swanson, founder of Genentech, who said early in that company's life that he believed it would grow to be a billion-dollar company by 1990. Realize that he said that in the early 1980s, and that no start-up pharmaceutical company had succeeded to such an extent since Syntex did it in the 1950s. Swanson did not hit his goal until later in the 1990s, but his achievement was nonetheless extraordinary, and Genentech's pioneering efforts helped pave the way for the entire biotechnology industry. Its 2008 revenues were more than $13.4 billion.

Mary was not the only analyst who saw committing to a specific long-term number goal as a reckless act. But remember my definition of reckless: when the risk is asymmetrical, meaning that the cost of failing is huge and the benefit of achieving the target is not sufficiently valuable.

In this case, the cost of failing was in fact huge, certainly to me personally. I was driving up expectations for us in a way some believed was unrealistic. If I failed to make that number, it could mean I would lose my job. But the reason I was willing to accept that risk was that I was not trying to energize the stock; I was trying to energize and inspire the *company*. I believed in the benefit of committing eBay to a big, simple goal, a goal we could cascade into every corner of the company in order to make clear how critical each and every group's input was going to be. That made it a risk worth taking.

In 2005, we did not achieve $3 billion in revenues.

We hit $4.5 billion in revenues.

That goal rallied the troops in a remarkable way. We looked across the entire company and broke down what had to happen: essentially 50 percent annual revenue growth per year for the next four years. We figured out the larger number, the gross merchandise volume that we had to meet, and we broke it down for every country and for every product category in every country. Suddenly a big company goal looks a lot more manageable if you are the person who handles electronics in Germany and you learn that what we need from you is total merchandise volume of $100 million. We challenged every manager to understand his or her team's responsibility to support our larger goal. It was a rallying cry, and it worked. You can make a big goal feel small by breaking it down, but you can't make a small goal big.

To do significant things, things that are important and worth doing, sometimes leaders need to take a deep breath and jump. The gravitational pull of mediocrity is strong. There is always a reason why you should go slow, wait for another quarter, hedge your bets. I like taking bold steps, and I am not afraid of making significant changes. That is the way you achieve things worth doing. If I had set a goal of $2 billion, would we still have hit $4.5 billion? We will never know. I think probably not.

Stretch goals are an important element of leadership. But they are something all leaders struggle with. As Gary Bengier pointed out, you want to put that fishing fly in precisely the right spot. You don't ever want to set such crazily optimistic goals that the people you need to pull together will be discouraged and turned off from the start. And you don't want to set goals that are too low, as people will back off and lose concentration if they are likely to attain the goal too soon.

This is not just a dilemma for executives running large enterprises. I think back on how many conversations I've had with other parents about how to motivate children to work harder in school, practice their musical instrument, or improve their performance in just about anything else. Do you hold up a real stretch goal, with the secret hope that the challenge will motivate the child to achieve far more than he or she otherwise would have, even if the goal isn't met? Or do you nudge along, focusing on each incremental effort— each additional hour of practice the child puts in, for example—and talk positively but vaguely of where that will lead? Clearly, what works for one family does not necessarily work for another. Personally, I am a fan of the stretch goal.

When we launched Auction for America in 2001 after the September 11 tragedy, we set a very ambitious goal: we said we hoped to raise $100 million in 100 days. That turned out to be overly ambitious, but keep in mind that when we set the goal we had absolutely no idea how this would work, because nothing like it had ever been done before. Americans were contributing so much money through so many avenues that I think eBay seemed like a less direct route than giving directly to the Red Cross or other public-service groups. Nonetheless, we raised $10 million in that period and provided important support to the victims' families. It was an extraordinary sum, and, as I mentioned, it led to a new vehicle for giving that continues to raise impressive sums for many different causes. Setting a high goal helped focus the eBay team to build that charitable capability, and it attracted the attention of the media and got those interested in supporting this effort to act quickly.

AS A CEO in a fast-moving industry, even if you eschew committing yourself to big, audacious goals, you nonetheless are constantly confronting big decisions that demand courage. There was a point in eBay's life in the spring of 2000 when we came within a few small details of being acquired by Yahoo. In retrospect, for eBay's sake, I am glad it did not happen. However, the deal made sense for both companies in a number of different ways and, based on our relative situations at the time, it *should* have happened.

Yahoo was one of the strongest Internet players emerging from the dot-com explosion, based largely on advertising revenues. It was the dot-com darling and around this time, U.S. market capitalization was very high: around $90 billion, about three times the size of ours. However, as I mentioned in my discussion of why we bought Skype, any company whose entire revenue stream, however strong, is dependent on only one revenue model is at risk. That's why Levi Strauss, despite the enduring appeal of its iconic blue jeans, has always made forays into other sectors of the apparel market. That's why Coca-Cola experimented with investments in the wine industry at one point, and why Pepsi bought fast-food restaurants. At a certain size, being wholly dependent on just one kind of revenue stream is riskier than forging into new areas.

Yahoo was anxious to develop marketplace capability, and even though we had competed intensely at various times, I had a good relationship with then-CEO Tim Koogle and the founders. We talked about merging the companies. I could see that despite eBay's incredible growth trajectory, it might make sense for us to be tucked inside a larger company where there might be different kinds of synergies and resources. Yahoo had a gigantic and enthusiastic community, and we had a vibrant community and a great marketplace. So we quietly went into serious negotiations.

Then we hit a weird patch.

For one thing, when the executives on my team began to meet with their counterparts at Yahoo, they found that there was an experience gap. My team was more seasoned, generally had a more consistent track record in delivering to plan, and by and large had more experience as businesspeople. They began to grumble that this merger might actually hurt eBay if they had to turn over responsibility to Yahoo executives. The Yahoo team appeared only to be looking at eBay's technical auction functionality, not at the bigger picture of the marketplace eBay had created. Still, I felt that we could manage through that, that our savvy would prevail.

Another issue was that the deal we worked out called for me to report to Tim Koogle. This did not sit well with Yahoo's COO, a young executive named Jeff Mallett. Despite Tim's support for the structure we developed, Jeff felt I should report to him.

We were literally within a day of announcing the deal. The press releases had been written. I was scheduled to go with my team on a Sunday afternoon to sign the final papers when I got a call from Tim asking me to come alone. Tim clearly had mixed feelings, but under pressure from the founders, Yahoo backed out. It was evident to me that Tim's team had also perceived the mismatches in management talent and were worried that they might not, in fact, prevail. Jeff Mallett had spent time with the young founders, Jerry Yang and David Filo, who suddenly listed an assortment of reasons why they were worried about eBay's prospects.

I thought they were making a mistake, and I told them so. What had happened confirmed to me the difference in the sophistication of our two management teams. As a CEO, Tim needed to stand up to Jerry and David and explain that the future of the company stood to be vastly better—not only by bringing eBay's technology, marketplace, and growth potential into Yahoo but also by bringing in more experienced management. Jerry and David were terrific, smart guys, but they were in their early thirties. Yahoo was their first job. The future of a multibillion-dollar public company was at stake. If they had appreciated the larger marketplace we had built and were continuing to expand, they would have realized that eBay stood to give Yahoo an important new dimension.

This was the beginning of a long, painful slide for Yahoo. Internet advertising collapsed, and with it Yahoo's revenue model. Within a year, Tim Koogle left, and Yahoo's market capitalization plummeted to well below ours. Except for a few years under Terry Semel's leadership, the company has struggled ever since. Had Yahoo mustered a bias for action and courage at that key moment, our respective futures could have been very different. Faced with a more experienced team, they lost their nerve to do the deal. That resulted in an outcome that was temporarily less risky for them personally but not in the best interest of Yahoo. Yahoo has faced a number of interesting challenges in recent years, particularly the emergence of Google and its dominance in the area of Internet search. The arrival of Carol Bartz as CEO in 2009 has brought the kind of hard-nosed "adult supervision" we've already discussed and the company's prospects seem to be turning up again.

COURAGE TAKES MANY FORMS. It is not always a bold or dramatic gamble. It also can be an act of quiet valor, a decision to do the right thing despite other options that are easier or cheaper. And courage is contagious. Whatever form it takes, people respond to authentic shows of courage from their leaders. In turn, leaders are empowered when they witness the courage of other leaders.

I think some people are born with a predilection for courage, just as some people are born with a bias for action. My mother, as I've mentioned, always taught us to try new things, even if there was some risk.

I am lucky to have another profile in courage in my own family. My sister, Anne, is an incredibly intelligent, well-educated woman and a wonderful person. After graduating from the University of Pennsylvania, she went to Harvard, where she got a Ph.D. in archaeology and anthropology, then followed that up with an MBA from Boston University. Although she was six years older than me, Anne always looked out for me and was a constant source of support and encouragement as I faced the new experiences that college brings. And, of course, I am forever grateful that she introduced me to Griff.

Anne embarked on a successful academic career, eventually landing at Harvard Business School, where she ran short executive education programs. She ultimately decided that she was more interested in administration and began moving along that path at Harvard. In 1984, she had a baby, Katie.

Not long after, her then-husband called me and said: "Meg, there are a few things you should know about Anne. She thinks she's going to be the next president of Harvard."

I said, "Well, she's ambitious, and she's held administrative positions, but I admit that does seem like a stretch."

Then he went into more details that made it clear that Anne's behavior had become erratic and deeply troubling. She had become convinced she was under surveillance and even that news commentators were speaking to her directly. Needless to say, I was angry that my brother-in-law had not started our conversation more directly. Clearly, my sister was in crisis. I flew to Boston and saw that Anne was in the grip of a manic episode. We had never seen any previous signs of this, but her doctors believed that postpartum depression had triggered psychosis. At the time, none of us was very familiar with mental illness and we all struggled to try to help her. It was a heartbreaking experience. After she took a six-week leave from Harvard and was doing much better, she returned to work only to be given an ultimatum: either resign or be terminated. It was then that we all became aware of the stigma that patients suffering from mental illness experience, even as they are struggling to battle their disease.

This situation was quite challenging for our family, as it would be for any family. As a stiff-upper-lip, don't-complain group, we didn't have the vocabulary to talk about mental illness even to each other, never mind to the outside world. The stigma associated with the disorder was considerable then, and Anne's experience trying to resume her work had driven her into isolation. My father was by then retired, and my parents moved closer to try to help her. It was not at all clear what we should do, which medications Anne should try first or for how long. For me—a drilldown, fix-the-problem kind of person—this was a new lesson in patience, as well as in the many forms of personal courage.

At first Anne was embarrassed, confused, and angry at what had taken hold of her. Instead of reaching out for help, she withdrew. Her husband left and she temporarily lost custody of Katie.

But despite these difficulties, she did not give up hope. Thanks in part to family support but also to the deep caring and commitment of some of her therapists and physicians, she began a very impressive journey.

The family bias-for-action gene kicked into gear. Within a year of losing her job at Harvard, she helped start the Bright Horizons children's centers, where her daughter was one of the first children enrolled. Then she successfully sold the concept of workplace child care centers to hospitals, real estate developers, and colleges.

She stayed with Bright Horizons for several years, but she felt a pull to work more directly with other patients and families coping with both mental illness and the stigma associated with it. And so in 1993 she and a colleague founded the Jonathan O. Cole, M.D., Mental Health Consumer Resource Center at McLean Hospital in Belmont, Massachusetts. The center is operated solely by people with mental illness and offers a broad array of resources critical to the mentally ill population. Today, the center is nationally recognized for the programs it offers, including back-to-work programs, educational lectures on mental illness, a referral service that connects patients with clinicians, and consumer advocacy and media outreach. The center also spearheads a program that helps first-year psychiatric students at McLean Hospital and Massachusetts General Hospital gain a better understanding of mental illness from the patient's point of view. It has given me great pleasure to support the Cole Center over the years.

But Anne didn't stop there. She subsequently broadened her efforts and is now also the co–executive director of the Metro Boston Recovery Learning Community, which is funded by the Department of Mental Health of the Commonwealth of Massachusetts. That program uses some of the peer-based support programs that have worked at the Cole Center to address a larger population. I see this as Anne's own Power of Many movement. Those involved are gaining strength and confidence from shared experiences. They are establishing meaningful human relationships that break the isolation that can be so devastating in mental illness. And they are benefiting from the very best sort of network—a community of people who understand one another's challenges and who are deeply interested in joining forces for the good of the group.

Anne did not just put this difficult challenge in her life behind her when she found the proper treatment and her condition stabilized. Her courage has enabled and empowered others struggling in profound ways to move forward.

I have a special place in my heart for those who overcome disabilities or medical struggles of any kind. Partly this is because of my experience watching Anne battle mental illness, but it's also because my own life began with a physical challenge. I was born with an unusual congenital bone defect: my left hip did not have a socket, a condition called dysplasia. The hip is a ball-and-socket joint, the socket being a curved enclosure that contains the top of the large bone of the upper leg and allows the leg to rotate and move. In my case, the surface of the hip against which my leg rested was flat instead of curved; the joint was inherently unstable, like balancing a book on the tip of a baseball bat. The condition occurs in four births for every thousand, and it is far more common in girls than in boys. Left untreated, a child with this problem would never walk normally because the leg bone would never sit snugly in the socket, constantly dislocating when it moved.

Our doctors discovered this issue when I was a newborn and my parents took me to a special hospital in New York City. And so at about the age when babies begin to crawl, family photos show me in a stiff metal brace and leather straps that literally pushed my leg into my hip in order to create the socket. I looked like a little baby-shaped weathervane, legs pointing straight out to the sides! My stroller and baby carriage had to be modified to allow my legs to point out sideways, and when I was not being wheeled places, I had to be carried everywhere. The strategy was to maintain a constant, steady pressure on those soft baby and toddler bones to create the socket. Amazingly, it worked. But it was challenging for the family. Even after the braces came off when I was two, I was not allowed to actually stand and put weight on my hips for another six months, my mother tells me, and that meant the family had to play its own form of man-to-Meg defense when it came to making sure that I, a rambunctious three-year-old, did not venture forth under my own steam.

When I finally got the all clear, the results were just as hoped. I could walk, run, and jump, just like any other child. I had no pain, and as all my class photos show, it did not slow my growth at all—I was always the tallest girl in class.

Almost from the minute those braces came off, I gravitated to playing sports with my siblings and on any team I could join. And I consider that opportunity critical to my eventual success in business. I'm a big believer that sports are a great place for young people to learn courage. Sports force you to make decisions in real time and live with them. There are consequences to winning and losing. Winning is always better (surprise). But when you make the wrong decision and you lose—well, the next day the sun comes up. The stakes are not so high that you can't brush yourself off, learn your lesson, and move on. I participated in many different sports as a child—tennis, figure skating, basketball, lacrosse, and competitive swimming. I liked team sports the best. When I'm pulling a business team together, I still use those basketball aphorisms I learned as a young person: "Let's pass the ball around a little before game time." "Do we need man-to-man or zone defense?"

As a young girl I was involved in sports at the early stages of what would be an explosion in sports opportunities for girls and young women. I don't believe it is a coincidence that so many successful women executives today were active—and in many cases are still active—in sports. In my case, I had to learn to handle competition more maturely, my mother reminds me. When I was a young child swimming in races, if I came in lower than first or second, I would emerge from the pool howling. Mom would hustle me off to the ladies' room, she says, where I would stand and keep crying, albeit with one ear poised for the buzzer that marked the start of the next race. While she would try to get me to calm down and buck up, she says, she could pretty much count on my unrelenting waterworks until that buzzer went off and they called swimmers to the block for the next race. The buzzer would sound, my tears would stop, and I would run out, leaving her to mop up the puddle and suffer the looks of the other swim moms who'd witnessed the show.

Several years ago I was sitting at my desk at eBay when I got a call from my high school basketball coach. We caught up and she shared with me a wonderful story I had never heard before. Apparently our local high school was running short of funds. Maybe Cold Spring Harbor High would just have to do without girls' basketball, school officials said. My coach was at the parent meeting where the budget was being discussed, and when it was time for questions, my mother raised her hand and asked the committee a very simple question: "If the girls can't play basketball in high school, how can we possibly expect that they'll play basketball in college?" In telling the story, the coach laughed at the memory of my mother's delivery. The administrators running the meeting, she told me, immediately realized that my mother wasn't talking about sports but about life.

Girls' basketball stayed in the budget.

I cannot imagine how my life would have developed had that treatment not worked and had I not developed the ability to walk, run, and play sports. Griff shares my appreciation for the power of sports: he played tennis and basketball in high school and rowed crew, like my father and brother, in college. I have seen my own sons mature and develop in so many ways thanks to both team and individual sports. Griff and I hosted our son Will's rugby team recently at our home, and it was great fun to see the camaraderie and close relationships that the team experience provides young people. There are just so many benefits from sports: discipline, time management, and, yes, even courage. You fall down, you pick yourself up. You learn from every failure, apply it to the next situation, alter your approach. When Will rowed on his high school crew team, I would look at the boys' faces in the last 50 meters of the race and realize that their muscles were burning and their lungs tight, but what better way to force yourself to learn that you have to power through and finish what you start? They were learning that the difference between success and failure, even when you've done everything else exactly right, is staying on course and powering through the final, hardest leg of any challenge. That takes resolve, determination, and courage.

To my delight, as eBay grew, it turned out that our company also nurtured courage. The particular tools and straightforward rules of eBay unleashed energy and resourcefulness in people with physical disabilities who might never have been able to achieve in a land-based world what they achieved on eBay. Like the members of a sports team, they united in a shared interest and pushed past their limits.

It took us a while to appreciate how much eBay meant to the community of people with physical disabilities. I credit the first eBay Live! conference in 2002. We organized the event as a combination trade show and celebration. There were booths where people who supported the community in various ways, from graphic designers to packaging experts, could set up, but mostly our community was just so happy to connect in person. We decided to hold a special reception on the last night, a Saturday, where we would have buffet tables and entertainment. That first year, people started lining up early to get in and get close to the stage. I and several hundred eBay employees were inside the doors dressed in the same color polo shirts and khakis, and we just sort of parted on both sides of it. Then, when the doors opened and the community members started excitedly streaming in, we began clapping. It was completely spontaneous. It was incredibly fun to stand there and applaud all these people who were so instrumental to our success. They had arrived with so much enthusiasm, and they clearly appreciated the validation we were providing.

But it didn't take long before we realized something else—many of these people had physical or medical challenges. There was a large number of folks in wheelchairs, on crutches, even on oxygen. The next year we had staff members circulate in the crowd to make sure that those with physical disabilities were given preferential spots toward the front so that they would not be jostled or injured in the rush as the doors opened. Being able to applaud the huge group of these special eBay community members is an experience that still brings tears to the eyes of eBay employees who have stood in what came to be called the "clapping tunnel."

As we mingled with them and heard their stories, we realized that eBay had made these individuals, who often felt isolated or disenfranchised, equal participants in our Power of Many. Some of them had had their own retail stores, antiques shops, or other kinds of businesses, but the physical demands of store displays and helping customers had become too great. With eBay, they could still run businesses they loved and make a sufficient profit that they could hire someone or get a family member to help them do some of the physical labor. They didn't have to put items on high shelves, travel to and from a store, clean a store, or close it when they had a doctor's appointment.

This was another insight into why eBay's bulletin boards and focus on community had become so important to our members. For many of them, the eBay Cafe really was their social life, a place to talk with friends and meet new people. Nobody had to know that they were in a wheelchair, or anything else they didn't feel like revealing. I once met a young man in a wheelchair with profound medical problems whose parents brought him to meet with me at eBay Live! I will never forget the way his mother looked at me, eyes shining, and said: "On eBay, he is not disabled."

The courage and grace of some of these community members was and is amazing. So often we would learn that a person who otherwise might have experienced life in a far more limited way instead had created an enormous network of friends and fans, often in part because of how generously he or she would help others with technical issues, such as how to take better digital photos of items. One of the most striking individuals was someone we knew for a long time only as Bobal. Bobal was a man who might have given up in the face of daunting challenges. Instead, he had the courage to jump into a whole new world.

Bobal passed away in October 2008, but he once posted his eBay story on his website, and he tells it better than I possibly could.

I have had seventeen operations in my sixty-five years. . . . I have lost one kneecap due to injury and also lost my right eye due to disease. In 1986, I was diagnosed with MS [multiple sclerosis]. It was the low point in my life. I lost all of my best earning years and in the next few years, I just got a little worse each year and the depression set in very hard. At one point, I didn't care if I lived or not. Then things kept adding to my life. I now have diabetes and from all of my smoking years, I also have emphysema and am on oxygen 24/7.

I also have a heart condition that usually puts me in the hospital at least once a year. Now I am getting arthritis in my fingers. Now you can picture a wreck, one that gave up three years ago because I was so lonely staying home alone while my lovely wife, Alice, went to work every day just so that we could live. She has been just a great love of my life even though I am getting to be more of a burden to her each day; she never once complains.

In April 1998, I found eBay, the largest and best on-line auction site that there is, and started to listen and ask questions on the Q&A board and the live support boards that we had then. I have a user name of Bobal and made a logo to use. We bought and sold lots of items and then prices dropped so we stopped buying and selling and I started to answer some questions even though I knew very little. I kept watching and learning from the many users that were and still are willing to help. I have got to the point that I live my life on eBay helping others. It has changed my life completely; when I see a happy user because of what I did to help them, I am on top of the world. I feel like my life is still worth living.

I have met so many friends on eBay, users like myself, and some of them have a little disability also and they help others because it feels great. I also have met many of the eBay staff and they treat me like family; it is wonderful.

Now you know my story, from feeling like a worthless person to one that now just takes whatever is passed my way and lives with it. I help new and longtime users on the photos/HTML board every day. Now if I can help anyone to understand that no matter how many disabilities you have, you can help make a difference in someone's life.

Some ways that you can do that is if you have a skill, share it with others so that they can learn and they will love you for it. If you are housebound, you can always call a nursing home and ask to talk to a lonely resident; you will be surprised how much that you can brighten up two lives at the same time. Then make it a weekly or a couple of times a week meeting; you both will look forward to your conversation. If you can get around, even by wheelchair, visit a hospital. There are lots of lonely people there who would love to have someone that cares to talk to; it doesn't take much. If you are able to get around and you are lonely, find a shelter or a food bank that you can help to feed those that have less than you; you will forget that you are lonely and look forward to helping others. Just look around and find out what you can do for others. Remember, if you can walk 10 steps, find someone that can walk 5, then together you can walk 7½ steps. I will guarantee that if you can help others, you will be the big winner because you will be paid with love. So remember, if I can do it, so can you.

Can you "manage" courage? Can you "teach" courage? I honestly am not sure. Bobal's thoughts inspired me, and who knows how many others, to want to be courageous. I do know that courage is enabled by and empowers every other value. You may yearn to act, but you will not do so without courage. You may want to know what others think of your ideas, but without courage you will be too afraid to listen, in case it's not what you want to hear. Never give in to the temptation to sit in the dark and scare yourself to death with all the possible scary consequences of an act that demands courage. Figure out the worst thing that could realistically happen and then move forward.

10

Be flexible. If you cannot scale,
you will fail.

Fast-growing companies are a bit like teenagers. After a frisky, fun childhood they always hit a point where reality bites. They must cast off some of the trappings and habits of their past that are no longer useful and grow in new, more mature ways.

In these situations, the question is whether the current management is up to the challenge of managing that transition. Can it retain the heart and soul of the company but also keep moving forward and effectively compete with other companies? What a company needs from its leaders changes over time, and entrepreneurs often struggle with this when they have to face the question. Their egos get caught up in the company and the idea of turning over control feels like abandoning their own child. But having worked in a variety of companies and seeing and studying managers during these transitions, I developed the opinion well before I joined eBay that the secret to management is always: right person, right job, right time. Inevitably, fresh perspectives and new skills will be necessary to keep reinventing an organization.

Analysts, investors, employees, and journalists are always quick to ask any CEO, particularly one who has had some success, "How long are you going to do this?" I can't remember exactly the first time anyone asked me this at eBay, but it seems like it was shortly after our IPO in 1998! What I usually said was, "I think ten years is probably the right amount of time."

I am not a person who makes elaborately detailed long-range plans. I typically am engaged by and optimistic about whatever I am doing, but I also always have a healthy respect for the challenge. When we moved west so I could run eBay, for example, Griff and I decided to rent an apartment for a year until we were sure both my new job and his were going to work out. With two new jobs and the 85 percent reduction in salary I took to move from Hasbro to eBay, we didn't want to risk a big mortgage. So we put the majority of our belongings in storage and rented a two-bedroom apartment across the street from Stanford Medical Center. Griff could walk to work. The master bedroom closet was actually bigger than the second bedroom, so we let little Griff have it for his room. (It was handy for me to have the Caribbean tool-shed story to trot out when I assured the boys how much fun all this was going to be.) My point is that I was optimistic, but I never, ever assumed that eBay's success would be automatic. We took it one step at a time.

As the years passed and eBay's results continued to be strong, the questions about my future began in earnest. But I was not following a detailed plan, public or private. I understood why I was getting the questions. Both eBay and I had had quite an extraordinary run. We had achieved something very unusual, and to get some perspective on it you have to appreciate a business concept called scale.

One way to think about scale is to imagine a digital photograph on a computer. When you want to make it larger, you manipulate its scale, either telling the program to increase it by a certain percentage or just clicking on the corner of the image window and dragging it to expand the image. When the original image is of good quality and detail, you can make it larger without distorting its integrity and shape. But sometimes there are flaws in the original image or the resolution is not good. Then you can't scale it. The image looks worse as you make it bigger, even indecipherable.

In the business world, taking the core of an idea and scaling it up is a much harder act to manage. As we discussed in the context of WebVan, many businesses don't scale very well. There may be flaws in the core idea, or what we call the "value proposition," or there may be a problem with how management executed the idea. For example, a novel product may be all the rage initially but then just run out of momentum. Beanie Babies were once 10 percent of the merchandise on eBay; hardly anybody talks about them anymore. It was a fun and successful brand for a while, but the idea had limits. Sometimes you can have a very successful small business, but when you try to expand, it doesn't work. The leap from owning one successful restaurant to opening another, for example, has confounded many a businessperson. You can't just replicate all the elements of the first success, from the chef to the location to the reliability of the waitstaff. Many things can go wrong.

eBay, however, proved to be incredibly scalable. The eBay model utilized the burgeoning network power of the Internet to bring a compelling, useful, even fun capability to ever larger numbers of people, and we figured out how to manage the attendant complexity and be profitable. By tapping the Power of Many, we created a virtuous cycle where the better our sellers did and the happier our buyers were, the more successful eBay was as a facilitator of all those transactions. eBay expanded in all kinds of interesting directions, but at its core is a business model that we scaled in a remarkably successful fashion, even exporting it to other countries and cultures.

All that said, eBay's success was never a foregone conclusion.

The outage in 1999 could have destroyed us. Fraud and bad behavior could have hurt us if we had not moved early to fight it. Not investing in the behind-the-scenes technology and innovative systems invisible to the outside world could have sent us back into the Bermuda Triangle at any time.

The result was a lot of attention on me, because it is not common for an executive who is good at running a $4 million business to be good at running a $400 million business, and then be good at running a $4 billion business, and then an $8 billion one. Each of those steps demands that you focus on different things, withdraw from certain functions while embracing others. Those transitions are hard. Executives develop emotional attachments to people and programs that they don't easily move past, even when they need to for the good of the company. That is the reason why boards tend to recruit individuals from outside a company as it grows, individuals who have experience at that next level. It was a tribute to Pierre's maturity and self-awareness that he realized that his core strengths were in the creative vision for eBay and in developing its foundational values and community. But at the $4 million revenue mark, he knew that he did not have the large-scale operating, marketing, or leadership skills and experience to take the company to the next level, any more than I could have sat down at a computer and invented eBay from scratch. He handed the reins to me, and that was the right call, as history showed. But when it became clear that eBay had become an established, global multibillion-dollar company, others became curious about what my next step might be. Would I want to take eBay to a new level or find my own new level somewhere else?

In retrospect, everything I had done in my business career prepared me to run eBay, but one of the most important elements of building the company was that I understood the human dimensions of how to manage growth and big organizations. I had run a $600 million division at Hasbro, so the first several years at eBay, as it grew toward that size, were familiar territory. I systematically added new skills and capabilities to eBay as it grew larger. Since I had worked for very large, well-run companies, such as Disney and Procter & Gamble, I had a good sense of the different techniques and the kind of focus that become more important as a company approaches $1 billion in revenues and beyond. I've discussed many of them in this book.

But unleashing and sustaining the Power of Many that propelled eBay was a constant exercise in managing scale. Scaling is all about flexibility and openness, understanding that what worked yesterday may not work today, and that to move forward you may have to let go of things you like. Scaling is about being comfortable with ambiguity and change. There is a fishing expression that applies: you never fish the same river twice. The weather changes, the current may be faster or slower. Different bugs are hatching, the fish are more or less active, or jittery, or hungry. To be a good angler, you must always adjust to conditions. What worked last week is not necessarily going to work today. To catch fish, you need the right fly on the right stream at the right time.

As the CEO of a growing company, you have to keep revising the scope of your attention as conditions change. In other words, you must *personally* scale. To do that, you must prune duties from your own portfolio. For most of my tenure at eBay, we were growing so fast and adding exciting new acquisitions to our portfolio at such a rate that every year I had to go through the process of asking, "What have I been doing that can be done by someone else? What new element or new priority now demands more of my attention?" It was a management version of "save to invest."

There were many things I did in the early years of eBay that over time I stopped doing. When I joined the company, there was no central calendar of events and meetings, so I put a paper calendar on my desk that became the common calendar. I was involved in every single document that we prepared to show to the outside world. I spoke with every person we hired; in fact, I saw virtually every employee every day. Shortly after I joined the company I sat down with then-CFO Gary Bengier while we tried to figure out something that sounds so basic: what shall we include in our cost of goods sold? We had to know where to list certain types of expenses in preparing financial statements to go public, but we looked at each other and scratched our heads. There really wasn't a cost of goods sold. We sold things, but we didn't make them, didn't inventory them, and didn't buy and resell anything. Eventually we decided we would list depreciation on our equipment and our customer service costs. This was usually a job for the accountants, but we were a brand-new kind of company, so we had to figure out these issues ourselves before asking them to approve it.

At Stride Rite I had learned that I could not indulge my love of marketing over broader concerns for the company, so I did not make that mistake. But it sometimes was hard for me to let go of one of my very favorite business activities: solving problems. I love to sit with smart people and figure out how to solve a problem. This harks back to my best-athlete training at Bain. I love the intellectual challenge; I love drilling down to the essential elements; I love reframing complexity as a series of simpler steps that will lead to success; and I like keeping an eye on the progress so I can make adjustments and keep fine-tuning the solution. This is a crucial activity for a CEO early in a company's life, but you have to make sure you recalibrate as the company grows. Within three or four years I had to reserve my attention for only the largest and most significant problems, the high-stakes acquisitions or strategic decisions, and let my very capable team use the same techniques to solve problems and craft strategies in their areas of responsibility.

This process of letting go of yesterday's pet projects and ac- tivities can be difficult. But if you can't do that, you can't scale. You can't take refuge in the comfortable and familiar; you have to grow with the job. You also have to get your people, when the times demand it, to cast off their own patterns and ways of thinking about their jobs so that they, too, can scale up.

As a leader, you work through other people. And therefore, in the context of the importance of scaling, let me say it yet again: there is nothing more important than finding the right person for the right job *at the right time.* People forget that last element. What we needed yesterday is not what we need today. Ultimately, this may bring you into conflict with your loyalty to team members, your appreciation for a heroic effort under tough circumstances, and your personal relationships and history. But it is the most power- ful scaling lever leaders have.

In my case, that elusive right-person equation involves many factors. Training, experience, and energy are the obvious starting points. Other elements are more counterintuitive. For example, I can't abide yes-people. I feel energized by other people with new and different perspectives from my own, not by an echo chamber. I also believe that one of Silicon Valley's great strengths is that we are a business community that does not consider a failure in an executive's portfolio to be a scarlet letter. There is an element of good luck in successful executives' lives and it's also true that an otherwise talented, smart, and high-potential person can hit a pot- hole of bad luck. The important thing is, what did the person learn? Has he or she been willing to process the larger picture of what went wrong in order to make sure the mistakes of the past are not repeated? Given a choice, I almost think I prefer the individual who may have endured a humbling experience over one who has failed to incorporate the contribution of luck in past experiences. Very few of us in the senior management team at eBay who drove the company through its most productive years had not suffered some kind of career speed bump or setback. Each of us had something to prove. Would I have been able to instantly appreciate the power of community if I had not spent a fairly unhappy two years trying to revitalize FTD? Probably not.

Another aspect to managing scale through your team is periodically taking responsibilities away from talented people and bringing in the right people from outside the organization. I think it is harder to do this than it is to fire people. Early in a company's life, individuals have to wear many hats. In many small companies, for example, the company's general counsel works on everything involving a contract, also becoming the de facto head of human resources, facilities, and security. As the company grows, you need to calve off some of those responsibilities or else the effectiveness and efficiency of those functions will suffer, no matter how good a job the person has done to date. The general counsel cannot simultaneously bulletproof a large company's legal strategy and efficiently develop and manage all the different aspects of the facilities, from leases to custodians to disaster plans. There is a point where you need a trained and experienced expert (remember the domain expertise I mentioned earlier) instead of the energetic, broad-shouldered team player who managed all those things when there was nobody else who could.

When you explain that you are going to take something away, however, the classic training of a business executive is going to kick in and set off disappointment and sometimes even anger. We are trained to believe that the surest sign of success and moving up the ladder is more—more responsibility, more people to manage, more money, more scope. If you look backward at the path most CEOs have taken to their job, that often appears to be exactly the profile. But when you look more closely you realize that a rescoping can be a moment of truth in a career—an opportunity to be the right person at the right time for a more specific and critical job. To scale as an employee you need to be flexible, take new opportunities and run with them, and earn the right to grow in a different way into more responsibility. The person who fixates on what he or she is losing cannot successfully scale.

During my tenure at eBay I built a tremendous team of people whose strengths I respected and whose friendship I still treasure. A strong management team is such a source of power, strength, and, frankly, fun that you don't turn away from that lightly. In fact, during my entire tenure at eBay, and despite many inquiries from recruiters trying to interest me in other positions, there was only one job anyone ever approached me about that I considered, and that was the CEO job at Disney in 2005.

In the early 1990s I had absolutely loved working at Disney despite the nonstop rugby match. I loved the quality of the people, their creativity, and their energy, and I loved what Disney did for its customers, finding ever new and more interesting ways to bring magic to children and adults alike. When I was invited to talk to Disney's board, I called Pierre (by this time he was no longer involved in the running of the company but was still a major shareholder and chairman of the board) to tell him I was going to do so. I said, "I really don't think I am ready to leave eBay yet"—I had three years to go on my original prediction—"and I feel like I have more to do, but this is the one company I would ever even consider joining after the whirlwind eBay has been." By this time Disney was faltering a bit again and the thought of restoring it to the creative dynamo it had been when I first worked there was quite appealing. I went through a round of interviews, but I eventually withdrew my name from that CEO hunt because I was not comfortable with some of the board dynamics. I was grateful for Pierre's understanding through that period, and I was more than a little touched by his relief when I told him I had withdrawn. It never would have occurred to me to have those conversations with Disney without telling him. That would have been a breach of trust in what had been a strong partnership and friendship between us. So many times, in his quiet way, he had stood shoulder to shoulder with me when a situation was difficult or demanded hard decisions.

When you are living the values you espouse, you tend to forge strong relationships that transcend all sorts of challenges or differences of opinion. When I recounted the story of Mary Meeker telling me I had done a really stupid thing in announcing that stretch goal, it might have seemed odd that I immediately added that she and I were good friends. We still are. Although our relationship started in a slightly rocky way, both of us still laugh about it, and Mary has told the story publicly many times.

Shortly after I joined eBay, David Beirne of Benchmark was trying to get Morgan Stanley to pay attention and start covering eBay. Mary and her Morgan Stanley colleagues were swamped with work and busy covering the highflyers of the time, such as Netscape, Yahoo, and Amazon, and were not even returning his calls. However, when we decided to take the company public, Morgan Stanley was one of the premier investment banks we interviewed to handle the deal.

When it came time for that meeting, Mary is the first to admit, Morgan Stanley "flubbed it." Compared to the other banks we had talked to, the Morgan Stanley team had not prepared a very good case that they understood us and could help us. Mary says that on her way back from this meeting, she realized that Morgan Stanley had made a terrible mistake and that eBay was going to be huge. So she and her team wrote a full report on eBay and how its business might evolve. After they pulled double shifts to get it done, she figured out where I physically was going to be, got on a plane, and hand-delivered it to me. She told me that she had seen the light.

I looked at the report and was impressed by Mary's personal determination to make this right, but I told her, "It's not fair to the other banks to add this to our decision-making process. You had your chance and they did a much better job. eBay runs as a democracy and it would go against our values of providing a level playing field." Mary didn't like that answer, but she understood, and she respected that I would have extended her the same courtesy. Down the road, we would do business again and we became good friends who respected each other and could tell each other the truth.

Personal relationships don't scale the same way business models do. Obviously, they don't get bigger, but they become richer with the passage of time and shared experiences, and that is its own important and valuable form of scale. They require tending and flexibility—not right person, right time, but right kind of attention or right kind of understanding or compromise.

This is how I think about my marriage. It is not so common for two busy people who marry young to "scale" a marriage through the kind of extraordinary experiences, intense pressures, and, frankly, good fortune that Griff and I have had over the course of our twenty-nine years together. It takes work and it takes flexibility. It takes paying close enough attention to the other person's mood that sometimes you just drop everything and say, "I think it's time we take a walk or go out to dinner alone, away from the distractions, and just catch up."

And it takes something else I mentioned earlier—a sense of humor. Griff and I try not to take ourselves too seriously. I always joke that one of my favorite quotes is "Behind every successful woman is an astonished man." Griff sees me start down some road unsure of how to go forward, unclear about whether I can pull it off. He asks good questions and he probes to understand the challenge but he is never discouraging. Instead, he says good luck and then he goes and does his thing, and I go work on mine, whatever it is. After I've made progress, he'll say with a big smile, "I can't believe this. At first you didn't have a clue and now you know more than the experts in this field." That makes it fun for me. He respects the work it takes; he knows success is not an entitlement. But he also has faith; he doesn't get so focused on the challenge that I have to prove myself to him, too. It's fun to impress him. It's motivating to me.

Griff and I are a type A couple. We are two people who are very happy doing many different things but who are deeply defined by our passion for our work. It's just who we are, and it has been this way for us almost from the very beginning. In the span of three days in June 1980, for example, Griff graduated from medical school, we got married, and he jumped on a plane for San Francisco to start his residency. Even by our standards, that was a fairly busy week.

I, meanwhile, did not join him on the airplane, because I was still at my job at Procter & Gamble in Cincinnati. Six months later, I landed a job at Bain in San Francisco. I know what you're thinking: "What, no honeymoon? Spending the first six months of marriage two thousand miles apart?" Yes, but we did have a wonderful, if delayed, honeymoon trip to Hawaii at the end of Griff's year of internship.

Griff and I share common values and a taste for adventure, but we are quite different in other ways. I love to socialize, love to team up. I'm an extrovert. When I was a little girl, my friends' mothers would sometimes call my mother in the middle of a play-date and plead, "Can you please come pick up Meg? She's worn my daughter out."

Griff is a quiet planner. He is deeply thoughtful and analytical about virtually everything. In his role as a doctor, his first concern has always been the care of his patients and delivering the very best treatment possible. For one patient, that might mean a fifteen-minute treatment with a robotically driven radiation beam, for another, an hour of explanation and reassurance, and for a third, a ten-hour microsurgical procedure. He is also appalled by the waste and inefficiency in our health care system, and his desire to better understand efficient management prompted him to complete an MBA, going to school on Friday nights and Saturdays in addition to being a full-time brain surgeon.

Like most surgeons, Griff is well served by having a different form of a bias for action. You don't want to crack open a skull and cut into the brain and then just wing it. In that realm, perfect is the *point*, not the enemy of good enough. You want to plan thoroughly and above all do no harm. In neurosurgery, it is bad to allow a bias for action to trump careful planning.

But time and again I have seen Griff respond to medical situations with confidence and authority. In a medical crisis, his usual quiet, even shy demeanor gives way to a calm yet assertive manner that enables him to take control of a difficult situation, direct a team, and make split-second life-or-death interventions. I have seen this in his management of the head injury of a friend, the seizure of a child, even the heart attack of a stranger in a movie theater. This ability to calmly make a difficult situation better has also been helpful as we deal with the unexpected challenges that every married couple and family faces.

Griff is a wonderful father and, as I have said so many times, I never could have managed a decade at eBay if, despite his own extremely demanding career, he hadn't shouldered a big share of the load of keeping our family running smoothly while I was at the office until the wee hours of the morning during an outage or visiting eBay's far-flung international operations. Both of our jobs are the sort that can invade and erode family life and, sometimes rather dramatically, turn plans upside down. Keeping some semblance of calm and order was not always easy, but we managed to be patient and flexible enough to take each situation as it came, analyze, act, and adjust until we arrived at the right solution.

Did I know when we started down this road that busy June week in 1980 that a Whitman-Harsh merger would scale so well? I never could have predicted the course we would take or the ways we'd be tested, but I think I did see that the Power of Two was going to be bigger than either of us alone.

BACK TO THAT QUESTION I kept getting as the years at eBay passed: how long did I plan to run eBay?

Arjay Miller, the former head of the Stanford Graduate School of Business, who also once ran Ford Motor Co., used to say that he thought leaders should "repot" themselves every ten years or so. The first time I heard that, it made perfect sense to me. I wish more leaders embraced that idea. Much more commonly, people stay too long at the top. There may be a lot of reasons for that— they may not yet consider themselves to be as financially secure as they wish to be, or they may identify so much with the company that they can't imagine not having it be a part of their lives. They may simply love the work or really enjoy their colleagues. All those things make the decision a personal one.

It was clear to me by around year eight or nine of my tenure at eBay that many of the elements so central to eBay's first decade of life had shifted. After a period in which we had beaten back early competitors to emerge as the unchallenged online auction leader, we had seen growth in the auction business slow down, and we had to embrace fixed-price retailing that involved formidable competitors, such as Amazon at one extreme and Craigslist on the other. We had seen the rise of Google and its extraordinary search capabilities, which play a larger and larger role in directing consumers to products. We were now a large company, and some of the idiosyncrasies of our first decade that had worked very well as a cultural inspiration had probably outlived their usefulness to the larger eBay ecosystem, such as the level playing field for all sellers, regardless of size. In the increasingly competitive world of search, the idea that the top item on every eBay category list was the one whose auction was about to end—whether it was someone posting a box of old bowling trophies from his attic or a high-volume sporting goods seller with hundreds of active listings—made less and less sense.

You simply cannot sustain good growth without making changes, adding new business lines, rethinking everything. As night follows day, the larger you become, the more slowly you grow. Google, for example, has slowed to single-digit growth—but on a revenue base of more than $20 billion, that is an enormous amount of money.

Nonetheless, as the CEO, you can't just sink into that rationalization. As A. G. Lafley proved at P&G, you can inject new life into an old organization and find new and dynamic ways to grow if you strip away the vision-limiting practices of the past. The trouble is, sometimes the need to do that finally outruns the existing CEO's ability to keep reinventing. (In fact, A.G. retired as CEO of P&G after just under ten years!)

As I started to approach years eight and nine, it became increasingly clear to me that eBay was going to need to reinvent itself again, and that it was time for both me and the company to "repot" if eBay was going to compete effectively in a new era. The company was going to have to shed aspects of my style and preferences that had been forged in the heat of countless battles and showdowns with companies trying to compete with or disrupt our auction business. Now many of those companies had given way to a set of new and powerful competitors determined to more effectively

sell items at a fixed price. New technologies with still unpredictable potential, such as Skype, were emerging. We could not afford
to look at all this through yesterday's lenses.

As I got closer to my ten-year target, I felt very confident about
eBay's future. I knew that John Donahoe had the skills and energy
to turn eBay inside out if he had to in order to prepare the company for its next phase of life. I actually expected him to do that.
When a CEO's successor makes changes, sometimes the media
like to play it up as a personal rebuke of the last CEO's decisions.
I don't see it that way. I made clear to John as I was preparing him
to take over that, just as I felt I had reinvented eBay several times
in ten years, he was going to have to do the same. When you operate in a technology-driven space, everything can change overnight, and you have to change with it.

As I prepared to turn over the company, however, I knew that
I still had the same energy that had exhausted my playmates when
I was a child. What *should* I do next? And then in 2007 I got a
call from another dear friend that would help set that course.

Mitt Romney fits squarely into the category of friends who
inspire me and give me energy and courage. He is a thoroughly
decent human being with a deep connection to public service. We
had breakfast together and he said, "Meg, I'm thinking of running
for president. I wonder if you would consider helping me." It is a
tribute to Mitt that I was able to set aside my previous exposure to
politics, which had left me a little discouraged, and agreed to be
national cochair of his fund-raising campaign.

I grew up seeing politicians as larger-than-life figures. I believed that they did what they did because they were inspired by
the idea of public service and wanted government to work in the
most effective ways possible. I had never spent any time with regulators or elected officials before I came to eBay. And at eBay I
was so busy with my career and with my family that, pretty much

until well after we went public, I had not focused on politics. I am deeply embarrassed to say that even my voting record during my eBay years was spotty at times. There were so many crises at work and so little downtime at home that I let this essential aspect of living in our extraordinary democracy drop down on my priority list, and there is no excuse for that.

But as time went by, and especially in the second half of my tenure, some interesting new challenges emerged that I now look back on as the political education of Meg, part one.

When you are driving a disruptive technology into a new market, you can and must expect that the existing industries you are disrupting are not going to like it. What started to happen to eBay was that state legislators and regulators who had constituents whom eBay was impacting were increasingly being pressured by their local industries to put the brakes on eBay's growth.

The growth of eBay Motors, for example, did not sit well with a lot of auto dealers. In Texas, the automobile dealers are an extremely powerful lobby, and they had some of the toughest rules in the nation about how cars could be advertised and sold across different regions. The laws were not just protecting Texas dealers from eBay; they were often about protecting Dallas dealers from poaching by Houston dealers. We faced a number of concerns from regulators there about our used-car business.

Professional auctioneers also were not keen on eBay. In California, we received an inquiry from state regulators suggesting that it might be necessary for each of our sellers to post a million-dollar bond, as auction houses had to do to be in compliance with state regulations. The trouble was, that regulation was designed for auction houses that took physical possession of large quantities of expensive goods, not for a mom posting a duplicate Beanie Baby her child received at a birthday party. If they had enforced such an interpretation—and we convinced them not to—it would have ended eBay on the spot. In 2005, the Illinois legislature threatened to pass a law demanding that in order to sell in Illinois, eBay sellers would have to get a special license, including the requirement that they pass a voice test by demonstrating the ability to say into a microphone, "Twenty dollars, I have twenty, who'll give me twenty-five?" etc. When I heard this I thought somebody was pulling my leg. I said, "They realize this is a virtual auction?" No matter. The point was, those legislators had constituents who felt threatened by eBay, and those constituents turned to their elected officials for help in protecting them.

We were quite successful in making our case in these situations, yet each of these developments was worrisome and distracting and demanded a careful response. It did not feel like we had a front-row seat to smart democracy in action. So often, the small-business owners who were the soul of eBay were buffeted by regulation, taxes, and bureaucracy that seemed designed to hold them back at the same time we were giving them wings.

At the federal level, meanwhile, we were facing various kinds of legislation, such as bills designed to both control and tax the growth of online commerce. We felt strongly that a transaction tax on top of an income tax was unfair to sellers and would inhibit growth. To express that concern, I asked eBay's first government affairs director to introduce me to some key senators on Capitol Hill.

In my very first meeting with an experienced, well-known, highly respected senator, I walked in and sat down, we exchanged some pleasantries, and I gave my introductory comments. He appeared to listen attentively (note the key term *appeared*), but then he put on a little dramatic show. He put on his reading glasses and looked at a sheet of paper in front of him, occasionally peering over the top at me and then back down.

"What I see here is that the political donations from eBay are running about 90 percent for [the opposing political party]," he said, ignoring everything else I had said. "That is going to have to change."

In the remaining few minutes of our meeting it was clear that he had delivered his message and was ambivalent about mine. His actual intention in meeting with me was to set the terms of any future conversations between us. I remember having a sort of sad, sick feeling in my stomach. When I left the meeting I turned to our government affairs director and said, "So it's all really just about the money."

He nodded glumly.

None of this did much for my faith in the political process. The degree to which money ruled Washington and the idea that people spoke so openly about the quid pro quo for support really bothered me. But it was my job to act in the best interest of the company, and after I thought about it, I saw that the senator had a point. I had not paid attention to eBay's political donations, and our former government affairs manager had skewed most of them to one party. I immediately realigned our government affairs posture and created a political action committee, or PAC, so that we were sure to distribute our donations more evenly and not close any doors to elected officials who might be in a position to influence our future. (Of course we made sure that any employee who wanted to direct where his or her donations went could do so.) This was the way the game had to be played, so eBay needed to play it.

It was not entirely bleak out there. I met other senators who were not quite so cynical, and some, like Senator John McCain, who did not strike me as cynical at all. In fact, Senator McCain particularly impressed me with his understanding of the importance of supporting small-business owners. However, it is safe to say that many of my interactions with both state and national politicians, not to mention my frustration with the congressional committee investigation several years prior, had not inspired me to get more deeply involved in politics. To be honest, for the most part I was disillusioned.

But when Mitt talked to me about his hopes and dreams for his presidential campaign, I could see that he wanted to run for president for what struck me as the right reasons. He was the son of a former governor of Michigan, George Romney, and he really felt the pull of public service. He wanted to bring in some of the rigors of business and financial analysis that we had both learned and seen work at Bain and put them to use in the cause of making government work more efficiently. He had already put some of those skills to use in Massachusetts. It was actually a relief—good grief, there were people in politics for the right reasons, and I had the chance to help one of them! I knew my values aligned with Mitt's and so I signed on to help.

Thus began part two of my introduction to politics. I raised a lot of money for Mitt, more than $12 million, and he never disappointed me in terms of his integrity and his desire to run for the right reasons. But I was troubled at the course Mitt's campaign took, particularly at the scrutiny and attacks he was subject to as a Mormon. They were so intense and became so defining that he could not establish a coherent campaign message. The media portrayed him as the "Mormon flip-flopper," which I thought was deeply unfair. Wasn't this country founded on the basis of religious freedom? When his father had run for governor of Michigan, his religion was not an issue. Mitt brought a powerful and proven set of skills to this challenge, and those were simply ignored in the heat of the name-calling and press coverage. We knew Florida was going to be a pivotal primary for his campaign. But when the state's popular governor, Charlie Crist, backed John McCain, that was it for Mitt. After Super Tuesday, he dropped out of the race.

Within a couple of weeks, Senator McCain called me at my home. As tough a battle as Mitt had fought against John, the irony for me was that John McCain and I also were friends. After our early meetings about taxation and other Internet commerce issues, he had restored some of my faith in public service. He had not checked his party donation sheet before he spoke to me. In fact, from the moment I met him, I felt like I was in the presence of a decent, honest, well-intentioned person of integrity. After Mitt dropped out, Senator McCain asked me if I would become a national cochair of his campaign.

What I have always respected about John McCain is his deep desire to understand the results of a vote or a position. What path was best for the country? Regardless of party affiliation or campaign donation, what would really happen to an American family, to our military, to our small-business owners, to our economy, as the result of a vote in the Senate? What was the right thing to do? He looked at the Power of Many as a way to inspire others to work for a cause greater than their own self-interest. I did not have to agree with him on every vote, every choice, but I respected the way he tackled challenges. To me, the right thing was to support him in running for president.

I campaigned for Senator McCain throughout 2008, but I was troubled that his campaign did not seem to have a clear and consistent message that summed him up. I put on my branding hat and thought about my own respect for John and what impressed me. Eventually I put forward the line that he carried into the summer campaign and to the Republican National Convention: "Country first." I remember his son Jack writing it over and over on a piece of paper the first time he heard it. "This is it; this is perfect," he finally said. I think he had that reaction because John McCain is just that—a man who puts his country first.

One of the myths about branding in both business and politics is that it is a superficial exercise. To the contrary, great branding comes from a deep understanding of functionality and features and a connection with human emotion. The perfect, authentic slogan always feels like it was sitting there all along, like you simply cleared away the brush and discovered it. Think of Nike's "Just do it." "Country first" was about John McCain's history, his tempering by fire, his daily operating style, and his love for America. This is a man who truly had devoted his life to trying to make sure his country's best interests were served.

So, based largely on the strength of personal relationships, I found myself caught up in a national political campaign as an insider. By the time I joined Senator McCain's campaign, I had retired from eBay. I spent a lot of time with his team and talked frequently and frankly with John about many things. I was not without frustration. When you have managed a big organization and thousands of people, you take for granted management basics such as respecting lines of authority and decision making. The lines of authority in the McCain campaign were constantly crossing, and there was much misfiring and battling for his attention. In a political campaign, I learned, the candidate simply cannot be the CEO of the campaign because he or she is on the road so much, meeting people, making appearances and speeches, doing media interviews. A candidate needs a firm structure, with the right people in the right jobs, and needs to keep aligning messages and evaluating performance. In something as fast-moving as a campaign, this is never a onetime chore.

John McCain really is a maverick, a fighter pilot to the core. But I believe deeply in every individual's need to scale to be successful. When the challenges increase, you have to take on new jobs and leave old ones behind, and you have to fill in gaps in your own skill set. When it came time to choose a running mate, for example, I believed that the times called for the skills of Mitt Romney, because he would have complemented John's inspirational leadership with the practical experience of having managed large and complex organizations, both in business and as a governor. Mitt was fluent in economics and deeply familiar with the workings of Wall Street, which would have stood the country in great stead. Instead, the campaign struggled as the economy unwound and Senator Obama ran a cutting-edge, highly effective campaign. But until the end, John fought the good fight, and I'm enormously proud of his courage and our friendship.

In the course of that experience, what I kept seeing was that, based on my own management experience, there seemed to be many ways for politics in general to work better. I don't just mean better ways to run a campaign, but better ways to campaign that lay the groundwork for better governing. Focus on the right issues for the time, and your campaign theme or slogan can scale into a blueprint for governing. It dawned on me that everything I had learned running the virtual eBay economy had prepared me to enter a new arena where I had some unique assets. I was not beholden to any special interests or to their money. I understood how to effectively run big organizations and manage people, and I understood the care that must be taken and the enfranchisement that must happen in the early stages of a turnaround situation. I knew how to analyze big problems and zero in on the best way to make a difference.

I had retired from eBay in March 2008, practically ten years to the day from when I first joined the company. The board honored me by naming the company's headquarters "Whitman Campus," which I deeply appreciated. I did not want a big splashy retirement party. I am generally a low-drama person and I had seen too many confusing, slightly chaotic transitions in other companies; I wanted it clear that the reins were in John Donahoe's hands. I did love some of the "analog" souvenirs I took away from my digital odyssey, such as the leather-bound books that had made their way around the world, in which hundreds of different employees wrote me kind good-byes and recounted favorite stories from the past decade. Together, we had empowered people to achieve more than they dreamed possible, and we had created a decent, well-lit place to do business in the process.

I don't think there will ever be another eBay for me. What we accomplished was so novel, our success so unprecedented, that other business opportunities pale in comparison. At eBay, values were a force multiplier—indispensable in building an empowering and successful community. I believe those same values have the power to transform not only the way we do business but our lives, our communities, and the world beyond.

Epilogue

W
hen my mother was a young girl growing up in Boston in the 1920s and 1930s, I am quite sure she could never have imagined that in just a few years she would be crossing the Pacific Ocean on a troop ship, bound for New Guinea. But like so many in her generation, when world events moved our country inexorably into World War II and she understood that we were in a fight to preserve our liberties, she was not the type to hang back. She felt a call to action and signed up to do her part.

So when I officially declared that I was running for governor of California in late September 2009, my mother flew out from Boston to cheer me on. She is eighty-nine and in delicate health, but you can't keep a bias for action down. She loved the excitement and commotion swirling around me, and as I looked at her in her wheelchair, ever the trooper, I thought about advice she gave me when I went off to college. "You should do what will make you happy and will make a difference."

A decade ago, neither of us could have imagined that such a desire would involve politics. Running eBay in the early years of an intense, fast-moving digital revolution demanded quick analysis and decisive action—the antithesis of politics, with its endless talk and slow progress. I faced the 24/7 challenge of figuring out what it meant to govern a global online community. One day it might involve a crash course in network outages, the next, beating back competitive attacks from companies, large and small. We wrestled with profound questions about free speech and censorship as we wrote the equivalent of a penal code for our diverse and boisterous marketplace. We encountered fascinating cultural habits and preferences as we expanded into new countries. And at all times I had to keep one eye on potentially game-changing new technologies.

Politics was outside my ken. In business, the rules are fairly clear: your numbers represent your report card, and all the spinning and arm-twisting and lobbying in the world cannot rescue a flawed business that is not making money for investors, or is failing to scale. At eBay, I worked the levers and techniques of management to lead and deliver results. Success demanded focus, setting those critical priorities that allowed you to maximize your energy and efforts for the most good.

But toward the end of my tenure at eBay, I had an awakening. I felt my own call to action. Once eBay's start-up dramas had subsided and we had become a big, global company, the hand of government in our community's activities, whether taxes or regulation, often felt encumbering. Because of our unique position dealing with virtually every state government on so many issues, it was clear that some states were more efficient and effective regulating certain activities than others. The National Governor's Association and both parties even have "best practices" study groups and efforts. But from the vantage point of a large company (one that depends on the energy and efforts of hundreds of thousands of small businesses and sole proprietors) it rarely feels like there is a concerted effort in government to streamline processes. Unfortunately, the practices that seemed to me as natural as breathing—

the idea of saving to invest, doing yesterday's activities more efficiently today, focusing on a more limited list of priorities so as to achieve a greater impact—are radical notions in the political arena.

But it's a point of view that is sorely needed. As I traveled with John McCain during his presidential campaign, it was clear that people were fed up, anxious to feel empowered again, yearning for their leaders to help instead of hinder their hopes and dreams.

I also realized that eBay's home state of California was headed in a dangerous direction. Prosperity never depends on one factor; it is always about having the right conditions for success. Silicon Valley offers a perfect example of that. Silicon Valley is an ecosystem. It developed because of very special conditions: a world-class university, a critical mass of entrepreneurs who realized they could achieve the most in the fastest period of time by working together, and an infrastructure that supplied the investment capital, equipment, legal advice, facilities construction, and countless other resources that build companies. Similar information technology ecosystems exist across the country—along Boston's Route 128; in Austin, Texas; in North Carolina's Research Triangle Park. And in other parts of our state there are robust and dynamic ecosystems clustered around fine universities creating other exciting new and effective technologies: medical devices, biotechnology, energy, and agricultural innovations.

But during my tenure at eBay, it was clear that this model of healthy ecosystems in California was breaking down. Ideas were percolating, but innovators and businesspeople were feeling the growing burden of regulations and taxes. Large and small businesses were fleeing the state, attracted by the promise of less onerous regulations and taxation in other states. Our K–12 educational system, once the envy of the nation, had slid to near the very bottom, leaving California's young people unprepared to take

advantage of our own fine universities. Layer upon layer of bureaucracy had left us with an enormous budget that was only sustainable when the economy was vibrant and growing, as it had
been during eBay's early years. That was a recipe for disaster, and
sure enough, California faces a budgetary and economic catastro-
phe today. What is so troubling to me is that our leaders can't seem
to figure out what every family knows: when times are tight, you
stop spending money. You find a way to do more with less.

Instead, a shocking number of people are advocating raising
taxes. That is a move guaranteed to keep our economy in a miserable doom loop. It will drive away even more businesses, destroy
even more jobs, and reduce consumer income even further, which
will reduce spending, which will lead inevitably to more layoffs.
If we do not focus first and foremost on restarting the economy
and reversing the direction of those trends, the human cost will be
enormous.

When I was running eBay, there came a time when I realized
that if we were starting eBay all over again, we would probably not
start it in California. It had become too onerous a place to do
business.

The Power of Many principles apply to virtually every aspect
of the challenge of getting this state out of its doom loop and
growing again. In fact, the same values we used to build eBay are
desperately needed across the landscape of public service today.
Let's go down the list:

Begin every endeavor with the faith that people are basically
good.

Stop dithering and act. Stop tolerating the structural problems
that have landed us in this situation—specifically, burdensome
regulations, unfettered spending, and excessively high taxes.

Nurture what makes California so authentically powerful: its can-do spirit, its many natural resources, its excellent higher education system, and its diverse population.

Wage an assault on waste by moving to sunset programs and budgets that no longer produce the return we demand. Create incentives for our government programs to work more efficiently and effectively.

Set specific targets for our most critical goals, which I believe should be job growth, reining in government spending, and reforming our K–12 educational system. Let's measure and adjust as we go, not just distribute the funds and cross our fingers.

Incorporate more listening and communicating, using technology to make many services more efficient. Transplant the idea of transparency from business to the political arena, which is too often a place of backroom deals.

Focus. Evaluate every program, every opportunity, and every idea by asking: Does it create or retain jobs? If not, we need to push it down our priority list until we restart our job engine. Even if it can create jobs, we must still ask: Can we do this more efficiently? That's the only way we can afford to overhaul K–12 education, fix our outdated infrastructure, and make the state more competitive.

Enfranchise. Reenlist our citizens in the larger cause of making our communities better through volunteerism and creating incentives for everybody, government employees and citizens alike, to come up with smarter, more efficient systems that get more done for less cost.

Be brave. This will be difficult. We will have to rethink some of the fundamental structures and processes of how we manage our state. But challenges open new doors, and I learned at eBay that nothing motivates quite so well as a big, stretch goal. I want to see California's educational system lead the nation again, as it did in the 1950s. If we don't rededicate ourselves to this goal with the same attitude Americans have applied to going to the moon and fighting wars, we will lose our ability to innovate and create the next generation of companies and jobs in California—to create the next eBay, the next Google, the next Genentech.

Finally, let's scale this. Let's cleave off those tired practices and inefficiencies that are draining our budgets for little return. Let's use the increased transparency and communication tools of the twenty-first century to govern our 38 million residents and our $1.8 trillion economy—which would rank in the top ten of *nations* if California were a country—more effectively, more efficiently, and more inclusively. All success in life demands constant reinvention. If you cannot scale, you will fail.

I am a problem-solver by nature. But I share a very human frustration and pain with other Californians in watching something that we love fall apart. California has a majestic, inspirational spirit that touched me even as a small child—when I was a little girl staring up at Yosemite's El Capitan, or walking through Disneyland, its own technology-rich ecosystem of creativity and dreams that the visionary Walt Disney built in a former orange grove. It has inspired dreamers but also doers. As the leader of one of Silicon Valley's biggest success stories, eBay, I was proud to play a role in the extraordinary Internet revolution that changed the way we trade goods and services, the way we work, and the way we communicate. I cannot just sit by and watch California fail. It's time to act.

ACKNOWLEDGMENTS

———————

This book was a Power of Many effort that really started with the employees of eBay and the eBay community. Together, we made business history while enabling millions to be successful doing what they love. I will always be grateful to Pierre Omidyar for inviting me to join his adventure, and I will always be so proud of what all of us accomplished together.

I want to thank my husband, Griff, who has accompanied me on our remarkable thirty-year journey, for his love, support, and encouragement. Griff has always been willing to stand in the background. This book offers me the opportunity to shine at least a little light on his good nature, unflinching support, and willingness, despite an extraordinarily challenging career of his own, to share the daily work of family life, from child-rearing to managing family finances to household chores. He was patient with the writing process and generous in revealing stories about our life together. Griff, you are the best!

I also want to thank my two strong, wonderful sons, who came of age with a constant spotlight on their mom and, because of that, on them as well. They have been supportive of every adventure and understanding and tolerant of my career. Griff and Will, watching you grow into the fine young men you are has been my life's greatest pleasure.

My family has always inspired confidence and an adventuresome spirit. I so wish my father, Hallett, had lived to see eBay's success because I know it would have delighted him. And my mother, Margaret; well, as you now know, I really am my mother's daughter. Mom, thank you for everything. My siblings, Hal and Anne, have always been there for me, supportive and fun no matter what. I think the three of us have made a great team. And I am quite certain I have the best parents-in-law ever. Craig and Griff Harsh have embraced and lovingly accepted me into their family from the earliest days; they are unfailingly kind and generous, and they are wonderful grandparents.

My very best girlfriends are a constant source of camaraderie and encouragement and fun. Thank you, Meg Osius, Linda Francis Knights, Gail Kittler, Carol Herman, Mary Meeker, Jaynie Studenmund, Diane Forese, and Solina Chau.

There are so many other remarkable people I have been privileged to know and work with over the years. You have met many of them in this book; each of them has taught me important lessons that ultimately shaped my beliefs about the power of values both in and out of the workplace. Former Massachusetts governor Mitt Romney, former California governor Pete Wilson, the late Frank Wells, A. G. Lafley, Tom Tierney, and Senator John S. McCain all set examples for me of courage and integrity, and they have truly inspired me.

In the very earliest days at eBay, the company's first president, Jeff Skoll, and our lead investor, Bob Kagle, were valued partners, setting a standard of integrity and accountability from the beginning. I have great admiration for all the directors who served on eBay's board throughout my decade there, and I am especially grateful to Scott Cook and Howard Schultz, who played such critical roles in the company's earliest days. Henry Gomez, for years eBay's senior communications chief, is one of my most trusted friends and colleagues. He not only delivers results, but his smarts, humor, and energy make any challenge, large or small, more manageable. My longtime assistant at eBay, Anita Gaeta, has been a key part of the team, often acting as air traffic controller, always with a positive attitude and unparalleled competence.

My gratitude to the executives with whom I worked closely at eBay is boundless: Rajiv Dutta, Maynard Webb, Mike Jacobson, Jeff Jordan, Matt Bannick, Bill Cobb, Brian Swette, Steve Westly, Mike Wilson, Gary Bengier, Alex Kazim, Mary Lou Song, Annette Goodwine, Simon Rothman, and Rob Chesnut all shaped eBay's history. A bit later, Bob Swan, Lorrie Norrington, Stephanie Tilenius, Scott Thompson, Phillip Justus, Jay Lee, Gregory Boutte, Michael van Swaaij, Jay Clemens, Josh Silverman, Marty Abbott, Lynn Reedy, Brad Peterson, Doug McCallum, Andre Haddad, and Michael Dearing, among many others, stepped up and added new strengths and dimensions to the team. I am especially pleased that John Donahoe was named eBay's CEO after me. I know John will take eBay to places we never dreamed we could go.

My talented, creative literary agent, Jillian Manus, saw the possibilities for an "outside the box" book and assembled a great team to pull it off, beginning with Crown publisher Tina Constable. Also at Crown, Rachel Klayman gamely and artfully shaped the text of a book that was not a typical biography or business book, and the result is something I think we're all very proud of. Thanks also to Tara Gilbride for her enthusiasm and commitment to the project. Joan Hamilton was the best collaborator I could have dreamed of. Her long career as a successful journalist and her ability to listen, synthesize, and inspire made this effort a success. Joan also deserves credit for chasing every detail down with determination and good humor. Joan is a true talent, and this book would not have been possible without her.